NARROW ESCAPE

"Oh, you live on a boat? I bet that's cold in the winter ... " "It must be great being so close to nature ... " "It must be fantastic to be able to go wherever you like, whenever you like ... " *Narrow Escape* sets out to dispel these common public myths. From how to avoid assassination by ninja stealth ducklings, through definitive proof that kittens are aliens and the best way to sleep at forty-five degrees, to the importance of having the right boating equipment (a child's plastic sledge and a never-ending supply of cotton-wool balls), this month-by-month account of one family's liveaboard year takes a firmly tongue-in-cheek look at the "idyllic" life on a narrow boat.

NARROW ESCAPE

MARIE BROWNE

LARGE
PRINT

First published in Great Britain 2013
by
Accent Press Ltd.

First Isis Edition
published 2016
by arrangement with
Accent Press Ltd.

A catalogue record for this book is available
from the British Library.

ISBN 978–1–78541–195–3 (hb)
ISBN 978–1–78541–201–1 (pb)

Published by
F. A. Thorpe (Publishing)
Anstey, Leicestershire

Set by Words & Graphics Ltd.
Anstey, Leicestershire
Printed and bound in Great Britain by
T. J. International Ltd., Padstow, Cornwall

This book is printed on acid-free paper

For Geoff; my partner in organised lunacy,
my rock, my voice of reason
and my very best friend.

Introduction

Over the last five years I have had so many people ask me what it's *really* like to live on a narrow boat. Not to travel around getting into various scrapes (our paintwork shows that we've had enough of those), but the ins and outs of coping with kids, school runs, work, illness, and all the other bits and pieces that come with twenty-first-century living.

The first thing everybody says, as soon as they find out where I live is, "Ooo I bet that's cold in the winter!" It always amazes me; there are so many more "issues" to living on a boat than the temperature.

This is not a travel book. Unlike *Narrow Margins* and *Narrow Minds* we don't have a new boat, we're not facing locks and, for once, we aren't intent on trying to sink ourselves (nature has taken on that job). *Narrow Escape* is a month by month, tongue in cheek account of *living* within a restricted space, on a restricted budget, and of our attempts to inject a sense of normality into our children's lives.

2012 wasn't that good for those afloat, especially in Cambridgeshire. The weather was, at times, extreme to say the least. Floods, high winds, snow, unempathic landowners, and panicked wildlife all took their toll this year. I have to admit I hope never to go through another like it.

Those that already live aboard will recognise many of

the adversities that nature tends to throw at those who reside on water. For those that may be thinking of indulging in this lifestyle, don't panic; I can assure you that this year has been one like no other. Yes, if you choose to live aboard an elderly "fixer upper" with children you may well face every single situation described within its pages. However, I can only hope that you never have to face them all within one twelve month period. Let me say again, this year has been EXCEPTIONAL.

I hope you enjoy spending a year with our family, friends and all the other elements that make up this odd life of ours.

Happy boating and don't forget, pirate coffee costs less than a session with a therapist. ☺

Marie x

CHAPTER
ONE

January Brings The Snow.
I'm Feeling Like An Eskimo.

"MUM!"

I jumped at the shout. Intent on giving our fire desperate CPR, I obviously hadn't heard my youngest trying to get my attention.

"What?" I yelled down the boat at him, "I'm a bit busy at the moment." Ignoring the muttering from behind me I turned back to my sulking log burner. "I can't believe I made such a damn rookie mistake." I poked at it and grimaced as my fledgling fire collapsed into a puff of sparks and cinders. "Oh, for goodness' sake."

"What's the matter Mum?" Sam, still yawning and dressed in pyjamas, three jumpers, and a lot of socks, had wandered down to see what all the swearing was about.

I jumped and hit my head on the blackened door of the log burner. "Jaaagghh!" was all I managed.

Sam winced and took a step back. "That wasn't my fault," he said.

"I never said it was." I sat on the floor and picked up my morning coffee, it wasn't very warm but, compared to the temperature in the boat, it was the closest thing I had to a hot water bottle. I stared up at the ceiling. My repeated unsuccessful attempts to light the fire had merely created rolling clouds of smoke that, hovering at ceiling height, effectively sliced the boat in two.

"I'm freezing." Sam stared at the cold, black fire for a moment. "Why is the fire out?"

I stared into my coffee cup and took a deep breath. Although I was fairly sure that screaming and throwing bits of wood around would warm me up, it would be a temporary solution at best. Taking a deep breath, I went back to chopping the wet kindling into the longest and thinnest slivers I could. "It's out because I didn't put enough coal on it last night. I was being lazy and didn't want to go out into the snow for a new bag so I hoped I'd put on enough to make it last."

"Never put off till tomorrow what you can mess up today." Sam solemnly intoned one of my favourite sayings.

I had to laugh. "Yes, thank you Sam," I said. "It would be a lot faster if I had some firelighters but I've run out of those as well, so maybe I should just concentrate on what I'm doing." I turned to give him my patent "now is not the time for daft questions" look. Unfortunately, my teeth were chattering so hard I'm fairly sure all he got was a "somewhat surprised" look. He got the message anyway and scarpered.

Thirty seconds later he was back.

I sighed and turned again as he poked me in the shoulder. "Sam honey, I can't do this with you sitting like a monkey on my back . . ."

2

He held his hand out. Curious, I took what he was offering. I was now the proud possessor of a handful of cotton wool balls.

"Very nice dear." I put the fluffy balls on the floor and wondered if the cold had finally leeched into his brain, I know *I* was finding thinking difficult.

He picked them up and handed them to me again. "Use these instead of firelighters," he said.

I stared at them for a moment and then put them down again. "I don't think so, Sam." I turned back to the fire.

"I saw it on telly." He piled them up into a little pyramid on the carpet. "They were showing you how to light a fire outside. They said that cotton wool was an excellent fire starter."

I peered up at him from where I sat on the floor. He didn't seem to be having a laugh.

He picked them up and handed them to me with a grin. "Go on, Mum," he said. "Can we just see what happens?"

I shrugged. Well, I might as well give it a go, nothing else I'd tried so far had worked and, at the very least, he'd learn that you can't trust everything you see on the goggle box.

Sam leant toward me and whispered in my ear. "You can also use erm . . ." he shuffled and looked around, obviously worried that somehow we had become a magnet for crowds of people eager to move away from their central heating and live in the frozen wastes of Cambridgeshire, ". . . Those towel things."

"Huh?" I had visions of setting fire to my tea towels. Actually, if this didn't work that might actually be a solution.

"You know, the ones women use." He gave me a sage look, raising his eyebrows and nodding at me in an effort to get me to understand without having to use the actual words.

"Really?" I removed all the charred sticks from the fire bed and dumped the woolly balls in a pile. Carefully covering them in tiny splinters and bits of twig I took a deep breath and struck a match. Firmly quashing the temptation to hold my hands over it for a moment I held the flaming piece of wood out toward him. "Do you want to do this, Mr Wilderness Wizz?"

Sam grinned at me and took the long match. Carefully inserting it through the open door of the log burner he set fire to the pile of cotton wool.

The fluff went up with a whoosh of blue flame which caused Sam to squeak and throw himself on top of me. Well, that was pretty much what I'd expected; there was no way that was going to burn for long enough to set light to the kindling, I waited for the balls to reduce to ash.

They didn't, they kept burning. For a couple of seconds I watched the little fire, too surprised to actually do anything useful. Then, as realisation settled in, I leapt about heaping ever bigger pieces of wood onto the flaming pile. I opened the bottom vent as wide as it would go, closed the door then sat back and thought good fiery thoughts at the whole thing.

An hour later, the contents of the wood burner were burning so fiercely the metal was almost glowing. And, with the Eco-fan spinning madly, sending waves of lovely warmth down the boat, I finally felt warm enough to start taking some layers off.

It had been so cold that morning that I'd just thrown on everything I could get my hands on. Wearing pretty much everything you own, while fairly good at keeping you cosy, does sort of label you "mad cat woman" and, with every layer I removed, I half expected to find felines hidden in the folds of clothing.

Handing Sam a mug of hot chocolate as he stood staring out of the window, I gave him a squeeze. "Good thinking about the cotton balls, Batman." I nudged him to take it from me. "There's an extra marshmallow in there." He took the mug with a smile but continued to stare out of the window, occasionally using his sleeve to wipe away the condensation.

"Mum, what do crows usually eat?" He absently took a sip, winced at the heat of the drink and then went back to staring out of the window.

OK, not a question I was expecting. "I don't know love, all sorts of things I think, why?" I turned back to the cooker and almost fell over our black staffy, Mortimer. Now that the temperature had reached an acceptable level, he had finally deigned to emerge from his nest of blankets in the hope that some marshmallows might end up inside him.

"Because there's one dancing outside." Sam wiped the condensation away with his hand; he merely succeeded in smearing the water across the glass.

"Um hmmm." I giggled at Mort who, with three small marshmallows stuck to his teeth, looked like he'd fallen out of the film "Deliverance". I half expected him to pick up a banjo. Finally Sam's odd statement made it through the haze to my frozen brain. "Sorry, what? I thought you said there's a dancing crow."

Sam nodded.

Picking up a wodge of kitchen towel I joined him at the window. I used it to clear the vast runnels of condensation that seemed to permanently cloud our view of the white world outside at this time of year.

Eventually, I managed to peer through the glass. Snow covered everything. At least eight inches deep it blanketed the flood defences and had blown up against our flimsy fence. The same colour as the sky, it created the illusion that you were staring into the abyss.

The only carbuncle on this vision of winter wonder was the incredible mess that littered the flats outside the boat. I cursed myself. The idea of trudging through the snow with a full bin bag last night had been just too much for me. So, preferring to sit in a lazy heap by the fire, I'd opted for slinging it outside with the intention of taking it down to the skip when I went to get the coal. I'd never gone for coal so, I'd told myself I'd do it first thing in the morning.

The crow had got there first.

A chicken carcass, vegetable peelings, tea bags, and all sorts of other unsavoury items were spread over about twenty square foot. The tea bags were gently staining the snow a horrible brown colour and, through the middle of all this, Eric rolled around and around, squawking and hollering in a suitably raucous manner. I had to admit he really did look as though he was break dancing.

Eric was a crow that Charlie, my daughter, had befriended a couple of years earlier. She had coaxed and cosseted it into taking food from her and it had taken the complaining might of half of the marina to get her to stop feeding the damn thing. He was beautifully behaved when she was around but, as soon as she went to school or turned her back on him for a moment, he would raid the neighbours' bins and turn the flood defences into a miniature landfill.

"Eric!" I hammered on the window. "Stop it. Go away!"

Sam looked up at me with a slightly condescending expression. "I don't think he's listening to you, Mum. I don't think he's going to listen to anyone until he finishes what he's doing."

"What exactly *is* he doing?" I peered through the window. I realised that Eric wasn't dancing, he was struggling with something. Performing the most amazing somersaults, he was screaming and pecking at whatever was beneath his feet. For a couple of seconds he would leap and cavort in and out of the snow, all mad eyes and open beak before disappearing beneath the white again. As we watched, completely dumbfounded at his antics, he flopped onto the snow, his wings outstretched and just lay like a feathered blackberry stain on a christening gown.

He didn't move. Sam and I looked at each other.

"Oh, for goodness' sake." That seemed to be my mantra for the morning. I grabbed my coat and began searching for my wellies.

As I left the boat, Mortimer mincing at my side, it began to snow again. Fat white flakes drifted down attempting to cover the garbage that had turned the flat white of the riverbank into modern art. The river itself was completely frozen over and also covered in snow, much to the consternation of the local swans who had taken themselves off into the fields to await the thaw. If it hadn't been for the line of boats marking the edge, you couldn't actually tell where the land stopped and the river began. We were all very careful when we stepped aboard *Minerva*.

"Leave it alone."

Mortimer, excited by deep frozen chicken had been adding to the mess. He dropped the carcass with a slightly guilty look and, after discolouring his own patch of winter, had tiptoed over to join me. Spying Eric lying in a crumpled heap he began a deep grumbling rumble. Both animals had met before and Mortimer usually came off the worse in their encounters.

"Oh shush you." I poked him in the rump. He totally ignored me, advancing stiff legged and fluffed toward the stricken bird.

"MORT!"

At my shout he subsided. Eric, warned that the dog was nearby, lifted his head and stared with menace filled black bullet eyes at his hairy nemesis. He opened

8

his huge strong beak and began a rumbling sound of his own.

Glad that the dog was there to distract the bird, I grabbed the feathered nuisance from behind. Lifting him out of the snow I realised that he had somehow managed to put his foot through some old ribbon. This in turn had become tangled with a length of cling film. He looked like a really badly wrapped Christmas present; presumably something the naughty would find in their stocking if the price of coal carried on rising.

As I lifted him into the air all hell broke loose. The big crow screamed over and over as he flapped his big wings and stabbed at my face with his beak. I held him at arm's length and began untangling the mess around his feet, all the while trying to find a way to still his wings. "Sam, SAM!" I yelled at the grinning face I could see through the window. "Get me a towel."

Sam rolled his eyes but disappeared into the darkness of the boat. Leaning forward I could see where the ribbon had split, trapping Eric's foot. Concentrating on the task, I forgot what I was holding and was reminded rather abruptly as Eric's beak performed a military tattoo across the back of my hand.

"Ow, you ungrateful little brute," I yelped as I tried to twist my hand away from the stabbing maw. "I'm trying to do you a favour. Ow, stoppit, OUCH!"

Mortimer had obviously decided that enough was enough. There was no way that smelly bag of feathers was going to attack his mum, so he launched an attack of his own. Twenty-seven kilos of over-indulged Staffordshire bull terrier shot up my leg and, after knocking me onto my back in the snow, landed squarely on my stomach.

Although being trampled and pecked I was very conscious that the dog must not get at the bird. I held Eric up out of the way as Mort unintentionally pinned me to the ground in an attempt to get to the screaming, flapping monstrosity.

Into this furore Sam arrived holding a tiny tea towel. Seeing absolutely no way that he could help without getting actively involved, he began flapping the towel indiscriminately at all of us. I swear the noise of dog barking, bird screaming insults, me shouting at the dog to back off and Sam just shouting must have been audible about twenty miles away.

Of course at this moment, Geoff arrived home. I wish I'd had a video camera as he came over the flood defences, his expression must have been priceless. On the other hand, if *he'd* had the video camera the footage would probably have been worth a fair amount of money from one of those home movie calamity shows.

Within thirty seconds my organised and useful husband had grabbed Mort and thrown him into the boat, come back out with a bigger towel, wrapped Eric in a big blue bundle, given me a hand up, and generally restored peace and tranquillity.

With Mortimer sulking in his basket and Eric lying trussed and furious on the table; my rather disgruntled husband finally had time to say hello. While I made tea he managed to unearth just Eric's feet from the towel and busied himself unwrapping the ribbon and cling film from around the bird's long black claws.

"But why did you let the flaming dog out with you?" he asked.

As I placed his mug of tea on the table, Eric swivelled his head with horror film precision and glared at me. He would have been fantastic as an extra in any Hitchcock film. Opening his beak he gave me the full view of his little pointed tongue then, with a clack that made me gulp, he snapped it shut and just continued his silent and accusatory stare.

"I didn't even think about it," I said, "he just came out with me like he always does; I didn't really notice he was there until he started eating the chicken." I shrugged.

"Hmm . . . well, he was nearly eating crow." Geoff smirked at his own bad pun and studied the bird's claws. "Why don't you go and clear up the mess while I finish this, then I might just be able to get some sleep." He gave a huge yawn and rubbed the back of his hand over his eyes, he looked like a ten-year-old that had been allowed to stay up too late.

Wincing, I remembered that he'd just done a twelve-hour night shift. I'm sure that the last thing he wanted to do was play cat's cradle with a sociopathic corbie. Dismissed and gently grumped at I went to do garbage detail. I didn't complain, if I hadn't been such a wimp and had done it last night none of this would have happened.

I was still picking up the frozen rubbish when Geoff threw Eric out of the boat. Ruffled and obviously in a foul humour the bird stalked across the snow toward me. I don't actually think he was really heading in my direction but I wasn't taking any chances, picking up the bin bag I high-tailed it toward the skip. By the time I'd crept cautiously back to the boat, expecting a whispered "Nevermore" in my ear at every step, Geoff had gone to bed and Eric had taken himself off only God knew where.

Seven hours later, full of fish pie, jam roly-poly, custard and tea, Geoff was back to his normal good humour.

"Why on earth did you try to pick the damn thing up?" He laughed. "I could hear you screaming as I got out of the van. But as Mort was barking I just thought he was up to no good and you were shouting at him. I couldn't believe it when I came over the floods. It looked like you were being attacked by some sort of dark angel." He sniggered. "There was just a ball of feathers and feet and dog and snow. I thought it was some sort of new extreme sport you were trying out."

Charlie looked up from her book. She'd slept through the whole thing and was very cross about it. "I hope you didn't hurt poor Eric," she said.

"Hurt poor Eric?" I rubbed the lumps and scratches on my hand that he'd dished out by stabbing me with that great beak. "What about me?"

Geoff, Charlie and Sam all turned to look at me. "Maybe you shouldn't deal with animals, Mum." Sam seemed to sum up everyone's thoughts. "You always seem to come off worst."

12

I decided to change the subject. "Was that the last night shift?"

Geoff gave a huge sigh of relief and nodded. "For a while, their electrician's back so I can go back to my normal hours, thank goodness."

Sam nodded. "Yeah and I can have my bed back."

This was rather an interesting conundrum. Geoff had been offered a week's worth of nights with one of his company's customers. The money for working anti-social hours was far too good to turn down and he'd accepted without either of us really thinking it through. It was only when he staggered home after the first shift that we'd discovered a rather sticky problem. When you sleep totally different hours to everyone else and you don't actually have a bedroom to go and hide in, where do you go? You either have to sleep in your bed, which for us is still in the middle of the living room and everyone else in the boat has to tiptoe around you (our bedroom is going to be one of the last places that gets built). Or you throw your son out of his room and use that. The whining from Sam had been growing with every passing day. I was glad that we'd soon be back to normal.

Charlie gave a big sigh.

"What's up, chuck?" I knew exactly what she was going to say but, as she had taken to whinging about this "problem" almost continually, I knew better than to ignore her.

"College," she muttered. "We go back on Monday and it's just going to be the same old boring rubbish we've been doing since I started."

I nodded. "That's the way things tend to go."

"Well I don't want to do them, I signed up to do art, my art, not study someone else's."

Charlie climbed to her feet and pushed her long dark set of dreadlocks out of her face, tying the front ones in a knot behind her head. "Why won't they let me do my own stuff?"

This same conversation had been going around and around for most of the Christmas holidays and I was now lost for something new to say. Sam, surprisingly, came to my rescue.

"How do you know your stuff's any good?" He gave her a big cheesy smile. "If you don't learn other things you'll just do the same old rubbish over and over again. By the time I go to college to take my A levels, you will have reached the heady heights of congratulating me on my results before asking me, 'do you want fries with that?' Art is such as waste of time, you should be doing something interesting, like maths."

Charlie glared at him for a moment her bright blue eyes turning icy and cold. We all tensed waiting for the inevitable. "You are such a little creep," she screamed. "Art isn't a waste of time, not everyone wants to be a geeky little nerd like YOU!"

Geoff held up a hand to forestall one of the scraps that seemed to be far more frequent these days.

Charlie ignored him. "I'm going to my boat, I hate living here and I hate this weather." She slammed out of the door and into the snow. Failing to shut the door behind her properly, she ignored it as it swung open letting a great blast of cold air into the room.

14

Sam got up to shut the door. Before he did, he leant out into the white flakes and yelled, "Don't forget to do that homework while you're there!"

I didn't catch the vague words that drifted back to us through the swirling snow, but the short sentence definitely included the word "off."

He closed the door and, sniggering, looked around the room. He was greeted with almost matching looks of disapproval from both parents. He gave us a theatrical shrug and a big smile. "What?" he said.

"I know she's been winding you up for years." I gave him a hard frown. "I know that you are now taller than she is and you've found your revenge bone . . ."

Sam smirked.

". . . But you have to understand you are dealing with five foot and two inches of pure rage there. If she gets *really* angry with you I can guarantee you are going to regret it."

Sam's smirk dropped and he looked a little uncertain.

"Just keep it in mind. If you push her too hard you are going to find yourself swimming."

"Or flying . . ." Geoff said.

Sam swallowed hard and gave the door a nervous look. "I think I'll go and read," he said.

Geoff nodded. "I would if I were you."

Our youngest gave the door another quick look and then scuttled off to his room. Geoff rolled his eyes. "That boy has no sense of self-preservation, does he?"

Since leaving school Charlie seemed to be either deliriously happy or heading toward psychopathic hysteria. We all found ourselves treading very lightly around her. She would morph into a screaming banshee at the smallest of things and I found myself trying to remember if I had been this psychotic at seventeen. From what little I could remember, I have to admit that I had probably been as bad if not worse. And we all say we'd like to be young again. No thanks, anything below twenty-two is just hormonal chaos.

The snow lasted another week before the thaw set in. By this time we were all heartily sick of the cold, the treacherous icy lane, digging vehicles out of the snow because they'd missed the road, and we were all generally looking forward to spring. It seemed we had a long way to go.

Just as there was a hint that winter might actually release its death grip on the land, the temperature dropped again. Everything that had been dripping and melting now, once again, became solid and slippery.

Since the first major freeze in November we had been struggling to cope with our pumps, pipes, and water tanks. Quickly installed as they were, it hadn't taken us long to find out that we hadn't put anywhere near enough insulation around any of them. I was fairly sure that, since the weather had taken a serious turn for the worse in December, we'd actually had only three days of running water. It wasn't just us, all the boats were affected. It wouldn't have changed anything even if our plumbing had been up to scratch; all the taps and pipes in the marina were also solid. The local supermarket was rapidly running out of big bottles of water and house-dwelling friends were getting used to us turning up and stealing fifty litres of water at each visit. I was sick to death of five-litre bottles. They lurked in the kitchen, in the bathroom, and lined up in military rows down the length of the boat. Unfortunately, most of them were usually empty.

Onc bitterly cold Saturday morning, Geoff trotted past with three hot wheat bags in his arms. Doing a bit of a double-take I rescued "Beddy Bear" from inside the steaming pile. Geoff's expression switched between guilty and irritated. "I need more heat." He reached for the hot, seed filled toy frowning when I held its dangling legs out of his reach.

"There is no way you are taking this into that smelly engine room of yours. I ducked as he made a swipe for it and stuffed the bear into the back of my big woolly shirt. Ooo, that was really nice and warm.

"Sam hasn't used it for years." Geoff grabbed the collar of my shirt and stuck a cold hand down my neck making me scream. "It just sits on the top of his wardrobe; I could give it some purpose in life."

"It doesn't matter." I sniggered and fell back onto the sofa trapping the hot toy between me and the cushions. "It's a treasured childhood toy and it would scar his little psyche to find it wrapped around a set of oily pipes."

Geoff grabbed my arm and tried to roll me onto the floor; his long fingers digging into the spots between my ribs making me laugh and scream. I retaliated by trying to poke him in the tummy button. Mortimer, wondering what was going on, decided to join in. He couldn't decide who to protect so he just jumped over both of us until we all fell off the sofa and lay in a screaming, giggling, and barking heap on the carpet.

The noise finally roused Sam from the model he was making. I looked up to find him standing above us, shaking his head and looking long-suffering. Reaching down he plucked Beddy Bear from Geoff's hand and, with a muttered "Mine I think," wandered off down the boat.

Geoff stood up and brushed himself off before pulling me to my feet. "Well I'd better go and try to defrost that stupid pump." He glared at me and gave me one last poke in the ribs. "And, now that you've stolen my teddy bear, I'm going to have to find something else to melt the ice with."

Standing by the door he pulled on another pair of thick socks, a pair of boots, his fleece, a waterproof jacket, hat, and gloves. Turning carefully so that his increased girth wouldn't knock anything from the top of our new TV cabinet he gave me a meaningful look. "Are you doing anything useful at the moment?" he asked.

I stared around the sofa, my book lay face down on the cushion and my empty coffee mug had been knocked over. The blanket that I'd been burrowing into lay in a heap on the floor, it didn't look like an area that was being used by a busy person. "Yes?" Well, it was worth a try.

"I thought not." He nudged the log basket with his foot. "We could do with some more fuel." Grinning at me from under his hat he turned and headed out into the cold.

Watching him go I considered if mutiny was an option. Grabbing my blanket I wrapped myself back up and sat on the sofa. Nope, I wasn't going to get away with this. Eventually I couldn't put it off any more and after faffing about clearing the coffee cups away I sighed and went to find my own outside gear.

The wood was cosy and protected inside a small log store which, like a lot of other things at this time of year, was also covered by a heavy tarpaulin. Every time we needed fuel for the fire we had to battle with this frozen covering which seemed intent on staying exactly where it was. The wood was being used up at an alarming rate during this very cold snap and I knew that I would have to get into the store on my hands and knees to get to the back. I shuddered, there was no end of multi-legged "things" that liked to live in the protective dark of the wood store. I peered into the coal scuttle. Oh poo, we were out of coal as well.

Trying hard not to think about *Cold Comfort Farm*, I peered under the tarpaulin and did a good job of ignoring the scuttling shadows that rushed away from the sudden influx of daylight. "There's nothing nasty in the woodshed." I told myself firmly and inched my way under the tarpaulin.

Holding the tarp up with my back and shoulders I reached in blindly and grabbed as much wood as I could and passed it out into the log basket. I knew from past experience that four handfuls of short-sawn planks would be enough to fill it. Something danced lithely over my knuckles, light and hairy, it was there and gone within seconds. I drew a breath in and stayed still while it tiptoed off into the darkness. Well that was the end of anything resembling sanity. Grabbing as much wood as I could I threw it into the basket, all the while trying to ignore the imaginary hairy little feet across the back of my neck. Finally, I pulled out from under the tarp and stood up; breathing hard. I could still feel something huge and hairy dancing its way across my neck and shoulders. I pulled my hat off and frowned at the mass of dust covered cobwebs that festooned the crown. I brushed ineffectually at them and then gave up. Shrugging I pulled it back over my hair, my ears were getting cold.

Sam and Mortimer arrived back from their walk and I called Sam over to take the wood into the boat. He gave a huge sigh and trudged through the snow toward me. Eventually he made it over to the wood shed and glared up at me from beneath his long fringe. "I don't see why I should have to . . . ."

He stared at me and whatever gripe he had been about to make died on his lips. The blood fled his face and his mouth dropped open. He took a step back, his eyes fixed on my shoulder.

Knowing how my big butch son felt about spiders I rolled my eyes at him. "It's just cobwebs Sam," I said. "We haven't got much wood left and I've had to dig about at the back of the shed."

Sam shook his head and pointed at my shoulder. "Gah!"

I looked down and swallowed hard. Now, I'm not particularly bothered by spiders, I can pick them up and put them out. I can brush them calmly off if they're playing their usual yoyo tricks in the boat and land on my head. But even I jump when I'm taken by surprise and, quite frankly, the size of the one currently sitting happily on my shoulder would have surprised anyone.

I copied Sam's example. "Gah!" Convinced that this couldn't possibly be the only one, I ripped off my coat and, after shaking the spider off, dropped the garment into the snow, moving it around with my foot in an effort to entice out the other suspected hordes of arachnids that were sure to be hidden in the folds.

"Mum, that was HUGE!" Sam, once again, employed his wonderful ability to state the flaming obvious.

I ignored him; I was too busy trying to get the shudders under control. I was convinced that I could feel little hairy feet dancing down my spine and forced myself to leave my other clothes firmly in place. Naked screaming woman in the snow I'd already done once, I wasn't in any hurry to repeat the experience. Although, I suppose, at least this time I wouldn't be covered from head to foot in cow poo.

Sam warily eyed the basket of wood at my feet. "Can I put that on the front deck for a while?" He sidled toward me and picked it up with the least amount of hand contact that he could get away with.

I nodded. "Good idea." I watched him carry the basket away and, as quickly as possible, put the tarpaulin back in place. Those things that wanted to live in the dark could stay there.

21

At least there shouldn't be anything living in the coal bag. The irritation with whoever had left precisely seven pieces of coal in the bag got rid of the last of the spider shudders. I sighed as I headed back out into the cold and over the flood defences and down to the car. I heaved the 25kg pack of coal onto my shoulder and then, after only two staggering steps, dropped it back into the snow. Geoff always managed to do this with such ease but he was far stronger than I could ever hope to be. He seemed to be turning into one of those wiry types, all grey hair and stringy muscles that, if pushed, could probably lift a small car without seeming to exert himself at all. I, however, as I got older, seemed to be turning into a small overstuffed cushion.

I kicked the bag of coal and wondered how on earth I was going to get it up the slippery, icy slope of the flood defences. Well I wasn't going to let a bag of rocks beat me. So I opted for a sort of drag and push routine. I would take three precarious steps up the hill, dragging the bag of coal behind me, then stop, pull the bag around me and push it ahead. With this sort of strange circling dance, me and my bag of coal made it up the hill. I was almost at the top when I slipped. My only thought as I slid backwards down the hill on my stomach was that I was glad the coal had managed to stay where it was.

Cold and wet I headed back up the hill, wishing that, despite it being full of evil vampiric spiders, I'd put my coat back on. At the top of the flood defences I stared down the other steep slope toward the boat and with a shrug decided that if I could slip and slide down a hill so could the coal, and gleefully kicked the bag off the top. It did slide, it slid very well. Straight down the hill, over the edge of the riverbank and onto the frozen river. I watched it closely as it settled on top of the thick ice, waiting for the crack that would signal its watery demise. Nothing happened and after holding my breath for a couple of seconds I sent a small thank you upwards and slid down after it. Leaning out over the ice I grabbed the corners of the bag and heaved, intending to get the coal back on to the bank. The bag split at about the same time as the ice cracked. Twenty-five kilos of coal headed for the bottom of the river, leaving me standing on the bank with an empty bag in my hand. The next thought I sent upwards wasn't so grateful.

Geoff stuck his head out of the engine room and waved at me. "Is that bag empty?"

I slowly nodded; there really wasn't anything I could say.

"There's some more in the car." He gave me a big smile. "Can you manage one bag? I'm a bit busy at the moment. I'll bring the others up later." He looked down at his watch and shook his head. "Good grief, it's taken you almost half an hour to get out here? If you don't hurry up that fire will have gone out and we'll have to light it again." His head disappeared back into the darkness.

The next bag took twice as long to carry up, and more than twice as long to carry carefully down the other side. By the time I got back inside the boat my fingers and toes felt like ice lollies but everything else was sweating up a storm.

Sam wandered past with his head in a book. "It's a bit cold in here."

I gritted my teeth and decided that, for once, I was going to follow my mother's advice. "If you can't say anything nice, don't say anything at all."

The only place I was truly warm was at work. Addenbrookes hospital must have a huge heating bill because the place always seems to be somewhere in the balmy 80s. Monday morning and, clutching a supersized cup of coffee I shuffled through the office shedding clothes as I walked. I must have got rid of at least three layers before ending up at the bright pink shirt that was part of my uniform.

Throwing myself into a chair I stared at the glum face of my boss. "Erm. Good Morning?" At the complete and utter silence I began to worry. "Am I late, did you have a bad weekend?" Still no response. "What on earth's the matter?"

Angela, the manager, handed me a memo. "More redundancies, I'm afraid."

I stared at the memo. There, sure enough, was a long explanation of the problems the company had been facing. The only way they were going to stay afloat was to get rid of more staff. The first wave of people had already been removed and now it was only Angela and myself that covered the entire hospital which consisted of over a thousand units. I wasn't really surprised, with the all singing, all dancing new units that had been installed, we still found time to watch telly and relax.

"Well I guess I'm looking for a new job." Angela had certainly been with the company longer than me, it was a foregone conclusion. "Damn," I muttered into a cup of coffee, "I don't want to get a real job."

"Well, you've got at least three months." Angela produced a bag of cookies from her desk drawer and waved them in my general direction.

I took a cookie and dunked it in my coffee. Damn it all, I actually enjoyed this job.

When I got home that evening I grumped at Geoff. "Where am I going to find another job like that one?" I said. "It was perfect, the hours fit beautifully in with Sam's school. Apart from that I really enjoy wandering around the wards fixing the televisions. It's easy, the patients are great fun to talk to and I get paid for doing it."

Geoff handed me a cup of tea. "Well, you do keep saying that you'd like to go back to university and get your MA," he said. "Maybe now is the time to do it."

I shook my head. "I don't think we could afford it, especially if I'm out of work." I sipped my tea and stuck my lip out at him. "Good grief, I'm going to have to get a proper job."

Geoff laughed at me.

Really, the man has no empathy at all.

"Oh the horror," he said and then, heaving himself to his feet, headed toward the bathroom.

I waited until he was quite a way down the boat before I stuck my tongue out at him. I looked back at the list I'd been making of all the things we wanted to buy for the boat. We were still a long, long way from being finished. Even the bits that had been built weren't completed, not a lick of paint had touched any of it.

One of the additions to our boat had been a new kitchen. Geoff had built the frame, the doors, and drawers. We had then, due to our restricted budget, covered the working surface in tiles. I hated it.

I'd been warned by a couple of friends that using tiles as a work surface was a bad idea as they were a complete pain to keep clean. Unfortunately, due to the strange angles and sizes of the work surfaces, tiles had been the best option. Despite their practical deficiencies they looked fantastic. British racing green and cream, we had set them in a random pattern and, against the natural wood of the cupboards, they glowed.

Poor Geoff had experienced a certain amount of trauma building the units as my design had incorporated cupboards set at a forty-five degree angle. The design certainly got the best out of the space available but really caused him some constructional headaches. He'd spent at least a week muttering, "45 degrees, 45 degrees," and rushing around with protractors, tape measures, and bits of wood. I suppose I had been a little unfair because the first time he'd complained about the design I'd stated loftily, "Oh you'll work it out, you always do." He'd really had no choice after that, and sure enough he'd come through as expected and presented me with a beautifully crafted set of units and drawers.

26

After it was all finished he grudgingly agreed that it was certainly the best use of space and that he was quite pleased with how it had all turned out. I really didn't want to tell him that I'd changed my mind about the working surface.

We'd lived with it now for a couple of months and it didn't matter any more how good they looked; those tiled surfaces were fast becoming my personal nemesis. Food and liquid settled in the dips between the tiles and, although I'd taken to scrubbing the wretched surfaces with a scrubbing brush and some bicarb., the cream grout was rapidly turning brown. In some places, where water collected, the dreaded black mould had already begun to appear.

One evening, after I'd sat down to immerse my scrubbed fingers in a pot of hand cream, Geoff snapped his fingers and said, "Oh, I forgot to tell you — Vikki and Neil are moving house."

Vikki and Neil had been friends for years. Neil is the world's greatest scavenger and the lord of re-use, he had sheds full of "useful" bits and pieces. Most people save things "just in case" but he, nine times out of ten, actually finds a good use for them.

"Where on earth are they moving to?" I asked. "It's going to have to be somewhere pretty spectacular to house all his junk."

"Hey, it's not junk." Geoff's eyes lit up. "But no, they can't take it all with them. Neil's taking the stuff he really needs and he's offered me the opportunity to see if there's anything I want." He grinned and rubbed his hands together with a little chortle.

I sniggered and went back to rubbing the cream into the dried-out husks that I used to call fingers. "Hmm and of course you said yes."

"Definitely." He picked up a book and, pretending to read, hid behind it. "You're working next weekend, aren't you? I said I'd help them move and then I could see if there was anything we could use."

"Just remember we're short on storage space ourselves, try not to go mad," I said.

"Of course." Geoff grinned at me. "Perish the thought."

Oh dear.

Geoff was absent most of that weekend but, as I was working, we passed like ships in the night. Sam and Charlie were old enough to do their own thing now and the whole family rushed in and out of the boat with various friends in tow. I'd found that, like cats, if I left food out they could be trusted not to kill themselves or anybody else for a couple of hours. It was quite an odd experience; it had been a long time since I'd been free of "small child" responsibilities.

As expected, Geoff came home with an assortment of "stuff", an entire trailerful to be precise, and he was very pleased with what he'd got. A lot of it was wood and, I had to admit, I was pleased to get the additional winter fuel. Some was in such good condition that Geoff had got building plans for it. We spent most of Sunday afternoon trudging through the snow carrying logs, fence posts, sheets of ply, and other bits and pieces.

"Well that's it." Dusting his gloves off he grinned up at the towering pile of old fence panels, bits of tree and pallets that he'd salvaged from the depths of our friends' shed. "That'll keep us going for a little while."

Lacking only a sad-looking Guy, the pile of wood gave the impression it was just waiting for bonfire night. I gave the whole thing a worried look; it appeared to be listing quite extensively toward the boats. "Will it stay like that? It doesn't look very stable."

"Don't worry," Geoff gave the nearest piece of wood an affectionate pat. I held my breath as the whole structure swayed alarmingly. "I'll separate it out and put away the stuff I can use and then reduce the rest to firewood." He gave me a big smile. "What's for dinner? I'm starving!"

"Nothing, I've been running around with you all afternoon carrying wood about."

"Oh yeah," he said.

I understood why he was being more vague than usual, his head was full of plans and lists.

Well this was an opportunity not to be missed. "Tell you what, I'll go and knock something edible up if you don't need me any more." My gloves were soaked and I couldn't feel at least four of my fingers.

He nodded. "Great, give me a shout when it's ready." Humming some Status Quo song he turned away to dive happily into his big pile of wood. "Oh," he said, turning back. "We don't have any use for three slabs of black slate do we?"

"Where did they come from?" I edged toward the warmth of the boat. The kids had given up on the wood moving at least an hour earlier. Back inside the boat, they had put the lights on and Charlie had stoked up the fire, it looked wonderfully cosy in there.

"They were the tops of old lab tables." Geoff shrugged. "You know Neil; they could have come from anywhere."

"Yes," I agreed. "They could also be infused with e-coli or something else equally terrifying."

Geoff glanced up as he began dragging out what appeared to be half a tree from his wood stash. "Is that a 'no' then?"

I held my breath as the tall pile teetered and tottered backward and forward, pieces of wood slid and bounced as they fell from the apex. Eventually the whole thing settled into a sort of half slump. "Yes . . . That's a no." I beat a hasty retreat.

Standing at the kitchen window I watched him trotting backward and forward with his "booty". He was entirely happy. I grinned and waved a mug at him, laughing as I got an enthusiastic thumbs up. Filling the kettle I carried it over to the stove and leant on the work surface as I waited for it to boil. I know he didn't like to let a good thing escape but slate table tops, really? I looked around at my horrible kitchen work surfaces and then imagined them in black slate. Oooh, that looked good, and there would be no cracks for food to fall down, and they'd be so easy to clean.

No! God only knew what had been on those work surfaces. Cambridge is well known for its rather experimental sciences. Wherever Neil had got them from they could have been experimenting with Anthrax or something.

But . . . they'd look so great, but then how would we get them to fit? That forty-five-degree angle would be a complete pain. All this and more swept through my head and I stayed, leaning on the units and arguing with myself until the piercing whistle from the kettle caused me to jump.

I looked up to find the kids staring at me.

"What?" I said.

"You've been muttering to yourself for the past five minutes." Sam was looking a little perturbed. "Are you all right?"

"Sam, I've told you before." Charlie gave me her sweetest smile; it didn't fool me for a moment. "They're getting old and mad and we have to expect this sort of mental deterioration."

"Thanks." I concentrated on making the tea.

After dinner Geoff flopped down onto the sofa beside me.

Grabbing his arm I wound it around my shoulder, the man was like a living hot-water bottle. "Am I allowed to change my mind?" I said.

"I thought it was mandatory." Geoff gave me a big grin. "So what exactly would you like to change your mind about?"

"Do you think there's enough slate to re-top the work surfaces?"

"Oh. I'm not sure we can make work surfaces out of it." He put his mug on the floor, then, grabbing a pencil and his pad, wandered over to stare at the kitchen work tops.

He does a lot of "staring at things": walls, floors, the cat's cradle he calls the electrical system and, being used to this sort of behaviour, I settled down until he had finished "mulling".

After about half an hour he scratched his head and then sighed. "Do you *really* think they'd look good?" he asked.

I wandered over to stand beside him. "Does that mean that you *could* get them to fit but you'd really rather not go through the anguish of doing it?"

Geoff nodded slowly and we stood in companionable silence, both studying the problem in our own way.

Oh great, two of us staring at inanimate objects! It's no wonder our children think we're "odd".

The slabs of dull black stone turned up the following weekend. After bribing the neighbours with rum-laced coffee and cake we managed to drag the wretched things up the steep flood defences and get them positioned in the "garden".

I waved goodbye to our small troop of "lift it" people as they happily staggered back to their respective boats, dumped the last drops of rum from my once-full bottle into my cold coffee and began to gather up the various mugs and plates that were strewn along the top of the boat.

Although we have found that the neighbours don't need an incentive to help, any nasty job we ask them to undertake always seems to be a far gigglier affair if I offer "pirate coffee" as it's been dubbed. I've sort of shot myself in the drinks cabinet because now it's expected. Anyone that turns up to help always has that sort of hopeful look about them. Luckily, Geoff doesn't drink, he never has, so at least there is one sober soul to organise the group of sniggering, staggering helpers. He occasionally gets a bit grumpy that every little job turns into a social affair and it takes us all twice as long to get anything done but we do have a lot of laughs.

"Right." Geoff downed his tea and studied the slabs of stone. They were very, very thick. Each one was about five foot long, three foot wide, and a good two inches deep. "I don't remember them being this big in Neil's shed." He nudged one with his foot, it moved not an inch. "Do you think they may have swollen in the damp?"

Two mugs of coffee had rendered me pretty much incapable of rational thought. It took me a good couple of minutes to realise that he was joking. "Are you actually going to be able to cut these?" I said.

"I think so," he said. "I need to take some measurements."

"You don't need me then?" I planned to wash up the plates and then probably go and lie down in a dark room for a little while until the world stopped spinning.

Geoff looked up at me. "Feeling a little wobbly, are we?" He poked me in the shoulder and laughed as I had to take a step backward to steady myself. "I think a bit of hard manual labour will get rid of that feeling. What do you think?"

"Erm . . ."

He pointed down at the slate. "I've got some great gritty stuff that you could use to give these a really good scrub, it will just take the top layer of the slate off and get rid of a lot of those marks and rings and things." He grinned at me.

"I hate you." I grinned back. Oh well he was probably right.

Three hours later I was well on the way to getting frostbite in my fingers. I had, in order of importance: a hangover, pink wrinkled hands, a sore back, wet knees, one soaked foot, and a beautifully matching set of matt black stone sheets.

Geoff had been puttering around making plans and taking measurements, he wandered up carrying a jigsaw and a notepad. He studied the outcome of my efforts. "Wow!" he said. "They look really good. Nice one."

I squatted back on my heels with a groan and threw my rather shredded sponge into the three inches of tepid grey water that was lurking in the bottom of my bucket.

He ignored my obvious pain as he poked and prodded at the little nicks and dips in the stone face. "Well I suppose I'd better bite the bullet and start cutting," he said.

I nodded and staggered to my feet.

"Tell you what," he said looking up at me. "How about I make a start after lunch?"

I nodded again. Seemed like a fair plan.

Geoff looked at me hopefully. "So, what's for lunch?" he said.

It was only with the utmost restraint that I stopped myself from pouring the contents of my bucket over his head.

Over lunch he outlined his plan to cut the stone. "I'll need to use two angle grinders," he said.

"Why?" I pushed the soup around my bowl and tried to tune out Sam's complaints about how much he hated vegetable soup, even the "homemade stuff that smells like Dad's feet".

"Because I can only make short cuts; even using a stone cutting blade it's going to heat up really quickly so I'll have to keep swapping tools and giving one the chance to cool down.

"So, do you need me?" I looked around the boat. Sam, bless him, had done the washing up and the table was strewn with unfinished History homework. Not his favourite subject, he'd obviously felt that doing the washing up would be a good way to get out of doing it and get him some brownie points at the same time. "I really need to go shopping, otherwise we'll be eating veggie soup for the next week."

"Oh great!" Sam leapt to his feet. "I'll come and help."

He rushed off to find his coat and boots.

I groaned and, leaning over, gently banged my head on the table. It always seemed to work for my husband when he was feeling overwhelmed.

Geoff sniggered. "It's your own fault, you know."

"I know." I muttered into the wood of the table.

A couple of weeks before Christmas, Sam had announced that he knew what he wanted to be when he left school. Geoff and I had looked interested, both waiting for the usual "IT developer" or "Games designer".

"An accountant." Sam looked around in confusion at the stunned silence.

"Erm . . . OK." I'd tried desperately to get my brain around what appeared to be a fairly sensible idea. "Why an accountant, hun?"

"I like maths and I like money and I think I'd be good at it because you keep telling me I'm a pedantic little pain in the neck." Sam had given us a big grin.

I'd looked around at our "interesting living situation" and thought ruefully about our sad and tiny bank balance. "This is some sort of teenage rebellion, isn't it?" I'd said.

Sam had just looked blank as his dad laughed.

"I think that's great," I'd said. Then I'd had a *brilliant* idea. "Tell you what; just to give you a taste of the lifestyle, after Christmas you can take over the shopping budget. Any savings you make you can keep half."

Geoff choked on his tea; he obviously could see the problems with this plan that I had failed to divine.

Sam lit up. "Deal," he'd said.

I lifted my head from the table and glared at my grinning husband. "You knew what would happen, didn't you?"

"Yep." He got up and began to put back the multiple layers needed to head back into the freezing outdoors.

I carried on glaring at him as he chuckled his way out of the boat and then starting getting myself together. This shopping trip was going to be one long ordeal. As good as his word, Sam had indeed taken over the task of cutting our shopping budget and consequently his pocket money had increased by an average of five pounds a week. To make that saving however, took at least a hour longer in the supermarket than I'd ever taken. Every product had to be scrutinised, weighed, and compared. There were big discussions about luxury items, unless of course they were what *he* wanted, and we'd had some fair arguments in the aisles. Just to save time, I'd taken to letting him sort out the basics. Anything on the luxury list, I snuck back and purchased while he was at school. He was going to make a great accountant . . . if he managed to live long enough to graduate.

By the time Sam and I returned, frazzled, fraught, and missing quite a few things I felt we'd need, Charlie had come home and was helping Geoff move the first of our new worktops into place.

Dumping the shopping bags I stood and stared at the new black work surface while the family stared at me, waiting for the verdict.

"Oh, it's just gorgeous!" And it was, the black of the slate was beautiful against the tiles of the splash-back and, even more wonderful, it had increased the height of the surface by at least two inches which for my height was just brilliant. "I love it."

Geoff grinned as the boiling kettle began its panicked hooting. "Good, I'm glad you like it. You can make the tea."

"Oh, OK." I made the tea and handed him the steaming mug.

"Erm . . ." He grimaced at me. "Could you just put it down on the floor and grab me a tea towel?"

I shrugged and put the mug down. "What's the matter, have you cut yourself?"

Geoff shook his head. "Can you put the towel on my lap?"

Curiouser and curiouser. I laid the tea towel across his legs and stepped back wondering what on earth the problem was.

Geoff winced and looked up at me. "You're just going to stand there and watch me aren't you," he said.

I nodded.

With a sigh he reached down and picked up the mug of tea. I was shocked to see how much his hand was shaking. Despite obvious attempts to keep it under control, he slopped the liquid onto the carpet, over the arm of the sofa and then proceeded to pour a fair amount into his lap. Gritting his teeth in concentration he attempted to get the vibrating, quivering mug to his lips.

"Whoa . . . WHOA!!" I grabbed the mug and held it away from him. "What the heck is all that about?"

Geoff reached for his mug his fingers palsied and quivering. "It's from the stone cutting." He grasped one hand in the other and it looked as though he was trying to shake a dice. "I was at it for two hours straight and now I can't stop them shaking." He bit his lip and stared at his hands as they twitched and fluttered in his lap. "I'm sure it will stop soon," he said.

"O . . . K." I took his tea away and poured it into a travel mug. Securing the top well, I handed it back to him. "Try that."

"Thanks." He managed to get the mug to his lips without burning himself although he did manage to bash himself in the nose and chin a couple of times before he got the cup lined up.

Trying not to giggle, I looked around at the kitchen. "Did you only get the one done?" I winced as I realised what I'd asked.

"Yes, Marie." Geoff's voice had a grating, irritated quality. "I *just* got the *one* done."

I leant over and gave him a kiss. "One is great," I said. Then found myself something to do, very quickly.

With the terrible weather, the dark nights, and the general pile of other stuff that took up most of our time it was another two weeks before the second work surface was even attempted.

Geoff managed to find all sorts of reasons to put it off. Eventually I cornered him and threatened to make him drink coffee if he didn't tell me what the problem was.

He sighed and slumped onto the sofa. "Do you remember the last work surface I put in?" He asked.

"Well, yes." I glanced at the new black stone surface. "It was only a couple of weeks ago, even I'm not that forgetful yet."

"No, you twit." Geoff rolled his eyes. "Not that one, the opposite one."

I glanced at the sink still sunk within the green and cream tiled surface. "Well it's there." I shrugged, "what's the problem?"

"If you think back you'd remember how much trouble that caused me," he said.

I thought back and, yes, he was right. He'd had to recut the surface three times because he seemed to have a completely blind spot about where to cut the hole for the basin.

"I seem to have a complete blind spot about holes in work surfaces." Geoff shook his head and shrugged. "I can do far more difficult calculations than this. Every time, I just get worried and it all goes wrong. If I mess this up we can't replace that length of slate without spending a vast amount of money. I'm just really terrified that I'm going to screw it up."

"OK." I wandered off, grabbed the keys to the storage unit and without another word went out.

It took me about an hour to find all the bits and pieces I needed. Staggering back into the boat I dumped them all in front of Geoff. There was a roll of lining paper for walls, a can of contact artwork glue, charcoal lengths, and a craft knife.

Geoff studied the pile for a moment then looked up at me with raised eyebrows. "Very nice, dear," he said.

I ignored him. "We're going to make templates," I said. "You make one, I'll make one, and then we'll lay one on top of the other and check that they are completely the same. If they are, we'll take one and lay it on the stone." I picked up the aerosol can of contact glue and waved it at him. "We'll stick the damn thing to the stone so that it absolutely can't move and just to make matters even more sensible we'll draw around it with this." I picked up a white chinagraph pencil. "I knew keeping all this art stuff from college would come in handy."

Geoff grinned up at me. "And if it goes wrong again, I won't feel bad because we're both to blame."

I nodded. "Or between us we'll get it very right." I raised a fist into the air and said in a flat voice. "Yay! Go team us."

Three hours later and we had another piece of slate cut out and laying on the frozen grass. We both stood and stared at the white circle that was drawn in the middle. In all honesty, I stood and looked at it while Geoff spasmed and flinched. He'd been doing the cutting and was, once again, twitching like a globophobic at a child's birthday party.

"How exactly are you going to get that piece out?" I asked.

"I'm going to drill lots and lots of holes all the way around the pattern." Geoff alternated between making fists and shaking his trembling hands in the air. "Then I *should* be able to put a jigsaw down one of the holes and just do a quick dot to dot all the way around."

"Hmm ..." I stared down at the piece of stone. "Would you like a cup of tea first?"

Geoff shook his head. "Nope, there's no point putting this off, let's just get on with it shall we?"

I swallowed hard and nodded. "Why don't you use one of the angle grinders?"

Geoff shrugged. "They're really not very good at doing curves," he said. "And, apart from that, I only have one left, the other one blew up."

"Oh." I really hoped it was ours that had died and not the one we'd borrowed from our neighbour.

Within an hour we were carefully carrying the stone through the front doors. Leaning the piece of stone against the side of the boat, Geoff wandered over and stared at the sink. "Now, I'll have that cup of tea," he said.

As the light faded he finally managed to remove the sink and all its plumbing from the old unit top. We stood, balancing the stone work surface between us.

"Well, let's see if it fits." Geoff had that little crinkle of skin between his eyebrows that always appears when he's worried.

I laughed. "It's too late to worry about it." I hefted my end of the stone up and, twisting, forced him to follow me until the stone was horizontal. We laid it carefully down on the top of the unit, let it go and stepped back to study it.

"Oh damn it all," Geoff moaned.

"What? WHAT?" I stared down at the surface, the hole appeared to be exactly where it should be. I couldn't see what was upsetting him.

"We've increased the depth of the surface by nearly two inches." Geoff stuck his head through the hole and peered at where the taps needed to be placed.

"So?"

Pulling his head out of the hole Geoff grabbed the mixer tap and brandished the end toward me, it had a long screw thread, about two inches of it. "It's now too deep for this to fit." Staring at the wall for a moment, he stood and ran the tip of his tongue over his lower lip, one of those little habits that always helped his thinking process. Eventually he turned to me and grinned. The little crinkle between his brows disappeared. "I can fix that," he said. Dropping the tap unit into the empty cupboard below the newly cut slate he headed for the door.

"Hey!"

He stopped and looked back at me with a quizzical expression.

"We got the hole in the right place though." I gave him a big grin.

Geoff gave me an obviously fake confused look. "I never doubted it for a moment." He shrugged at me. "Why, were you worried about it?"

"Get out." I threw a cushion at him as he ducked out of the door and into the darkness.

CHAPTER
TWO

February's Sleet And Ice. Peace And Quiet Would Be Nice.

Saturday, the 4th of February and I found myself staring out of the window with a vaguely melancholy air. Of the twelve, February has always been my least favourite month. March isn't much better for weather, but at least it has the occasional promise of spring. February has nothing to recommend it at all. Rain and wind sweep across the flat Cambridgeshire landscape. With no hills to break up the view the vast grey skies seem to go on for ever. Staggering around in the ankle deep mud with the frigid wind whipping the tip of my nose and my ears into luminous red pain I couldn't find anything to enjoy at all. Even the wildlife wasn't bothering to venture out from whatever bolthole each animal had found for itself. The days, although short, seemed completely endless.

On this particularly unexciting February morning, Sam was playing some convoluted game on the computer, Charlie was still asleep, and Geoff was trying to find the enthusiasm to go and pump out the bilges.

As the kettle boiled my mobile chirped. I picked it up and grinned. Maybe my oldest, Amelia, would have some interesting news.

I didn't hear from Amelia as much as I really would like but, as she always reminds me, she is an old married woman, I have to accept that she has her own life now.

The luxurious wedding had taken place the previous July and had been terrifying, irritating, and positively gorgeous in equal measures. It had been a classical wedding with a marquee in the garden of Amelia's new parents-in-law. I was terribly grateful to Doreen, Chris's mother, for taking on a lot of the trauma. She was wonderfully organised and there was no doubt that without her input and skills the whole thing would have been a very different affair.

I have to admit at being torn between being horrified at the overall cost and slightly jealous that we just didn't have the funds to put more toward the opulent affair.

On the day, Amelia had gracefully stepped down the aisle toward the man who would shortly become her husband. I surreptitiously checked Chris's face for the telltale signs of possible flight risk but there were none. His whole face was just alight with happiness. Charlie, unusually decked out in a deep purple satin dress, stilettos and flowers, looked both uncomfortable and elegant. It's a real shame she shuns this sort of outfit — it suits her so well.

Helen, my paramedic friend, is a keen amateur photographer and had been drafted in to do the wedding pictures. She'd proved to be not only a great photographer but, when an elderly relative collapsed at the dinner, she and her paramedic husband, Dave, were able to get her sorted out and keep her comfortable until the ambulance arrived to take her away. They were certainly the heroes of the day.

Seven months later and the newlyweds seemed happier than ever.

"Hey, Mum." Amelia sounded a little upset, maybe I'd got it completely wrong, I hoped I hadn't.

"What's the matter?"

"Nothing, why would you think there's something wrong?" she asked.

"Just a little intuition: one, you're phoning me on a Saturday morning, two, you have your voice pitched just a little higher than usual, you sound slightly breathless and you're snapping at me," I said.

"Oh." There was silence for a couple of moments then she sighed. "Don't freak out, I'm pregnant."

Six entirely separate thoughts crashed through my mind at the same time. In no particular order they were: you're only twenty-four, you're too young, you can't afford it, aww a baby, you haven't finished your degree, but you're still *my* baby.

There was another thought however, that, growing in ferocity, it repeated and repeated, getting louder and louder until it drowned out all the others: I'M GOING TO BE A GRANDMA . . . NOOOOOOOOOO!

"Mum?" Amelia's voice broke the shocked cycle of panic that was threatening to reduce me to a puddle.

"Say something. Oh damn, I knew you wouldn't be happy."

"NO! No." I took a deep breath. "I'm fine, it was just a bit of a shock and I had to get my thoughts in order before I said anything." I picked up the thought that was threatening to make me cry and firmly squashed it. "Are *you* happy about it?"

"YES!" her voice changed completely, "Well, I am now that I've stopped being sick."

"So when is it due?"

"He, it's a him." She laughed. "I'm four months pregnant and I've had my first scan, the nurses wouldn't commit to telling me if it's a boy or a girl but I'm fairly sure it's a boy. He's due in June."

Arrrgh! That's only four months away. I was going to be a grandma in just four short months. I took another deep breath and forced a laugh. "That's great, really great! We get to buy the pram. I call dibs."

We chatted happily about baby stuff for another fifteen minutes or so and then she rang off, relaxed and cheerful.

Geoff handed me a cup of tea as I carefully placed my phone on the work surface. "Are you all right, Grandma?" He gave me a cheeky grin.

"I don't know why you're laughing." I took a big gulp of tea. "*You* get to be *Grandpa*."

Geoff blinked. "Oh yeah, I suppose I do. Well, how about that?" He wandered off with a smile.

The next morning I stared at myself in the mirror. Despite knowing full well that I was indulging in every tedious cliché that I could, I checked very carefully that

I hadn't been visited by the "granny fairies" overnight. No, I still didn't have a perm and my hair wasn't blue. I didn't feel the need to wear a pastel cardy, or learn to knit, and I already wore sensible shoes so that really wasn't going to be an issue. Being told that you are going to be a grandma does some very strange things to your psyche. You can fool yourself into believing that you are still young and daft until "that" word starts getting tossed around. Suddenly you worry about falling and breaking a hip. You worry that you are forgetting things more than usual and there is a vague acknowledgement that all the wrinkles that have appeared over the last five years have inevitably been leading up to "this" particular moment.

Luckily, two days later, I had Charlie to pull me out of my decline.

"Hey Mum!" She leapt through the doors of the boat and after throwing her helmet and leathers onto the sofa came rushing over and gave me a hug.

I hugged her in return and then stepped away. "What have you done?"

She gave me a big and obviously fake smile. "Nothing! Why do you always think the worst of me?"

"I don't think the worst of you . . . I know you." I bent down and gave her a hard stare. "Now, tell me . . . what . . . have . . . you . . . done?"

"Oh, all right." She flung herself onto the sofa, landing on poor Mortimer who rolled over and tried to suck her ears. "Now don't freak out . . . ."

Well this was a déjà vu moment. "Oh God, you're not pregnant are you?"

She laughed. "I really don't think that's likely, do you?" She ran her hand over the shorn sides of her head. The dreadlocks had recently come off after she'd found a spring from a biro and a dead spider matted in them and she had completely freaked out about it all. She now sported a short and wide blonde Mohican with dark sides. Like everything it looked good on her even if it was a little extreme. Being an art student pretty much meant she could get away with any style she wanted to.

"Drugs?"

"No!" She looked slightly horrified.

"Alcoholic? Armed robbery? GBH? Running away with the circus? Joining the Army? Murder?"

"No . . . Mum, for goodness sake let me finish." She got up to put the kettle on. Obviously the family habits do go down through the generations. "Actually . . . running away with the circus sounds quite like fun." She gave me a big smile.

I shut my mouth with a snap and perched on the edge of the sofa. I gave her an expectant look and made sure I said nothing at all.

She wandered up and down the boat for a couple of minutes while the kettle boiled and then made coffee. She handed a steaming mug to me. "Just watch that," she said. "It's hot and if you jump up and down you'll burn yourself."

Ah, so that's why we give people hot drinks; they act as a safety feature.

"How about you just stop prevaricating and tell me what you need to tell me." I took a sip of my drink.

"I'veleftcollegeandgotajob." She shut her mouth with a snap and winced, obviously waiting for the hammer to fall.

"What?" I put the coffee down. "I didn't get that at all, you've done what with college?"

"I've quit." She stared at the toes of her big boots.

Silence fell. I really couldn't trust myself to say anything supportive so I forced my lips together and just waited until my brain stopped shrieking.

Charlie, surprised by the silence, looked up. "I sort of expected some sort of melt-down."

"I am melting down." I forced the words between clenched teeth. "Just very, very quietly. How about you give me the whole story?"

She nodded. "I just got so fed up with the stupid rules and things I had to do. I'm fed up with having no money, I can't afford to run my bike, I can't afford to go out, the amount of homework means if I get a part-time job I don't have enough time to put into making the art really good." She sat down next to me. "I went to the college and sorted myself out an apprenticeship." She grinned. "I still get qualifications and I get some money and I really like what I'm going to be doing."

"And what exactly *are* you going to be doing?" I imagined that maybe an engineering apprenticeship or an apprenticeship at the hospital would probably be worthwhile, I could live with that.

"I'm going to be working at a crystal shop that specialises in holistic treatments and I'm going to be looking after their feet-eating fish!" She gave me a huge smile. "It's going to be great fun and I'm going to get a retail qualification which I can use anywhere. I really don't think I'm cut out for further education."

Feet-eating fish??? I wondered if she'd like to think again about joining the circus.

"Right." I took a long look at her. I could see a lot of downsides to this but, of all my children, Charlie was the one that was going to have to learn things the hard way. She wouldn't be told, she wouldn't learn from others' mistakes, she was going to carve her own way through life, swim against the tide, and she would, with sheer determination, bludgeon a life for herself despite being told she was probably going about it all wrong. If nothing else, I had to give her credit for sorting it all out for herself, at least she didn't just quit and then look to me for support.

"Well, I can't say I think it's the right thing to do," I said. I held up my hand as Charlie's face fell into her usual mutinous expression. "But I think you've done well to sort it all out for yourself and if it's what you want . . ." I shrugged.

"YES!" Charlie jumped up and after giving me a rather damaging hug headed out of the door toward her own boat. "Thanks, Mum." She gave me another hug.

"Hey, don't be so rough, us grandmas are fragile, you know." I laughed.

Charlie stood up and regarded me for a long moment. "I wouldn't do that if I were you."

"Do what?"

"If you start thinking of yourself as a poor old fragile grandma, you will become one . . . Self-fulfilling prophesy and all that." She gathered her helmet and leathers together. "You're no older than you were before Amelia called you," she said. "But I bet you feel a lot older now don't you?" She headed toward the door, then turned and looked at me. "You would do better to just think of yourself as young and fit, which you are." Opening the door, she climbed out and was away.

I stared at the closed door for a moment then shut my mouth with a snap. She was right, and with that sort of insight maybe, just maybe, she was heading in the right direction after all.

"Don't forget to budget for the new mooring fees." Geoff was wading his way through a pile of paperwork.

I couldn't help but pull a face at him. "Don't wanna." I muttered into my coffee.

"Well, that's an adult response." Geoff looked up from his bits and pieces.

"I don't wanna give you an adult response." I hesitated for a moment. "In fact what I want to do is stick my tongue out and waggle it every time I see the new owner."

Geoff snorted. "I'm sure that would go down extremely well."

The marina had been "given away" to a member of the previous owner's family as a present. Or at least that was the rumour that had been moving around the boaters. All we knew for sure was that, once again, we were "under new ownership". It wasn't going well.

Since they'd taken over in December, I'd only had the "pleasure" of meeting the new owners once and had been sadly unimpressed. I'd said to Geoff at the time, "If that woman has ever been on a boat it would have been large and white. There would have been Martinis (dirty of course) and the captain would have had the name of the boat etched onto the brim of his fake sailor's cap". With each passing missive that was issued by the poor put-upon administrator in the marina office, my statement was being proved more and more correct.

Tall, dark, slim, a look that said "I understand the rules of lacrosse" and with an accent that could have only been privately purchased, Mrs Owner had managed to irritate nearly everyone she had talked to.

She and her husband had their "big plans" for the place. That much she was more than willing to tell us and everyone else. Anyone that came away from talking to her and her "agreeable" husband (he seemed to agree with everything she said) came away with a slight twitch, it became known as the administration glare.

The fees rose, complaints were made to the boaters about how scruffy things were, and warnings that come spring "something would be done". She seemed to be going out of her way to make our lives as difficult as possible.

"Oh, hello there."

The next morning that cheery, cut-glass voice hailed me over the fence. I sighed heavily and for once didn't stop Mortimer trying to love someone to death. Her dog, which looked strangely like a skinny sheep on a piece of string, panicked at the heavy onslaught from the other side of the frail fence and tried to run on the spot, turning Mrs Owner in circles. I let it all carry on for a couple of seconds before my innate sense of fair play got the better of me and I hauled Mort away and sent him inside.

"Oh . . ." She huffed and untangled the sheep's lead from around her legs. "Thank you, he's a bit boisterous isn't he?"

I nodded. "Sorry, he's still a baby and he doesn't realise how heavy he is when he's being . . . *enthusiastic*. Luckily the fence keeps him in so at least he's not out terrorising the neighbours."

She gave a little laugh. "Yes of course, um, I wanted to ask you about the car parking."

"Oh yes?"

"Yes," she said. Frowning at me she took a deep breath. "You know we've asked people not to park on the flood defences. Come and have a look at it, look at all those deep grooves from the cars, it's becoming very messy."

I opened the gate and, drifting up the steps, joined her at the top of the floods.

She was right, the land beyond was a deep mire of heavy pits and troughs which were filled with water. It was a mess.

"You do realise that all those deep trenches were made by the electricity people when they came to put up the new pylons, don't you? Those over there . . ." I pointed to another set of pits and troughs, ". . . they were created by the railway trucks that were here putting in the new crossing last month."

54

"We don't want people parking on the grass, look at the mess."

I hummed experimentally; maybe I'd lost my voice. She certainly didn't give any indication that she'd heard me say anything at all. "Yes," I said, "I understand that, but we're not the ones making the mess. We have been parking there for six years and we don't do it in the winter, we don't want to get stuck in the mud."

"There's a nice car park down at the marina." Her voice became just a little more shrill. "We want you to use that."

Oh dammit all. I was obviously going to have to be a little more direct. "We don't want to use that." I turned and looked at her. Maybe if I maintained eye contact she'd listen to what I was saying instead of just running through her pre-planned monologue. "Can you imagine carrying a week's worth of shopping from the car park to here? The place is a complete mudfest. It's like a bad Glastonbury festival at this time of year. Five bags of shopping and a child weighed down by school stuff and in his school uniform. None of this is what I want to drag through the muddy swamp that is between the car park and here." I paused for a moment. "Would you?"

Her eyebrows shot up and she paused. I don't think that the idea of carrying shopping bags any distance at all had even occurred to her. She shook her head. "No, I suppose not."

"It's not just shopping." Feeling I might be actually making a point I ploughed on. "It's wood, it's coal, and it's coming home in the dark and the rain. You're suggesting that we all walk along the top of the floods? You've just come that way, look at your boots."

She stared down at her expensive leather boots; sure enough they were muddy to the ankle. "I see," she murmured.

"We're not trying to be unhelpful, but we have to live in this mud and we have to try to run normal, day to day lives." I wanted to add "We don't climb into our four by fours and drive away at the end of the day" but I stopped myself. "We have jobs, we have school runs and shopping to do. We don't all sit in our boats contemplating our navels until spring comes around and then float off to have fun, you know."

Mrs Owner studied me for a moment. Obviously the possibility of us having to "do" things hadn't occurred to her at all.

"What if we built a new car park down there?" She pointed to where the little road turned a sharp corner.

I nodded and treated myself to a silent cheer. "That would work very well and we'd be more than happy to use it, we could walk up the gentle slope to the railway line and then along the top. I think everyone could deal with that.

Her face broke into a big smile. "There, I knew there would be a compromise."

I nodded and grinned back at her. If every conversation went like this maybe the new owners wouldn't be so bad after all.

Both smiling at each other we headed our separate ways and looking up I was about to give her a wave when she spoke again.

56

"Oh, there was one other thing."

I tried to ignore the rolling, sinking feeling in the pit of my stomach. I was reminded of the 70s detective, Columbo, the man in the mucky mack. He always said "Oh, just one more thing" before delivering a stinging accusation or pointing out the huge gaping hole in the main suspect's alibi.

"Yes?"

"All of these fences have to come down." She turned to walk on.

What? No, no, no that would be a very bad idea, poor Mortimer would have to be tied up and that would just be terrible for him.

"Why?" I called after her.

"Because they're untidy," she said. She turned with the same look that I use on Sam when I'm having a long-suffering day and trying to get an obviously sensible thought across to him.

"I'm sorry you think so." I looked along the lengths of green wire held in place by long, thin steel pegs. The winter hadn't been kind to it and yes, if I was honest with myself, there were some places that could do with being a little more upright. "We could reset it all so that it's neat and tidy again."

She sighed. "I don't mean the fence is untidy, it's all untidy, the whole place. In the spring we want to start mowing these banks so that they're all the same length, take down these terrible steps and put nice new ones up, and all the boats will have jetties." She smiled and shrugged as though that concept was so obvious even a three-year-old would get it. "Don't worry," she called back toward me. "It doesn't have to be done until spring. But then everything will have to go, not just the fences." Gathering her dog/sheep up she walked briskly away leaving me fuming behind her.

I was still fuming when Geoff arrived home. "We need to leave." I bellowed at him as soon as he stuck his head through the door.

Geoff, obviously used to this type of behaviour nodded and walked calmly past me heading toward the kettle.

I bit my lip until he was settled and attentive then launched into a tirade. He heard me out and let me run out of steam before he spoke.

"We can't," he said.

Not really thinking the whole thing through, I again launched into the myriad of reasons why we should. No marina fees, no electricity to pay, freedom to do as we liked and go where we liked and, the biggest reason of all, not have to kowtow to the upper classes.

He nodded again. "All excellent reasons for heading out of here," he said. "I can't argue with any of them but we do have a few downsides that you seem to have forgotten."

"Like what?" I dropped onto the sofa and gave him a mutinous glare.

"Well, we've been concentrating on doing up the inside so that we can live in here," he said. "We really aren't equipped to be without an electricity hook-up just yet. I'd have to make all sorts of changes to get her completely self-sufficient."

I glared at my coffee.

He continued, wagging a finger at me. "The prop shaft is in bits." He began ticking points off on the finger. "We will need a generator. The lights will all have to be changed. We will have to lose the freezer. There will be no short walk to a washing machine." He peered at me just to check I was keeping up.

I muttered at him to show that I was.

"If we move, what do we do with the cars? With Charlie's little boat? How do we get Sam to school? Are we going to have to walk miles from where the car can park to home?" He shook his head. "We'd planned to get this all done by the time Sam went to college. We have three years before that happens, we're just not ready. If you wanted to seriously travel we should have done things in a different order and concentrated more on the systems rather than the comfort."

Having dumped a huge steaming heap of reality onto my fury he waited for me to get to grips with it all. Eventually I groaned and fell over, face first onto the sofa. "I hate changes; I like this the way it is, mud and all. I don't want it to become all 'homes and gardens'. First it will be the grass and the parking and fences, then she'll start moaning that the boats are looking skeezy."

"Well, ours does look like a wreck." Geoff grinned. "She has that sort of battered tin can thing going for her. It's a strange fashion but it might catch on."

I threw a pillow at him.

The next morning was a Saturday and we had been looking forward to a very long, warm lie-in. Not a chance. About nine o'clock we were woken by a hammering on the roof.

"Whasafufup?" Geoff surfaced from beneath the covers and struggled to keep his face away from the enthusiastic greeting of Mortimer who had once again managed to sneak into bed between us. How on earth does he keep doing that without us noticing?

I stuck my head under the pillow. "I don't know, but I can guarantee if they are hammering with that much urgency and at this ungodly hour in the morning it's not going to be for me."

Geoff groaned and fell over the end of the bed. He stuck his head out of the door. "Hang on, I'm naked," he shouted through the gap. There was a snigger from outside and a string of abuse. Geoff laughed and shut the door.

"Who?" I peered out at him from under the pillow.

"Drew," he said. He dashed about getting some clothes on and then disappeared outside.

I settled into his warm spot, irritating Mortimer who was lying there with his head on Geoff's pillow, comfortably cosy under the covers. He looked very human and happy. Tea, I needed tea, and obviously my husband wasn't going to do the honours.

By the time Geoff came back inside, the tea was made, Mortimer was sulking in his basket and the bed had been put away.

"What's going on?" I handed him a cheese and jam sandwich and a mug of tea.

"Some bloke's boat is sinking down the line." Geoff took a big bite of his favourite snack.

I winced at his obvious enjoyment of the horrible-tasting butty. "Whose?"

He shrugged. "Don't know him, he's the guy that lives in London and bought it to do up."

"What that really old blue thing that's now where Steve and Jude used to be?"

I stared out of the window at the sleet and wondered how our old friends were doing. They'd moved to Australia the previous year and occasionally posted pictures of vast blue skies and long golden beaches, happy children, and bouncy dogs. I really hoped they weren't having a terrible time.

Geoff nodded. "He bought it and then the weather's been so bad he hasn't really been back to look at it." He snaffled another mouthful of sandwich and washed it down with a gulp of tea.

"And?" I prompted him. Any time now I was in danger of getting a point to all this.

"Well with all the rain and snow the water's cascaded down from the back deck and filled the engine room."

"Oh dear."

Geoff nodded. "Drew's been trying to help but the electricity's cut out and they can't get the bilge pumps working."

"Ah." Oh well it all made sense now. "And I suppose they want you to go and sort out the sparks?"

Geoff nodded and drained his mug. "Yup."

For the rest of the day Geoff and Drew clattered backward and forward over the flood defences carrying odd bits of kit. At one point they both dashed off with a hoover. I felt that sorting out this guy's carpets might just be taking the neighbourly bit a smidge too far.

Eventually they both fell through the doors and collapsed on the sofa. I put the kettle on.

"How did it go?" I handed Drew a black coffee and went back to mashing Geoff's tea.

"Well, it's not sinking any more," Geoff said.

"Thing is . . ." Drew took a gulp of coffee and pulled a face at it. "If he doesn't keep an eye on it and come back to visit it more often it's going to sink again."

I sighed and waved my nearly empty bottle of rum at him, he brightened almost immediately.

"What's he going to do with it?" I tried to pour just a little alcohol into Drew's coffee but he pulled such a sad puppy-dog face that I topped it up. Well, that was another bottle in the recycling.

"He doesn't do anything with it," Geoff said wrinkling his nose at the all-pervading smell of alcohol. "He bought it as a project, something to do up and relax on."

I laughed. "Right, because these things are so relaxing to be around." I leaned on the kitchen unit and thought about all the "relaxing" times we'd had. Looking down at my hand I realised I still had the scars from some of them.

Drew laughed. "Narrow boats are like kids. Most of the time they're fine but take your eyes off them for even a moment and you can guarantee disaster, especially with the older ones." He grinned at Charlie as she dropped into the boat.

"What have I done now?" She sat on the step and stripping off her socks placed them carefully on the top of the log burner where they proceeded to steam.

"Nothing." I stepped over all the legs and removed her socks before they burst into flame then hung them on the back of the chair. "Have you ever considered putting shoes on to walk from one boat to the other?" I asked.

She shrugged. "My boots are wet as well, I've just come from the marina and there's a huge row going on in the car park."

She looked up from examining her toes as we all fell silent. "What?" she asked.

"Row?"

"Oh yeah. Some bloke's having a right go at the new owner." She went back to examining her pink wrinkly toes completely oblivious that we were hoping for more. Eventually the continuing silence made her look up again. "What?"

"Which bloke? What are they rowing about?" Honestly, teenagers would try the patience of a saint.

She shrugged and stood up. "I don't know." She rolled her eyes in exasperation at our stupidity. "I didn't hang around to find out." She sauntered into the kitchen and began turfing out the cupboards looking for something to eat.

Drew shook his head. "I hear all the fences have to come down."

I nodded.

He studied Mortimer who was currently splayed out on his back with his legs in the air in front of the fire.

"What are you going to do with 'stupid-head' over there?"

I shrugged. "I suppose he'll have to be tied up. If I don't restrict him somehow he'll be fine until some jogger or walker goes past then he'll be all over them like a cheap suit."

Drew snorted a laugh. "By the time he's finished with them they'll just be one quivering heap of trampled drool."

Mortimer snored and twitched, completely unaware of his upcoming restricted lifestyle.

Geoff shrugged. "He gets a lot of walks, he'll cope as long as we put him on a long enough lead." He frowned for a moment. "Actually I could put a long running line down the boat and we can link him to that, he'll have almost as much freedom as he had when the fence was up."

Drew shook his head. "I'll bet you a tenner he spends his whole life getting wrapped up in his own lead and you spend the rest of yours untangling him."

Well, I knew how bright Mortimer was, there was no way I'd take that bet. I jumped as Sarah, Drew's wife, hammered on the door. Mortimer also jumped at the sound and managed to bash his head on the log burner.

Sarah, commonly known as "Bill", battled her way through Mortimer's over-enthusiastic greeting and settled down on the sofa. I'd only just managed to refill the kettle and put it on the stove when there was yet another knock at the door. I winced, four adults, two kids, and a dog shaped like a piano stool was more than enough to fill any narrow boat, it was now standing room only. Keeping Mortimer back with one foot I opened the door and stuck my head out to see who was brave enough to walk all the way down the line to us in a wind that was rapidly becoming more than a little frisky. A bulky figure was silhouetted against the sky.

"Here, just a little thank you." A heavy bottle was pushed into my hand and with a wave the figure turned and walked away.

"Oh, erm, thanks," I called. He gave me another wave, then head down and collar up he made quick progress back toward the marina.

Back inside we studied the bottle. Large and black, it had a cork held down by wire. Worried by anything that has the potential to go "bang" I regarded it with a raft of suspicion.

"Is that champagne?" Bill peered over my shoulder as I was trying to work out what I'd been given.

"No, it says Cava." I looked up at Geoff. "Can you have ten-year-old Cava?"

He looked blank. "How on earth would I know? I haven't had a drink since I was eighteen." He took the bottle from me and turned it around in his hands. "I'm not even sure I know what Cava is." He handed it back to me.

We all looked at each other then shrugged. "It was for you as well, and Geoff doesn't drink, do you want it?" I held it out toward Drew.

He shook his head. "Nah," he said. "You keep it, but I'll tell you what, put the kettle on again and see if there's any more pirate coffee. I'm almost certain you have another bottle in that cupboard of yours."

An hour later and we were all far too relaxed. "That's not going to be the end of it you know." Bill drained her hot chocolate and stared into the flames that were flickering red and orange behind the glass of the log burner.

I giggled. "It will have to be, unless we drink the Cava, I've definitely run out of rum now."

"No, you goose." She climbed to her feet and began fishing around for her hat and gloves. "The fences coming down, I think that's only the start of the changes they want to make around here." She pulled her hat down over her long ponytail with a decisive movement. "I have a horrible feeling, she's going to want to make some big alterations and we're all just going to be in her way."

I peered up at her. "You don't think she'd want the live-aboards out of here do you?" My happy fuzziness faded at the thought.

Bill scratched her hat. "I don't think we fit her idea of how life should be."

Geoff shook his head. "There's been a boating community here for at least fifteen years, longer I think. I can't see her getting rid of it, how would she pay the bills?"

Bill shrugged and dragged Drew to his feet. "I may be wrong, I hope I am." She grinned down at her husband who was having problems fitting his fingers into the right holes in his gloves. "I think we'd better be off before my best beloved decides it's time for a song."

Drew, coming from a robust Scottish family, was well known for falling into a giggling heap from time to

66

time. The first time I'd met him we'd been attending a re-enactment show. I'd threatened to do him actual bodily harm if he didn't stop singing outside my tent. Sam had been about three months old at the time and I'd just managed to get him to sleep, it was four o'clock in the morning, and I hadn't slept at all.

Unlike a lot of people, Drew doesn't get aggressive when he's had a little too much. He smiles, wants to be everyone's friend, then he falls over and starts singing. It was all rather sweet and predictable.

We waved them off and watched them go up the steps and along the rise toward their own boat parked two down from ours. As I turned, the lilting sound of some Scottish drinking song could just be heard echoing back on the wind. I laughed and shut it out. "Do you think she's right?"

Geoff had sprawled out on the sofa and was yawning hugely; it had been a long day. "No." He shook his head and then, closing his eyes, settled himself back on the cushions. "I can't see any reason why they'd get rid of all the boaters . . . some of them, maybe. Not all of us though, we're an easy source of income."

As his snores, and those of Mortimer, filled the boat I began looking for something to make dinner out of. I hoped he was right but there was just this little nagging voice that told me, this time, he was wrong

CHAPTER
THREE

Hooray It's March, The Sun Is Back. Beware Of Duckling Sneak Attacks.

Boaters, it has to be said, are a lot more like gophers than we would care to admit.

The first sunny day of March had everyone out and about. People we hadn't seen since the previous autumn suddenly decided to take a sunshine-filled constitutional. In little groups they wandered along the top of the river bank in an attempt to get some vitamin D and presumably to check that everyone was still where they'd last seen them and not at the bottom of the river.

All along the bank spring cleaning suddenly began. Various people decided to throw out clutter that they'd been refusing to acknowledge in the cold dark days of winter and small piles of grot began to grow outside each boat. It was quite sweet that there seemed to be a fair amount of grot-swapping going on. I had no doubt that the same would happen in the summer when the next round of cleaning out cupboards began.

Donna and Steve, tanned and relaxed from spending a winter in Thailand, arrived home and probably

68

wondered why we were all a little grumpy. They had only had a couple of weeks of the new order before they'd, very sensibly, hightailed it out of the country and had settled in the sun while the rest of us had battled snow, ice, and various other trials and tribulations.

Donna, normally small, dark-haired, and pale-skinned, seemed to have become a negative of herself. The woman grinning at me from across the fence was almost blonde, and her skin had turned a glorious coffee colour. For just a moment I was tempted to dump her in the river, I was so jealous.

"So, how was the holiday?" I leaned on the woodpile and winced as she shivered in a huge woolly jumper. "You should have been here, it's been wonderful," I said. "You missed all the snow, the cars that wouldn't start, the mud, the coal runs, and the frozen water systems." I gave her a big grin. "I just don't know how you could have let yourself miss all that."

Donna laughed. "I swapped it all for empty beaches and long swims in warm seas." She spent the next ten minutes telling me about beach huts and travel through exotic climes. She obviously missed it all and coming back to this swamp must have been a little horrific.

I wondered, is it better to not go at all and stick with it or, is it better to leave and just come back to the tail end in the hope that things are going to get better? I thought about for a while then went back to being jealous. No, it was definitely better to head south for the winter. Let's face it, thousands of birds can't all be wrong.

"So, how's it going here?" Donna peered over at the new car park. "When did that turn up?"

"No more parking on the flood defences, evidently we're making it scruffy." I couldn't resist just a slight dig.

"But, we didn't make it scruffy, it was all the lorries and trucks when they were putting that new pylon up." Donna frowned.

"Fences have all got to come down as well and all the gardens have to be cleared."

"Ack!" She stared around at all the junk we all had piled beside and on top of boats.

"It's all right; we don't need to do it yet." I shrugged. "She just said, 'spring'."

Donna rolled her eyes and huffed, "Well that's just going to be great, isn't it?"

I shrugged and nodded.

"Hang on," she said. "The fences are going to have to come down?"

I remembered that my next door neighbour had an almost incapacitating fear of dogs; it really didn't matter if the dog was large, small, vicious, or stuffed. She would go rigid and forget to breathe if there was one in the local vicinity. "Don't worry; we'll make sure Mort stays away from you."

She grinned in relief, "Thanks."

We chatted for a few more minutes then she disappeared back inside Steve's boat. I waved goodbye and then turned my attention to the woodpile. It had seriously decreased since the beginning of winter. Lifting the tarpaulin, I peered into the empty darkness.

Even the multi-legged things seemed to have moved out. Well at least we wouldn't have to re-locate all that wood. Peering around the back of the shed, I was a little disconcerted by the amount of "stuff" stacked there. There was far more than I had expected: large logs that were waiting to become firewood, bits of plumbing, saggy old walls that had been removed to make way for open plan living. It was all stacked neatly and had obviously been put there with the mental label of "To be dealt with later". Obviously, much later. I wandered away, if I ignored it maybe it would never happen. It was a method that had worked before and I was fairly sure it would work again.

There was a clatter behind me and Charlie, Sam, and Mortimer all leapt from the boat with matching grins.

"What are you lot up to?" I gave them a piercing look. "You all have that 'don't ask me what I'm doing because you won't like the answer' look."

Charlie shrugged. "Nothing . . ." she said.

Sam bounced up and down and cut her off. "We're going to get the push bikes out of storage and then we're going to tie them together so we've got four wheels and see if Mort's strong enough to pull us." He finally had to stop talking in order to take a breath.

Charlie thumped him on the head. "Sam," she shouted.

"What?" He rubbed his head and then promptly fell over as Mortimer took off after some walkers, dumping Sam on to his back in the mud.

I grabbed Sam's arm to pull him up and watched as Charlie rescued the walkers from a severe bouncing. "Well he's probably got the strength to do it." I paused for a minute then shouted up at Charlie. "Try not to break my dog?" I sighed as she grinned and waved then disappeared over the defences being towed by an over-eager, over-stuffed staffy.

"Hey! Wait for me." Sam shot off after them.

Geoff appeared from inside the engine room. "Was that all the kids disappearing?"

I nodded as he sidled across the grass and put an arm round my shoulder. "Does this mean we have some time together, just the two of us?"

I nodded again, I knew exactly what he had in mind.

"Good." He planted a big wet kiss on my cheek. "I think it's about time we cleared out underneath the dinette, there are things in there that haven't seen the light of day since we bought this wreck."

Yes, that was exactly what I'd expected him to say.

Two hours later and both of us, plus most of the floor of the boat were buried in damp mouldy paper.

"This is disgusting!" I moaned at him as he passed me yet another pile of old paperwork, green and grey with mould spores. The smell was making me positively nauseous. "Why is it all so wet?" I gave the paperwork a brief once over before dumping it unceremoniously into a black bin liner. I could almost feel the mould eating away at my fingers. I had to really work hard not to run screaming into the bathroom where I could use a scrubbing brush and bleach to get rid of the horrible feeling.

"It's just condensation." Geoff dragged out another handful of old paperwork. "That, coupled with our terrible habit of keeping every piece of paper we've been sent, is beginning to make papier-mâché down here."

I peered into the dark recess of the box that made up the seating part of the dinette. "This isn't going to get any better until we can get some ventilation in there, is it?"

Geoff shook his head. "No, and putting the new dinette in is going to be difficult because I have to try and incorporate a bed, and wardrobes and drawers."

He ran a hand over his short silver hair. "There's just so much to fit in."

I'd been struggling with his idea of putting in a replacement dinette for a while now. The problem was that I really didn't want one. I don't like them. I know that they are absolutely classical narrow boat fittings but it really didn't fit in with our lifestyle and, more than anything, we needed a place to put the computers and create somewhere to work.

Nonchalantly tying up the last black plastic bag I wandered over to put the kettle on. "I don't suppose there's any leeway on your thoughts about that dinette you want to make is there?" I turned and began washing my hands in the sink. Then I washed them again, just to make sure. The smell of mouldy paper had given the boat that second hand bookshop aroma.

"Possibly," Geoff peered over the table. "What did you have in mind?"

"How would you feel about not having one at all?"

"I can't see how that would work." Geoff leant on the wall and stared into space. "What would you suggest we put here instead?"

I handed him a cup of tea and joined him against the wall.

"What about an office?"

There was silence for a moment.

"Go on," he said.

"Well if we take out the table and the seats, we'd have more space for a wardrobe and we could have drawers and shelves. We'd have space to put in that washing machine I've been lusting after and we could move the freezer from the grot cupboard by the bathroom into a space of its own."

"Hmmm." Geoff stared at the wall.

"Then we could have a desk and put the computer stuff underneath so that we don't keep tripping over it and they'd be all tidily away." I patted the partition that made up the short wall to the kitchen. "We could have a storage unit here for all the bedding and attach the desk to the back of it." I paused and looked at him. "It's a terrible idea isn't it?"

He was silent for a couple of minutes. "No actually. It isn't."

Well that was a surprise.

"I need some time to make some plans," he said.

That was my cue to hop it. "I'll go and find something to do then shall I?"

He nodded vaguely, completely lost in plans and space restraints.

I wandered off down the boat and wondered what I could do with myself for an hour or so. I had a new book that I wanted to read and there was that DVD I hadn't watched. I actually had some time to do something relaxing, which would be nice. Luckily I was saved from apathy by Sam crashing through the door holding what looked like a brake lever and some trailing cable.

"MUM!" He jumped down the step and held on to the door frame as he panted and heaved.

He'd obviously been running hard.

"Charlie . . . *puff puff* ran over Mortimer . . . *puff gasp* and she's on the ground . . . *puff puff* and this fell off her bike."

Geoff looked up from his plans and as one we almost trampled Sam into the carpet in our rush to get outside.

Charlie was still flat on her back in the grass. Geoff and I slid down the flood defences and my hammering heart slowed as she groaned and sat up. Mortimer slunk out from behind one of the cars in the car park that was about twenty yards away and came over to hide behind my legs. Geoff was lifting Charlie to her feet so I checked the dog over, he seemed fine.

"What happened?" I wandered over to them with Mort at my heels.

"That stupid dog tried to KILL ME!" Charlie shook Geoff off her arm and, reaching down, dragged her bike upright. "Look at this, he's trashed it, where's the bloody brake gone?"

"Sam's got it, he brought it in to show us." I clipped Mortimer to his lead. "So, what happened?"

"Mort was running beside me. Sometimes we were going at the same speed and sometimes he was giving me an extra bit of whizz." She winced and, pulling up her sleeve gazed mournfully at a beautifully grazed elbow. "Anyway, it was all going well, when stupid here decides just to turn left." She groaned as she pulled herself upright. "Ouch. I feel like I've been trampled." She glowered at Mortimer who was currently sitting on the ground scratching his ear, his long tail wagging gently and his mouth open in that classic, pink-lipped staffy grin. "So, he shoots right between the front wheel and the back, obviously he doesn't fit and we all come to a very sudden stop. All I remember is going straight over the handle bars as the back wheel went over the dog."

"You. Ran. Over. My. Dog." I gave her "the look".

"I didn't run him over, he ran under me. He tried to commit suicide and take me with him." She tried to take a step and moaned again. "Ow! My knee."

"Come on," Geoff said. He picked the bike up and put it over his shoulder and then let Charlie grab his other arm. "I'll give you a pull up the floods."

Charlie turned, "Is he all right?"

I nodded. "He's fine, but I think this may be the last dog/bike experiment, don't you?"

She laughed. "No, I think we ought to do it again but next time have a video recorder set up."

Geoff began to haul her up the hill. "Killing yourself for prize money really isn't the way to go," he said.

I watched them stagger off and shook my head. It had to be Charlie that got broken and it was always Sam that watched her do these insane things. When she'd fallen out of the tree in France and broken her coccyx he'd been the one that picked her up. He was also there when she'd decided that having a new pair of roller blades would give her superhuman abilities. She had put them on at the top of a steep hill in Durham and just let herself go. Sam had watched as she'd face-planted herself into a cattle grid at the bottom. It was no wonder he was a cautious child, he never saw his sister succeed at doing something dangerous and stupid. Well, there could be worse ways to learn a lesson, I supposed.

By the time Mortimer and I got back to the boat, Charlie was dabbing at the abraded bits of herself with a wet cloth.

"Do you have any actual punctures or is it just shallow cuts and grazes?" I wandered over to check her knee.

"Just grazes." She made a face as the water in her bowl turned alternately brown and then red.

Taking my Aloe plant from the top of the fridge I selected a sacrificial leaf. Collecting a sharp knife and my chopping board I laid the leaf down and carefully slit it lengthways revealing the juice and slime within. "Here, rub this on when it's clean."

Charlie nodded; she was used to this sort of behaviour.

Cuts and grazes were all right, all I ever did was rub gunk on them. Sore throats had to be really bad for either of them to tell me about it. The first thing I did was reach for the tincture of myrrh. It was a terrible-tasting substance. If they were willing to take that, I knew they were ill. Strangely enough they weren't ill very often.

By the time Geoff had completed his revised plans for the new office area, night was beginning to darken the sky, and I'd just finished making the dinner.

Charlie was in full flow moaning about her various scrapes and bruises and Sam had disappeared into computer world.

"Do you want to have a look at these plans?" Geoff wandered over to where I was studying the pile of washing up.

"Erm . . . Yeah." I picked up my big saucepan that was full of hot water from cooking the potatoes and groaned silently, I'd just filled the sink with bubbles and now I didn't have anywhere to throw it. "I just need to throw this outside."

Geoff nodded and went back to drawing cupboards.

It was cold on the front deck and, not wanting to spend any more time than necessary outside, I put one hand on the gunwales and began to tip the water into the river. A startled "quonk" stopped me in my tracks.

Peering over the side I squinted into the twilight. A group of very young, very early ducklings peered back at me. I panicked and, worried that I might inadvertently cover them in boiling water, I pulled the pan back quickly, and dropped it.

Boiling water splashed across the deck turning the whole thing into a hot and slippery nightmare. One foot went one way, the other decided not to join it, and down I went, the last thing I remember thinking was, it's a bit early for ducklings.

I woke up with a royal pain in the back of my head and Geoff's face looming over me. It had obviously taken him some while to realise that I hadn't come back in as I was frozen to the bone and soaked through. There were also various parts of me that were bright red and beginning to blister.

As he helped me to stand my stomach turned over and I had to rush to the side of the boat to be very ill over the side. My head throbbed and there was a warm, wet sensation in my hair. I put my hand to my head and it came away dark and wet. Geoff looked a little sick and for a moment I thought he was going to join me at the side of the boat.

"I think we'd better get you to A&E," he muttered.

I nodded and then desperately wished that I hadn't. The world swam like ink in oil and once more I headed for the side of the boat.

Accident and Emergency at Addenbrookes was, thank goodness, quiet and it didn't take long before a very young doctor was poking at the back of my head. Thankfully the nausea and the psychedelic vision had now subsided; all I had left was a raging headache.

"You were lucky." The nurse, who had taken over after the doctor had decided I'd got no brains to rattle, was applying steri-strips to my skull.

"I suppose I was," I said and winced as she applied another strip. "I could have decorated the front deck with all the pink and gooey inside my skull."

She laughed, "It's grey actually," she said. "I was thinking that it was lucky you fell backward. If you'd bashed your head and fallen forwards you'd have been in the water and unconscious."

"Eaten by ducklings, they were waiting for you to do just that, you know." Geoff put on a hollow voice. "There would have been no trace; just a set of very fat ducks and one, sad, floating slipper."

I would have given him a gentle slap but it was too much effort to raise my hand. "Anything left would have drifted ashore and Eric would have eaten it out of spite." I yawned. "I'm really tired. My headache's getting worse."

"Haven't you had any pain killers?" The nurse looked a bit startled. "I'll get you some; I'm all finished back here."

As she wandered off I put my hand to the back of my head. I couldn't feel anything, there was a big gauze patch on it. "How lovely," I muttered. "Draw a circle on this and I'd have a target."

Geoff sniggered, then his smile fell. "Are you all right?"

I nodded slowly and carefully, then grinned as the nurse came back holding a white paper cup containing tablets. "I'll be much better in about fifteen minutes," I said.

The children's concern lasted about twenty-four hours, the incredible headache lasted twice that.

Amelia was horrified. "You could have died." She screeched down the phone at me. "I don't need that sort of upset right now. I've only got two and a half months left."

Well, that brought me up very short. Ten weeks! Ten weeks and then I was going to be a grandma. My headache came back and I had to go and have a lie down.

Amelia had taken to pregnancy very well, far better than I ever did. Every time we saw her, she got a little bit more round and a little bit happier. I wondered if this state of affairs would last into the final days. The baby's due date was around Sam's birthday in early June. As Amelia had asked if I'd come to Cardiff for the birth I'd had to do some fast talking to get Sam to take a later birthday celebration. He'd taken it very well considering. Ever the one to make the most of the situation, he'd held out for a much more expensive birthday celebration than the one I had planned for him and had agreed to the compromise that I could say *when* but he had the final say in *what* we did on the day.

Geoff wasn't at all concerned about his upcoming change of status. Using the last of his holiday he set about building the new office and storage space.

As with most builds the initial creation of the desk, the cupboards, and the bedding storage should have taken about ninety per cent of the total time required. The reality is that you set aside some time and get ninety per cent of the work done. The other ten per cent takes at least another ninety per cent of the allocated time, or just never gets done at all.

Some of the work HAS to be done when the sun shines. Painting is one such job: the weather has to be warm as every window and every door needs to be opened as wide as possible. Meals have to be taken outside and the secondary job is occasionally rushing back into the boat to pick the dead mosquitoes and other suicidal bugs out of the wet paint. I have to admit I'm not keen on this job and in our last boat we had a vast array of tiny bumps in the paintwork. Each one marked a glossy bug tomb.

Geoff, however, was more than happy pottering about building the office. Apart from the slanted side of the boat there weren't any odd angles.

"It's so much easier when some pest isn't demanding forty-five flaming degrees." He punctuated each word by rapping me gently on the head with an old school wooden ruler.

I caught the rule and with a slight tug took possession of it. "I don't want anything at forty-five degrees this time." I gave him my sweetest smile and, holding one end of the ruler onto his new desk, I gave the other end a flick making the foot long length of wood go *boiiiiiiig*.

He grimaced at me and winced as I kept flicking the ruler, making odd noises.

"Good." He took a swipe at the flapping measuring stick and tried to stop me from being irritating.

I manoeuvred myself around so that he couldn't reach the ruler. "No, I want . . ." I stopped flapping the ruler and turned to face him with another big smile. ". . . a curve."

"Gimme that!" Geoff snatched the wooden stick away from me and waved it triumphantly over his head. "Mine . . ." He laughed and held the ruler onto the ceiling. After a couple of moments his face and the ruler fell. "What did you just say?"

"A curve." I marked out where I wanted the desk. "Look it could start here." I held my hand about two foot from the new bedding store he'd just finished building. "And it could sweep around the side of the boat and meet up with the edge of the new storage unit behind." I refused to look at him knowing full well that he would be going puce about now. "It would look lovely."

"No, no, no, no." Geoff stuck his fingers in his ears. "I did not hear you say that, therefore I don't have to take any notice."

I stuck my lip out at him and ignored his frantic humming. "But it would look fantastic. We could put shelves underneath and have books and all the paperwork that we needed in box files. We wouldn't have to worry about it all turning to mulch because it would all be nicely organised and out in the open." I knew he hadn't wanted to put shelves there because of the damp.

"Anything but a curve." Geoff gave me an anguished look. "I'm an electrician not a flaming chippy, I just can't do it without doing dovetail joints and all that sort of thing. It would take ages and I'm not convinced that the outcome would be very good." He stared at the wall for a moment. "Tell you what, how about a compromise?" He looked hopeful. "I'll take the panelling down, and reline that wall. Then I'll put the shelves there and I'll bring the desk around like a little plinth but it will have an angle not a curve." He scratched his head with the ruler, looked at it in surprise and then stuck it in his back pocket. "How about it?"

"Oh all right." I grinned at him. "I really would like shelves there."

He stared at me for a moment and then groaned. "That's what you wanted in the first place, wasn't it?"

I nodded and shrugged.

"There are times you know . . ." He left the implied threat hanging and wandered off to get a hammer to start taking down the panelling.

Mortimer had wandered up to see what all the fuss was about. I looked down at him. "I have a feeling I should make myself scarce for a little while. The sun's shining, fancy a walk?"

He wagged his tail and stared blankly at me.

I pointed at the door. "Where's your ball?"

At the word "ball" he bounced and took off down the boat like a rocket. Braking with all four feet just before he hit the step he scuffled around under the sofa and backed out holding his bright orange ball in his mouth. He doesn't understand every word I say but there are times when that dog understands just enough.

It was a nice day. There was still a hint of chill in the air but outside the world was taking advantage of the sunshine. Elaine and Dion next door had a gaggle of grandkids leaping in and out of their boat. Dion, completely unfazed by the furore that was going on around him, was calmly sitting on top of his boat with a fishing rod in his hand.

"Have you caught anything?" I hailed him as I waited for Mortimer to finish his investigations of the undergrowth.

"I'm not fishing." He took a sip from a can by his side.

"Oh?" I stared pointedly at the rod in his hand. "So what are you doing, gnome impressions?"

He laughed. "I'm staying out of the way." He checked to see if all the kids were still in sight. "Up here I can keep an eye on them and they're still too small to reach me." He gave me a happy thumbs-up.

I laughed and headed off toward the reservoir with Mort.

There is something glorious about walking in the sunshine with a happy dog. We stopped occasionally to skim stones across the sun-flashed water. Mortimer, who isn't very bright, decided that I needed a large stone from the bottom of the lake and kept sticking his head under the water to look for one. He finally selected a huge slab of slate which he dragged on to dry land. Being rather muscle-bound he didn't realise that it was longer than he was and proceeded to run around in circles, one end of the stone between his jaws the other embedded in the soft mud of the bank.

Leaving him to it I wandered off beside the water. Looking around I could see for miles. I always loved it here. There wasn't a house to be seen, boats chugged slowly up the river and occasional tractors could be seen puttering backward and forward planting whatever the farmer decided was optimal for that year. But it never changed; year after year the same things were done. It was one of the most restful places I'd been able to find.

Eventually, after I had managed to separate Mort from his rock and we'd completed a couple of circuits of the large reservoir, I headed back toward home.

The grandkids next door were keeping Jake, Dion's dog, occupied by rolling his ball down the flood defences and then laughing hysterically as the happy spaniel rushed up and down collecting it for them to throw again. He would lie on the top of the bank and if they ignored him for more than a split second he would pick the ball up, carry it over to one of the children and drop it on their bare toes, then sit back, white feathery tail waving frantically waiting for them to throw it yet again.

Into this happy group Mort arrived like a bowling ball hitting a bunch of skittles. Children scattered, giggling, in all directions. Jake, momentarily nonplussed, opened his mouth and his ball rolled down the flood defences and towards the boat. Hitting the concrete step that Dion and Elaine used to access their boat it bounced and with a little flip headed straight into the river.

I put Mort back on his lead and headed down the steps to retrieve it.

"Don't worry." Dion climbed down from the roof and picked up a child's bright green fishing net. "I'll get it." He shook his head. "He only drops it in there about twenty times a day."

I laughed and turned to see why Mort was pulling so hard on his lead. There was a huge splash and when I turned back most of Dion had vanished, all that was left were the soles of his feet sticking up over the riverbank.

There is an odd moment in any situation where your brain refuses to process what your eyes are seeing. Then all the information comes crashing in all at once.

At my panicked yell Elaine appeared at the boat door.

"What? WHAT?" She looked around, obviously counting grandchildren. When she had come to the number she was expecting, she looked down as Dion's wet head appeared over the side of the bank and sighed.

"It had to be you." She leaned over the side of the boat and watched him clamber, dripping and shivering, on to the grass. "I knew it wasn't one of the kids because Marie only gave a small screech, she'd have made a lot more fuss and there would have been a second splash if one of them had gone in."

"Are you OK?" I stepped forward and offered him a hand. It was really difficult to walk and laugh at the same time and my hand shook.

With a wet huff Dion ignored it and clambered out on his own. "You're laughing, aren't you?" he accused me as he shook himself like a dog. I noted that both dogs flinched and moved out of the way of the water, neither of them had dived in to save him. Lassies they are not.

"No, no I'm not laughing." I knew for a fact that my face was bright red and that I was shaking with the suppressed mirth. "Are you hurt?" People falling in the river is funny but there is a multitude of hidden dangers under the water.

He checked himself over and then shook his head. "No, just a scratch on my arm and seriously dented pride."

"Good." I gave him a big grin. "Now I'm going to laugh."

Dion stuck his tongue out at me.

"I am sorry about one thing though."

"What's that," he said.

"I just wish I'd had my phone out when you fell, I could have got that on video." I laughed again as, kicking his flip-flops off, he began picking waterweed and tiny snails out from between his toes.

"Thanks, Marie." He flicked a bit of weed at me.

"I'd have shared the money." I ducked and fled as he reached for a larger clump that was floating by his boat. Definitely time to make a sharp exit.

Talking to Elaine over coffee later, I did check that Dion was entirely in one piece.

She was definitely more concerned about the changes currently happening at the marina so I assumed he was fine.

". . . and not only that but I hear they're going to instigate a hosepipe ban," she said.

"What? Sorry, I missed that, the owners are saying no hosepipes? How the hell are we supposed to fill up with water?"

Elaine laughed. "No, you dafty," she said. "It's going to be county-wide. Evidently we haven't had nearly enough rain for the last two years and they're really worried about East Anglia. They haven't given a date yet but it looks as though we're going to have a water shortage."

"Oh, it won't affect us." I couldn't see how we could be stopped from filling our boats with essential water. Even at our worst we used far less than any normal household. "It's not like we all go out on a Sunday and wash our family saloons, is it?"

Elaine shrugged. "It's probably just the changes going on at the moment but I just have a horrible feeling that this is going to be one long and awful year." She laughed. "Well, that was positive of me wasn't it?" Gathering up the coffee cups she sighed. "Maybe I'm just feeling a bit down but I just have this sense of impending doom." Giving me a wave she headed back inside her boat.

Well that was two people that had a bad feeling about the upcoming months. I wondered whether Bill's sense of nervousness was spreading. One thing was sure, we didn't like change. I'd noticed that since the new management had taken over "the grumps" had been spreading like a virus. I resolved to not get involved. It would be far too easy for a mob mentality to emerge and when, one voice turns into many, it can be really difficult to separate real problems from the noise of outraged and possibly unjustified screaming.

The next day was a Sunday and I was awoken from a rather nice lie in by the boat swaying. I looked through the curtains expecting to see a stupidly fast boat disappearing into the distance. Instead, I was confronted by the odd sight of someone walking down the riverside gunwales. I jumped and suppressed a yell, I had no idea who it was, all I could see was a pair of legs.

"Geoff." I called down the boat. "Geoff!"

The legs bent at the knee and my worried-looking husband peered in through the window at me. "Yes?" He looked slightly alarmed at my yells.

I knelt on the bed and peered up at him. "What on earth are you doing out there?" I wiped the condensation from the window so that I could study him a little better. "And why are you holding a hammer?"

"Put the kettle on and I'll come in and tell you." Geoff stood up and the legs moved away toward the front of the boat.

I slumped back into the pillows and reminisced about the days that I was woken up by the clink of bottles from the milkman or the sound of post through the letter box. Those days were long gone.

Ten minutes later and the tea was made, the bed put away, and my husband was waving a hammer at me.

"This is all your flaming fault you know," he said.

Well, most things around here were so I just shrugged and tried to think of what I'd done that would need a good clobbering. I shook my head. "Sorry, you've lost me. I haven't poked anything recently, I haven't broken anything, and I'm fairly sure that nothing's dropped off."

"I want shelves on that wall." Geoff mimicked me. "It won't take long, just a couple of shelves."

I shrugged again. "I'm still at a loss how my wanting shelves means you have to cavort up and down the outside of the boat waving implements of mass destruction." I took the hammer away from him and placed it carefully on the work surface.

"Because that wall's damp." Geoff rolled his eyes as if that made the whole thing clear.

"So . . ."

"I took the cladding off the wall and found that all the insulation was completely soaked." Geoff ran a harassed hand through his hair. "So then I found that all the water was coming through the window above the new desk."

"OK . . ."

"So now I have to take the window out, reseal it, reseat it and make sure I've stopped the leak before I can put new insulation up and replace the wall." Geoff took a gulp of tea and glared at me.

I thought about it for a moment. "But, that's a good thing, isn't it?" Surely getting rid of as many leaks as possible was what we wanted.

Geoff picked up the hammer again. "The window's riverside, Marie," he said. "I don't really want a four-hour jaunt to turn the boat around just to do one window." He gave me a big grin. "So I'm going to do it while standing on the gunwales."

Now that was NOT a good idea. Trying to wrestle out a fairly heavy lump of aluminium and glass while perching on six inches of steel could only end in disaster. I was certain that Geoff could see this so I sighed. "I get it, bad idea. I know you planned to remove and reseal all the windows this summer, so we'll just wait until we do all the others."

Geoff sighed as well. "Actually, those shelves would be really useful, much as I hate to admit it. I don't want to replace that wall without doing this window and I can't really build the other bits I need until this wall's sorted out. I think it will work as long as you give me a hand."

Oh great! My sense of balance is possibly second only to my night vision.

An hour later and Geoff was ready to take out the window. Luckily he hadn't wanted me out on the gunwales with him; he wanted me supporting the window from the inside. I was more than happy to accommodate him.

I removed the top pane of glass and set it carefully down. The window wobbled alarmingly and I held on to the aluminium spar that ran horizontally across the frame and held the main piece of glass in place.

"Right." Geoff wiggled his fingers around the outside of the frame and gave a gentle tug. The frame came away from the boat and he let it lean at an angle on the bottom edge. "When I say *lift* we'll both lift together and then we'll angle it so that it can come through the space and you can take it into the boat, all right?"

I wasn't convinced about this idea. Because of the glass I only had a fairly tenuous grip on the bar, if this thing slipped away there was no way I'd be able to hold it. I pointed this out to Geoff who was busy studying the edge of the window.

"Don't worry about that," he said. "All we really have to do is swivel it while it's leaning on the boat and then you can move your hands to the edges and take it inside."

Oh well, that made sense.

"Where are you going to store it?" He studied the muck and old sealant that was hanging off the upper edge of the window frame. "You might want to put some newspaper down, if we get this on the floor we'll never get it off."

Leaving him holding the window I scuttled around putting newspaper down. Mort, obviously remembering this routine from when he was a puppy, came and sat in the middle of it. I took another five minutes to shoo him outside; a sealant-covered dog wouldn't be good.

Back at the window again Geoff and I took a deep breath together.

"Ready?" Geoff peered at me through the glass.

I nodded.

"OK," he said. "One, two, three, and lift."

For once, the disaster that followed wasn't my fault, it really wasn't. As we lifted the window from its housing Geoff caught his hand on something sharp on the roof. The first I knew about it was a spray of bright blood spattered across the glass in front of me.

Geoff yelped and pulled his hand away, letting go of the window frame.

As the window swung away and down Geoff stepped back to avoid being hit. He missed the gunwales and staggered, one foot dangling in mid-air. Letting go of the window he made a grab for the rail on the roof and hung there. The sudden weight of the window pulled it out of my fingers and away the window went down into the muddy brown waters.

Geoff clambered back on to the gunwales and took a moment to calm his breathing. He studied his hand and we both watched as bright droplets of blood chased the window toward the river bed.

There was silence for a minute or so.

Geoff edged his way to the front of the boat and, holding his hand to his chest, stepped in through the front doors. "I think I'd better wash this," he said.

I nodded and wondered if Dion and Elaine were at home. The last thing I'd dropped into the river had been the ash pan for the fire, their big magnet had dragged it out within seconds, very useful. As I walked up the boat realisation dawned on me. The window frames were aluminium — I could throw a hundred magnets into the river, that window wouldn't stick to any of them.

Deciding to deal with one issue at a time, I dealt with Geoff's hand. We didn't speak until the wound was cleaned and dressed and then only after I put the kettle on. "So what do we do now?"

Geoff wiggled his fingers and winced. "We hope that the fates are smiling on us and that window hasn't hit anything sharp on the way down," he said.

94

I poured boiling water onto tea bags. "Geoff, that window's aluminium, how the hell are we going to get it back without one of us going into the river?" I stirred the tea. "The river's about eight foot deep there, I'm not looking forward to going in and I'm really very unhappy about you even attempting it." I handed him a mug of tea. "And you certainly aren't going in with an open wound."

Geoff peered at me over the rim of his mug and gave me a great smile. "How long have we been doing this now?"

He didn't seem anywhere near as upset as I thought he'd be. "Coming up on seven years, on and off," I said.

"And how many things have we dropped in the river over those years?"

I started to think back and then decided there really wasn't much point. "Too many," I said.

"So, with all that experience, do you not think I would have a contingency plan?"

The man looked way too smug and my worries started to dissolve. "Probably," I said. "What did you do?"

He put his half-finished mug of tea on the side and waved me over to the empty space where our window used to be. "Watch and be amazed," he said.

I stood back as he leant out of the gap and rootled around outside the boat. Moving very slowly he pulled his arm back through the window space and smiled hugely as he showed me a piece of white string.

"You tied the window frame to a piece of string?" I supposed I shouldn't have been surprised; we had dropped a considerable number of items into the river.

Geoff nodded. "While you were getting newspaper, I noticed Sam's old broken kite on the top of the boat. I decided that it might be a very good idea to use the string as a safety line so I tied one end to the top of the frame and the other end to the anchor." He gave me a happy smile.

"Very clever, oh wise one," I laughed as within minutes I watched him pull the window frame up from the depths. We were in luck; the glass hadn't smashed on the way down.

It took Geoff about an hour to scrape off all the old sealant and apply the new to the outside of the boat. Eventually he gave me a shout to bring the window back. I'd spent a lot of time cleaning it while he was working outside so the window now sparkled and looked almost new. Resting the very edge of the frame on the hole in the metal wall I refused to push it any further out until Geoff re-attached the kite string. I was no stranger to the same thing going wrong twice.

Luckily there was no need. The manoeuvre was slick and tidy. Within half an hour Geoff had finished screwing the frame back into place and, after wiping away the excess sealant, was once more standing inside admiring his handy work. "Ta da!" he said.

"Hmm," I muttered non-committally at him as I studied the window. "I think you need to go back outside."

"What?" Geoff's smile fell away. "Why, did I miss a bit?"

I shook my head. "No, it's just that one clean window makes all the others look terrible. If I give you a bucket of hot water and a sponge and squeegee could you clean all the others?"

Geoff opened his mouth and, before he exploded, I shot away up the boat.

"You can go off people." He shouted after me.

CHAPTER
FOUR

Broken Neighbours, Tensions Brew. Thwarted Ducklings Plan Phase Two.

As our next door neighbour predicted, the hosepipe ban came into effect on the 5th of April. There was, as expected a lot of confusion about what we could and couldn't do with hosepipes. After about two days of discussions and worrying we all just gave up and carried on as usual. There didn't seem to be anything set in stone about filling up water tanks on boats. Without that water we wouldn't be able to drink or wash so we all just figured that we came under the "health" section of the ban and were exempt.

It didn't really matter, merely days after the ban came into effect it started to rain and it just didn't seem to want to stop. There were a lot of bad jokes about water shortages as we all sloshed about in the rain.

My poor car was definitely showing signs of leakage. There was at least an inch of water in the front passenger foot well and the children were beginning to moan about trench foot. It was definitely time to get another car as there was no way my current conveyance would pass its MOT.

I had to admit that particular car had been showing its age for nearly six months. Things had fallen off, the car was more rust than paint, and it was beginning to be an embarrassment on the roads. The only problem was that, despite the outside falling apart, the engine was excellent and I was more than a little loath to swap it for one that might well be prettier but might die on me at any time.

The day the MOT ran out, Geoff and I stood in the rain and waved goodbye to it as it bumped its way down the drive on the back of a flatbed truck. I turned to look at the new car. Charlie, who had just arrived home, came to stand beside us.

"What the hell is *that*?" She frowned at the new car as it squatted in a rapidly spreading puddle. "Have you ever considered buying something that isn't laughable?"

I studied the new car. A silver Kia Rio. We'd managed to pick it up for a song because, although its engine was excellent, at some point in its chequered history someone had tried to do a home paintjob on it and had only got as far as rubbing it down and painting it with silver primer. It was definitely spotty. It wouldn't have been so bad if the spots had been an entirely different colour but they were just the wrong shade of silver. It looked as though it was suffering the early stages of automobile leprosy.

"Do we always have to look as though we live on other people's giveaways?" Charlie snorted her distaste and stamped away up the flood defences.

Geoff looked at me. I looked back. She was right, it did look silly but, it was reliable, a good size, and it hadn't cost the earth. Really, looks weren't everything; at least our feet would be dry. I figured that if it kept on raining like this that was something we were really going to come to appreciate.

With my date for being made redundant rapidly approaching, I had spent a lot of time trying to find another job. Because we lived so far out in the sticks I didn't really want to work full-time. It would make Sam's day very long and of course it would mean leaving Mortimer to his own devices for a significant amount of the day which usually resulted in most of my clothes being used to make a "nest".

There was one position that stood out. It was full time, but it was a short-term contract for a huge drugs company. Due to start at the beginning of May, it would finish on the same day as the summer holidays started. Being a contract it was rather well paid which would give me the money to take the summer off with Sam and Charlie. I discussed it with Geoff and it was decided that the benefits far outweighed the drawbacks so I started the tedious application process.

I have to admit that I was more than a little nervous. This was a "proper" job in an office and I'd need to find some clothes that actually didn't make me look as though I'd fallen out of the pages of "Middle-aged, grunge, stinky diesel woman magazine". I tried to put it all to the back of my mind, after all, it was unlikely that I'd have the experience they were looking for. I hadn't done anything accounts-worthy for about ten years.

It was still very sad to be leaving the hospital and I was almost continually being stopped by people who said, "Oh, I hear you're being made redundant, that's awful, I'm so sorry." I'd met far more people than I'd thought was even possible. I was really going to miss them all and it made me quite maudlin. I had to accept that although I had to apply for this job I didn't really want it.

Geoff, happy in his job, had decided that shelves were quite a good idea and was now lining the corridor with bookshelves. He was in his element, happy to be building something and didn't really give me a lot of sympathy.

"Oh do stop moaning, it's done and there's nothing you can do about it." His voice, coming as it was from under a shelf inside a new cupboard he was building next to the bathroom, sounded hollow and muffled.

I addressed his wavering backside. "I know, it's just sad. Ever since we've been here we've just bumbled along and we'd got that bumbling down to a fine art. Oh well, if this is the biggest change this year, I suppose I can cope."

His response was too muffled to understand except for the swearing; *that* was quite audible. Evidently a piece of his wiring system was playing hard to get. He was trying to pull wires through the new woodwork in an attempt to bring light to the darkness in our grot cupboard. It was taking all his attention.

Feeling unloved and misunderstood, I sighed and wandered off to put the kettle on.

Charlie had been in her new job for about two weeks and was clearly enjoying the freedom. Arriving home with strange books on holistic healing or the powers of crystals she had turned into a sixties hippy and would give me long lectures on the importance of "grounding" on your anger chakra or something like that. I did try to keep up, I really did, but as soon as she suggested laying sparkly stones all over me and humming over them I have to admit I made my excuses and did a runner. Sam however, had completely fallen in love with her feet-eating fish. She had treated him to a foot treatment one Saturday. The shop had eight tanks with a small shoal of Garra Rufa fish in each one. The tanks were placed below plush seats and from the slightly worried looks of the women *enjoying* their treatments I decided to decline. Sam, after shucking his shoes and socks, shuffled onto one of the seats. He studied the fish that were currently swimming below his quivering toes.

"Don't think about it," Charlie instructed. "Just plonk them in."

Sam swallowed hard and after taking a deep breath pushed his feet into the fish-filled and tepid water. As the little fish fastened themselves to his feet his eyes widened and I could see it was taking all of his self-control to leave them in the water.

"How does it feel?" I watched as the shiny little creatures nibbled away at his toes.

Sam thought for a moment. "Like putting your feet into really bubbly lemonade," he said. "It's quite nice actually." He gave a little giggle as one little fish swam between his toes.

Leaving him to it, I went to have a look around the shop: cabinets full of crystals, books, and jewellery lined the walls. Stands of incense flanked the entrance to the treatment room and huge paintings of Buddha smiled benevolently down on those beneath.

Sam's giggles grew louder and although he tried to stifle them the tickled laughter kept breaking through the gentle sounds of whale song that were drifting through speakers set high in the ceiling.

A tall woman dressed in white poked her head out from the treatments room with a frown.

Sam ignored her and, gripping the cushion on the chair he was sitting on with both hands, howled with laughter. He rocked backward and forward in an effort to force himself to keep his feet in the water.

Thinking he was a paying customer, the woman shook her head and pulled back into the treatment room.

Sam's laughter was obviously infectious. The woman with her feet in the tank next to Sam's also started laughing, then the woman across the room. The sound of people giggling was really quite loud.

The curtain was pulled back with some force and the woman in white stepped into the room. Her lips had thinned and two small red patches marked her cheekbones.

"I'm trying to meditate," she hissed at Charlie.

Charlie shrugged. "Laughter is the best medicine."

The tall woman gritted her teeth and glared at my irreverent daughter. "I'm going for a coffee," she said. "I'll be back when the hootenanny has ceased." Turning on her heel she stamped toward the door.

"Sorry." I waited until the door had swung back with a jangling of distressed wind-chimes before I apologised to Charlie. I didn't want to get her in trouble.

"Ah, don't worry about it." Charlie shrugged and carried on measuring out fish food. "She always acts as though she's got a big stick up her ar —"

"Mum?" Sam lifted his dripping feet out of the water and studied them. "The fish have stopped eating me, does that mean it's all finished?"

I glanced at Charlie who nodded. "Get your socks and trainers back on." I really wanted to be out of there before the healer came back.

Sam shrugged and began to put his socks on. "That was really good, Mum, can we do it again next week?" He thought about it for a moment and then asked. "What would happen if I just dangled my feet in the river outside the boat?"

Charlie gave him her sweetest smile. "That pike that lives under the boat would remove your toes."

Sam swallowed hard, he'd seen those teeth only once. Last year they'd fleetingly formed a ring around a tiny duckling before snapping shut and dragging it to its watery death. He looked down at the fish swimming slowly around their tank. "Thanks for that mental image, Charlie," he said. "I've sort of gone off the idea now. I think I'll find some other way to keep my feet healthy."

104

Health was obviously on all our minds and Amelia was concerned about hers. As the baby grew she was finding it more and more difficult to dash about and, with her exams coming up and her energy levels dropping, I was definitely getting a lot of moaning phone calls.

One fateful day, around the middle of April, she called to tell me that she was in hospital.

I panicked.

"It's fine. It's fine!" she soothed me down the phone as I bombarded her with every question I could think of. "He just isn't moving too much and they want to put me on some machine that goes 'ping' for a while just to make sure he's doing what he should."

"Do you want me to come over?" I started listing things in my head that I'd need to take.

"Don't be daft, it's a two-hundred-mile journey. I'll be out of here before you even make it halfway." She laughed which turned into a bit of a cough. "I'll be fine." She heaved a heavy sigh down the phone. "I've got to go, Chris is here, I'll call you when I get home."

With that, she was gone.

I spent the rest of the day completely failing to do anything useful. With all the traumas about my job I'd forgotten how imminent the baby's arrival was.

Two days later she called me.

"Are you all right?" That was the first question I screamed at her as I answered the phone.

"Er . . . Yeah?" Amelia sounded puzzled and then her voice changed. "Oh damn, I was going to call you when

I got out of the hospital, wasn't I?" She groaned. "Sorry, Mum, I completely forgot."

"I've sort of had this low-level panic going on for two days," I said. "I've been trying to call you but it just goes through to your answerphone so I assumed that you were still in the hospital." I huffed at her for a bit. "I was just about to call Chris's mum and see if she knew what was going on."

"I'm sorry, I'm sorry." Amelia sounded genuinely regretful. There was silence for a moment and then she changed the subject. "So what are you up to?"

"I'm standing in a leaky boat, staring out at the rain and wondering if my daughter and grandson are OK." I wasn't going to let her off that easily.

There was silence on the end of the phone.

"Shall I call you back some other time?" Amelia sounded on the verge of tears.

I caved in immediately. "No, no. Now is good and I'm not mad at you. I was just worried."

"Chris knew what was going on," she said as if this was some sort of defence against my being forgotten.

I didn't want to upset her so I backed off a little, changed the subject and things were fine again.

It was only later that I realised that now, more than ever before, I was no longer her first port of call when the storm winds rose. Her husband was now her anchor and with a baby on the way that state of affairs would cement them into something really strong.

It's a hard thing to finally let go.

Geoff, for once, had managed to get home early and as usual was using any time that he had to work on the boat. I suppose I shouldn't have been surprised when I was handed a paintbrush and invited to help with the varnishing of the new desk. As we were slapping on the sticky substance, I noticed that a dark stain had crept across the ceiling.

"What is that?" I gave it a bit of poke, much to Geoff's annoyance.

"Condensation," he said as he gently slapped my hand away. "This boat is a terrible condensation trap and cooking with gas doesn't help: that just adds to the humidity."

"Does that mean it can't be stopped?" Condensation had been our biggest problem since the day we'd bought this boat. The windows always ran with water and, with the lack of heating in the bathroom, every time someone had a shower, the steam would condense on the ceiling and then a gentle rain would fall on us from above. The only way we were going to stop it would be to strip back to an empty shell, completely re-insulate the whole boat, fit new windows, and find an alternative fuel for our cooker. As we didn't have that sort of money to spare, the chance of this happening any time soon was minimal.

Happy go Lucky, our previous boat, had been much better ventilated and used diesel for cooking and heating. After a few leaks had been got rid of she had been a lovely dry and warm haven. *Minerva* was older and much less forgiving about giving up her full complement of interesting moulds and spores. I spent a lot of time washing down mouldy walls and cleaning the dirt caused by a mixture of condensation and smuts from the fire from between the metal runners on the windows.

"So how are we going to fix that?" I stared up at the ceiling.

"That's where I took out that old light you hated." Geoff studied the small damp patch above his head. "I think I've got something that will cover it. Tell you what . . ." his fingers rasped over his beard as he considered the problem, ". . . you pop down to the marina and pick up the post and I reckon I can have that fixed by the time you get back."

Well, that seemed like a good deal.

As I trudged through the rain I could hear Drew's ancient Honda motorbike making its way down the long drive. I waved to him as he came past me. But soggy, windswept, and intent on getting home, he didn't see me and I lost sight of him as he went over the hill and down into the marina.

As I rounded the corner, I could hear the bike engine screaming and watched as people ran across the gravel of the marina car park. Increasing my own pace I found Drew lying in a heap on the gravel and "Swampy", his ancient green Honda, was flat on her side with her wheels in the air the engine revving as though trying to take off. A long gouge in the gravel marked the point of upright failure and the subsequent slide and fall.

Stepping over the tantrum-throwing motorcycle I hit the kill switch and the engine sputtered into silence. Bob, one of the boaters that lived in the pond, was already checking Drew over. He looked up at me. "I'll call an ambulance," he said.

I nodded and wandered over to talk to Drew who was lying, groaning gently, on the grass beside the track.

I looked into his face and checked that he was conscious. I've known this man for a very long time and I know how many bike accidents he's had. "What's broken this time?"

He gave a shaky laugh. "Shoulder, maybe both but definitely one wrist." He winced and hugged the particularly injured arm closer to his side.

I nodded and we chatted for a while about what had happened as we waited for the ambulance to arrive. Eventually I looked up as flashing blue lights turned into the long drive. They were still just under a mile away but from our vantage point we could watch their slow progress down the drive. "Cavalry's nearly here," I said.

Drew nodded. Gritting his teeth and scrunching his eyes in pain. He tried to get to his phone. "I need to call Bill."

I stilled his searching. "I'll go and pick her up from work; they'll be taking you into Addenbrookes. We'll meet you there. I've got her number, I'll call her now and if she doesn't answer I'll just go and hammer on the door."

Drew gave me a shaky grin. "Hey," he said. "I asked you to do all that without moving my lips."

"Oh, shut up and get in the ambulance." I watched as Bob chivvied the paramedics into a decent parking place and then stood away. While the two paramedics checked Drew over, wincing all the while at his terrible jokes, Bob and I pulled Swampy upright and stashed her out of the way. She didn't look good and how he'd managed to crush both the left and right handlebars, I'll never know. "Did you actually see him come off?" I asked Bob.

He shook his head. "No. I heard the scrape and crunch and a complete dictionary of swearing and when I looked up he was face down in the gravel." He shrugged. "Why?"

"Well it's weird, look at the bike, it looks as though he's hit both sides of it. Did he flip it? Did it bounce? How on earth do you managed to crush both sides in one accident?

We stared at the bike and then at each other. Well, I doubted if Drew would remember what happened. Leaving the mystery for another day, I waved the ambulance off and, heading to the car, called Geoff to say he would have to pick up the post himself.

Within an hour Bill and I pulled into one of the staff parking places at the hospital. I waved to the nurse who had bandaged my head the night of the duckling-avoidance manoeuvre and she trotted over to see us.

"What have you done this time?" She stared at my head.

"Not me this time, we're here with her husband." I gestured vaguely at Bill who was hopping from one foot to the other. "Motorcycle accident . . ."

"Another one," Bill grumped with an irritated air.

". . . came in by ambulance probably less than half an hour ago?"

The nurse nodded. "Come on, I'll take you through to him."

By the time we found him, Drew had taken a fairly large dose of pain killers and was alternating between being in pain and terribly giggly. "I'm really hungry," he said.

"We'll get you something when they've patched you up." Bill shook her head at him.

Within a couple of hours Drew was sporting two rather nifty wrist braces and had one arm in a sling.

"Are we done?" I looked up at the doctor and started gathering my things together.

He nodded.

"Is he all right to have something to eat?" I could hear Drew's stomach rumbling from where I stood about five foot away.

He nodded and shrugged.

"Great, thanks." I waited until he had wandered off before muttering. "Very informative."

The hospital has a very large food court and soon Drew was ordering a burger and chips. With Bill holding the food we wandered back to the car. Drew clambered into the front and Bill hopped in the back. We positioned the food on his lap and made sure he was well belted in.

Munching away he seemed very chatty and bright. We drove through Cambridge and headed onto the A14. Concentrating on the road I wasn't really listening to Drew and Bill's conversation. It was only when she said, "What the heck are you talking about?" That I swung around to take a look at him.

The hand holding the chips dropped to his lap and, as he passed out, he was, silently, very sick.

Heaving in sympathy I hit the warning flashers and pulled the car on to the hard shoulder of the slip road. Bill and I leapt out of the car and between us man handled a completely unconscious Drew out of the car and into the recovery position on the grass verge.

A large set of headlights pulled up behind us and two very wary police officers climbed out of their car.

It must have looked very suspicious; two women dragging an unconscious man out of a car and towing him toward a dark hedge. It probably looked as though we'd murdered him and were trying to hide the body. It didn't help that I was still heaving and trying to control my stomach and Bill was desperately trying to get Drew to come round.

The silence continued for a moment. I honestly couldn't think what to say. Eventually I got my stomach under control and approached the female police officer. "Can you call an ambulance?"

Both police officers stared at me and then glanced at Drew then at each other. One took a step forward and asked, "What's going on?"

"Oh, for goodness sake," I yelled at them. "He had a bike accident this afternoon, he's been in A&E, they've

112

just released him, I'm taking them home, and he threw up and then passed out again." At this they sprang into action, one called for an ambulance the other trotted over to have a look at Drew.

Within five minutes the ambulance had arrived. I couldn't believe it, it was the same flaming crew that had picked him up from the marina.

"Hello again," one of them said as they stepped from the cab.

"Not again," said the other.

After a brief conversation with the paramedics the police took off and Bill and I followed the ambulance back to Addenbrookes.

"This is ridiculous." Bill stopped me as I was about to get out of the car. "You go home. We could be here for hours."

I got the feeling that worrying about me being bored and fed up was playing on her mind so I nodded. "OK, just make sure you ring me when you need a lift home."

She gave me a hug and took off back toward the emergency department. I was just getting back in the car when my phone rang.

"Hello?" I didn't recognise the number.

"Oh hello." A cheery female voice on the other end of the phone chirped in my ear. "You're on call this week and we have a blaring unit on the children's ward can you attend?"

I sighed and then laughed. "Well, yes I probably can."

"ETA?"

"About three minutes." I laughed.

"Really?" My answer shocked her out of her professionalism. "Have you moved? It usually takes at least an hour for a call-out."

"No, I haven't moved." I locked the car and trotted back across the road toward the back entrance. "The hospital has become sentient and is exerting an unusually powerful force on me tonight. I can't seem to get away."

"Well you were either in A and E or the staff bar," she laughed.

"Bingo!" I slowed down as I walked past the travel agents and the solicitor's office, Addenbrookes is a large hospital and has its own tiny village. "A and E."

"Oh dear," she said. "If you're sure you're all right, I'll tell them you'll be there very soon."

It took me about an hour to fix the television. Under normal circumstances we were just supposed to cut the power and leave it till the morning but leaving a child without a television just seems to make the parents crazy. Before I left I called Bill to find out if she needed a lift home, she didn't.

"They're keeping him in," she said. "He's asleep."

At least some of us are, I thought. I stifled a huge yawn and checked my watch. Midnight, wonderful. "I'm working here tomorrow — give me a shout."

She said she would and let me go. I staggered back into the boat at about one o'clock in the morning. Geoff was fast asleep and even the dog only opened one eye and then ignored me. My last thought before oblivion took me was that my car was still full of very smelly substances and that would all have to be cleaned out before I took the kids to school.

"They" do say that no good deed goes unpunished. "They" may well be right.

Bill and Drew turned up the next evening. With two broken wrists, a mashed shoulder, and high as a kite on prescription pain killers it didn't take Drew very long to run out of steam. Bill helped him back to their boat and then popped back for the shopping that she'd left on our front deck.

Helping her with the bags I had a sudden thought. "I take it this means that Drew won't be working for a while?"

Bill shook her head. "I'm not really worried about him working," she said. "With no hands and a broken shoulder he can't do '*anything*'." She frowned. Not one to usually let the irritating little dips in life get her down she was obviously worried about this. She turned to look at me. "This is going to be very difficult I think."

I contemplated all the things that we do on a day to day basis. She was right, it *was* going to be very difficult. I looked up at the cloud-filled sky. It had rained yesterday, today, and more was forecast for the rest of the week. So much for a drought, we were rapidly turning into a swamp. Without the use of his arms and hands Drew was going to find even simple things like climbing out of the boat and walking down the hill to the cars impossible. He'd do it, no doubt, but he would be in very real danger of face planting himself into the mud and breaking something else.

"Whatever you need." I handed the shopping bags over the front deck to her. "Tell you what, I'll give your number a different ring tone so that I know it's important and won't ignore you like I do everyone else."

"Oh!" She raised her eyebrows in mock outrage. "So that's why I can never get hold of you, is it?"

I decided to just pass that question by and laughed. "Any time for anything, OK?"

She nodded. "Thanks. I'll see you at the weekend."

With a wave she disappeared into the dark depths of her boat, no doubt in an attempt to go and put Drew to bed.

I stared at the side of their boat. A broken Drew was very likely to be a grumpy Drew. I hoped the pain killers kept him asleep for a good long while, otherwise Bill was going to have her hands full of frustrated tantrums.

As I wandered back towards the lights of *Minerva* it started to rain again. This life is great as long as you are completely fit and healthy. It's hard enough to do what we need to do with all limbs working. It's no wonder that a lot of us are rather obsessive about safety. One false slip and it's not just a case of sleeping in an armchair for a week. It's your whole life that gets thrown into disarray. I thought about those that boat alone, and, unusually for me, just sent a little request to anything that might be listening that they'd be kept safe.

The next morning Geoff was all smiles.

"What's got you so cheerful?" I'd just peered into the coffee container and found only damp smears at the bottom; I was not a happy bunny.

Geoff dug around in one of the cupboards and emerged with a dusty box of "real" coffee in one hand and an ancient cafetiére in the other.

Oh, you had to love the man.

"I'm working at the RSPCA today," he said.

"Which one?" I stared at the thick black liquid in the cafetiére, willing it to brew faster, the smell was fantastic.

"Wildlife," he said shortly. "I'm cleaning out their extractor fans and replacing some lights. I always like it there. Last time they had some seal pups in and a young fox."

"Lucky you." I finally managed to get a mouthful of coffee, it was bliss. "I'm taking Sam to the dentist, then back to school, then I'm going to the launderette, then I'm walking the dog, doing the shopping, bringing up those last two bags of coal, going back to pick Sam up from school, and then we've got a doctor's appointment to see about his nose bleeds. Wonderful day."

Geoff laughed. "What are you moaning about? It's your day off." He scuttled out of the boat before I could decide what to throw at him.

Standing in the launderette I realised that we didn't really get "days off". Living like this you just have to group everything together and do it whenever you can. Hoping that no one would mind, I dumped all my washing into one of the big dryers and then did a very fast supermarket run. The only way to fit everything in is to make sure you have excellent time management. I got back just as one elderly lady was about to take my dry washing out of the dryer.

"I'm sorry, I'm sorry." I panted as I rushed in. "I hope it wasn't in there too long."

"You can't just leave your washing in there and wander off you know, it's very selfish." She glared up at me from about four inches below my chin and then shook a gnarly finger at my nose. "We're all waiting for that dryer."

I looked around, there were at least four other dryers standing empty and silent. "I'll keep that in mind," I murmured at her.

"Make sure you do," she snapped at me. "I'm just going across to the shop to get some washing powder. I'll expect you out of that dryer when I come back, it's the best one you know and you're hogging it."

Well, there wasn't really anything I could say in the face of such righteous ire so I nodded and watched her leave.

"Don't mind her." A woman reading a newspaper spoke up. "Your washing must have finished about a minute before you walked in through the door; she's just a cantankerous old misery."

"Thanks for telling me." I gave her a smile. "I thought maybe I'd miscalculated and it had been about half an hour or something." I began taking the dry washing out of the machine and piling it on the side ready to be folded and put away. "Mind you, I'm not going to argue with her, scary little thing." I folded a towel and placed it in my basket. "It was like being told off by the wicked witch. I half expected her to wave a stick and turn me into a toad; I bet she's a demon with

118

her family. Husband terrified, kids buried in the back yard." I laughed.

"She's my mother." The woman glared at me.

The following loaded silence obviously helped me work; I'd never packed up washing so fast in my life. On my way out to the car I decided I probably needed to find another launderette. Or at least fit myself with a muzzle.

When Geoff walked in that night I couldn't wait to tell him about my mishap with the witch in the laundry and moan that if we had a washing machine like normal people this sort of thing wouldn't happen. I recounted the story and he laughed.

"One of these days," he said, "you're going to just keep your mouth shut."

"Well it's been nearly fifty years, I haven't managed it yet," I said. "You look a bit ruffled yourself. Did you have a rough day?"

"I did a bit." He took a long sip of tea.

"Oh yeah?" I plonked myself down next to him on the sofa. "So who did you mortally insult?"

"No one." He sighed. "I got taken captive."

"What?"

Now, to most people, this would be taken as a joke but I was the office manager for a maintenance company when one of our engineers was held at knife point. The rather confused lady on the other end of the very large, very sharp knife, rang me to tell me that I could have my engineer back when the parts for her boiler were delivered and not before. We'd had to get the police involved. I'm sure this sort of madness

119

happens more than people can believe. "I thought you were at the RSPCA, what grabbed you, an injured badger?" I was being serious, I've been backed into a corner by a grumpy badger — those things can be quite scary.

"Ducklings," he said.

Silence fell for a good thirty or forty seconds.

"Sorry, for a moment there I thought you said you were taken captive by ducklings." I swivelled around to get a better look at him. He didn't appear to be joking.

He nodded. "I was up a ladder replacing an extract fan in a pen with about thirty orphan ducklings in it."

"O . . . K." I was still baffled to see how little fluffy ducklings could have grabbed him. I mean, knock you unconscious and try to steal your soul, sure, but captive? They were certainly branching out their nefarious activities.

"Well I was up there about ten minutes," he said. "When I'd finished, I looked down and the ducklings had decided to climb the ladder. They were completely packed on to the two bottom steps. Those that couldn't get on were just running around and around the ladder. Those things move pretty quickly you know."

I started laughing. I tried to keep it to myself but I had this mental image of my rufty tufty husband stuck up a feather filled ladder, I knew exactly what he was going to say next and sure enough I was right.

"Well, I couldn't jump over them because with my great feet I was sure I would land on one of the ones that were rushing about trying to get on the ladder. I certainly couldn't climb down the steps because they were all packed on to them like little fluffy sardines, so there I was — stuck."

I snorted gently.

"The staff were at lunch and every time I called for help, it startled the ducks and they all shifted about, one was pushed by the others and it fell off," he said.

"Oh no!" I couldn't help it, I just couldn't keep a straight face. "Was it all right?"

"It seemed to be." He took another swig of tea and shuddered. "It just bounced down the steps, fluffed itself up at the bottom and came around and started climbing the flaming ladder again." He shook his head. "It was like that flipping penguin run game where the penguins climb up the iceberg and then slide down and another takes its place."

My face began to hurt just a little bit. My poor husband looked so mournful it was hard to keep it straight.

"So anyway, there I am, stuck at the top trying to whisper for help, I can't move because I don't want to shake the ladder, I've got a box of tools that's precariously perched on the top with me." He paused for a moment and rubbed his leg. "I was up there for about half an hour. I'd just got to the point of attempting the long jump when they started feeding whatever was in the next pen. With one clatter of a pail all the ducklings leapt off the ladder and rushed over to the door." He frowned and settled himself deeper into the sofa. "One of the staff came in and just looked at me, I must have looked completely insane, white and shaking at the top of these flaming steps. She asked me if I was OK, well there was no way I was going to tell her what happened so I just nodded. She gave me a very odd look as she walked out."

That was it, I howled with laughter and spilt my tea.

Geoff looked hurt. "That wasn't the end of it, my next job was in with a woodpecker."

"Well they're only little." I managed to get the words out between taking gulps of air, my sides hurt and my cheeks felt stretched.

"Little and angry." Geoff widened his eyes as he remembered his day. "I walked into the pen and this thing started screaming at me at the top of its little lungs. You could tell that it was using every woodpecker swear word it knew. It didn't shut up once the entire time I was in there, just kept screaming and swearing. By the time I left I had the shakes and a headache." He held his cup out with a sad look. "More tea?"

I managed to stop laughing long enough to take the mug.

"Thank God I don't have to go back for another month," he said.

I handed him his refilled mug. "I thought it was me that any wildlife, big or small, wanted to traumatise. I didn't realise it was a family thing," I said.

"I'm going to need all that time to get over the nightmares," he said. "I think I have post-duckling-stress-disorder."

I laughed and rubbed my head where the dent was still evident. "Don't we all, honey," I said. "Don't we all."

As the rain continued to fall we began to notice a strange smell permeating the boat. As soon as you walked in through the door this faintly sickening odour hit you in the back of the throat. I began to use scented candles, joss-sticks, and even aerosols. Anything that didn't smell of rotting meat.

Eventually I'd had enough. "What the heck is that smell?" I finally cornered Geoff.

He looked faintly surprised. "What smell?" He sniffed the air. "I can't smell anything."

Sam looked up from where he was doing his homework. "I can't smell anything either."

"I can." Charlie got up from where she was watching a film and opened one of the kitchen cupboards. She peered into the darkness. "I thought maybe some veggies had escaped and begun to form their own civilisation in the back of here, like last time." She got up and dusted her knees off. "But there's nothing in there."

Charlie and I wandered about sniffing like bloodhounds while Geoff and Sam watched us, both wearing identical looks of bemusement. They are very similar in looks and obviously neither has a good sense of smell.

"It's definitely here." Charlie tapped her foot on the front step.

"I think you're right." I stooped to take a final sniff of the step. "Is it the carpet, do you think?"

Charlie shook her head and took the top of the box that formed our front step. She wandered into the kitchen and sniffed at it. "Nope just smells like dusty carpet."

"Is it really that bad?" Geoff wandered over and began sniffing. "I honestly can't smell a thing."

I nodded. "It is that bad. What's under this box?"

Geoff shrugged. "Just those water catching mats, and then there's the floor and below that we're into the metal bottom of the boat." He lifted the box up and took it away. The sweet, nauseating stench wafted up at us.

"Oh YUCK!" Sam grabbed his nose. "I can smell it now."

Geoff looked irritated. "I'm going to have to get that bit of floor up," he said. "There's a possibility that a mouse or a rat has managed to get in and then couldn't get out and died under there."

The rest of the family all took a good couple of steps back.

He looked up and grinned. "I take it that means that the man with no sense of smell is on his own for this one?"

We all nodded frantically. If you'd put us in the back of a car we could have sold insurance.

"Whoever makes me a cup of tea doesn't even have to look in the hole," he said. There was a rush and scrabble as we all leapt toward the kettle.

"You're all pathetic." Geoff laughed and went to get his jigsaw.

It took him about an hour to find the source of the smell. A mouse; a very long time dead mouse by the level of decomposition that had already happened.

Unfortunately, all that was left was lying in about half an inch of water which, presumably, had managed to get in via the same hole as the mouse. It was a stinking soup.

By this time the smell was so bad that Charlie, Sam, and I had taken refuge in Charlie's boat. I took the opportunity to complain about her lack of housekeeping and irritated her by collecting stray socks that seemed to be trying to inch themselves under every available surface.

"Oh for goodness' sake, stop it!" Charlie grabbed the socks from me and shoved them into her dirty washing bag.

On the front of the bag it read, in stages, "One week, two weeks, three weeks, naked". By the way it bulged Charlie should have, by rights, been running about in the buff at least a week ago.

"You always do this, you always come in and take over," she said. Glaring at me she folded her arms across her chest. "This is why I'm moving out next week."

I nodded and coaxed another sock from beneath her sofa.

"I am!" She snatched the sock away. "One of the healers that comes into the shop said that I can rent a room from her if I hate living with you lot so much."

That got my attention. "You tell people you hate us?"

Charlie had the good grace to blush and, dropping the sock, she hurried over to give me a hug. "I don't tell them I hate living with *you*," she said. "I just tell them that I hate living so far out in the country. I want to live in town."

"But you're only just seventeen," I said. "You're supposed to hate living with us, can't you put up with hating being here until you're at least eighteen?"

Sam, sensibly deciding that the stench of dead rodent was probably preferable to the fracas that was just about to erupt, made a quick exit.

Charlie sighed and plopped herself down on the sofa. "She's a really nice lady, she's married and they have a spare room that I can have for fifty pounds a week," she said. "It's only available for three months and we decided that it would be a good way to try moving out and see if I can manage."

I wandered over to her rat cage and peered inside. Three pinched little faces of varying colours peered back at me. "I'll need to talk to Geoff about it," I said. I was really just playing for thinking time.

"What's the point?" Charlie stared down at her feet. "I'm going to do it. There's really nothing you can say to stop me. I'm going to be safe so you can't use that old chestnut to keep me here. I'm going to be warm and close to work. I really can't see what you'd have to moan about."

Taking a deep breath I decided to ignore that faintly facetious tone she always used when she felt I was trying to hold her back.

"I'm not trying to 'keep you here' as you so delicately put it. Good grief, you make me sound like a jailer. If you think you can cope on your own I won't stop you but here's the deal," I said.

126

Charlie glared at me, pinched her lips together and huffed.

I silently counted to ten and kept my expression very blank.

"What?" She began picking her fingernails.

"I go with you to take your stuff and if it's a pit or it looks like there's something dodgy going on you come out of there and home with me immediately," I said.

Charlie thought for a moment. "Fine," she muttered.

It wasn't a victory but it was as close as I was going to get.

Later that evening, with the kids in bed, I was restless and couldn't help myself. I paced up and down our tiny saloon. On the fifth or sixth pass Geoff grabbed my hand. "Will you sit down?" he said.

I sniffed and then wished I hadn't, the smell was still lingering and I held my breath for a moment to stop my stomach from rolling.

"I'll put the kettle on." Geoff heaved himself up from the sofa.

"Can you set fire to a couple of those scented candles while you're there?" I stole his warm spot. Mortimer stood up, stretched and then, mincing along the sofa, climbed on my lap. Well at least I didn't have to worry about the smell any more. A dog that heavy sitting on my stomach meant that I couldn't actually breathe at all.

Geoff leant on the sink and laughed. "Do you realise that you've gone bright red?"

I nodded and pushed my rather disgruntled hound back onto the sofa. "Is this going to happen again?"

"What, a mouse dying under the floor?" At my nod he shrugged. "I think I found where the poor little devil got in but I can't guarantee that I blocked it up completely," he said. "It was right in the corner, under the television cabinet. I was lying flat on the floor with my arm underneath the boards and trying to keep my face out of the smell. I'm not convinced I did as good a job as I might have done under easier circumstances or if I'd had the right tools."

"The right tools?" I tried to imagine what on earth he'd need to block a hole over an arm's length away.

He nodded. "A gas mask would have been good. At those close quarters even I could smell the wretched thing."

I sniffed and then wished I hadn't. "How long do you think it will take for the smell to go away?"

He shrugged. "I got as much water out as I could but it's going to take a couple of days for the dampness to dry out." He sniffed the air and Mortimer looked up at him in surprise. "I can't smell anything at all now," he said.

It has to be said that neither of us can boast a full set of senses. However, it seems that for those we have lost the others have tried to take up the slack. I am completely blind in the dark, I have no night vision at all (much to the amusement of my family) but I do have a fantastic sense of smell. Geoff on the other hand seems to be able to see as well at night as he can during the day but unless something is stuck up his nostrils and has a really damaging aroma he doesn't even notice it. I count myself lucky, due to his lack of ability to

128

smell, he doesn't have much sense of taste either. This caused quite a few sulky moments when we were first married and I needed to be complimented on my cooking. It never happened. Years later I'd worked out I could serve anything but unless it was tainted with scotch bonnet chillies or had alcohol in it, he would only ever comment on the texture.

"Well at least if it gets worse I'll be able to bunk in Charlie's boat," I said.

"I don't think Charlie would be very pleased with that arrangement," Geoff said.

I took a deep breath, I was actually going to have to say the words and acknowledge reality at some point during this conversation. "She won't care, she won't be there, she's moving out," I said.

Geoff did what he normally did under these circumstances and went silent. I had nothing else to say about the matter so there we sat for a couple of minutes. Eventually Geoff nodded and leaning over put the kettle on again. "She *has* been straining at the leash for a couple of months now," he said.

I nodded and felt glum.

"Is she going somewhere nice, is she joining the army, or has she found a squat?" Geoff frowned at the kettle.

I explained all that Charlie had told me and Geoff listened in silence. When I had finished he shrugged.

"We can stop her, we have that legal right until she's eighteen," he said.

He held his hand up as I opened my mouth to argue. "No, I don't think it would be a good idea to stop her,

I'm just saying that we could." He thought about it for a moment. "They all have to fly the nest sometime, some earlier than others. All we can do is catch her if she falls and make sure that when she does fall, and she will, she can't afford this, she feels that she can come back with no teasing or micky taking."

I looked up at him annoyed. "I've never teased her about things that go wrong," I snapped at him.

"I know that. You know that." He handed me a fresh mug of coffee. "Charlie, however, always feels that we are out to sabotage her life. It's normal, I think."

I sighed. "We'd better keep next weekend free for moving duties then, hadn't we?" I said.

Geoff nodded. "Two down, one to go." Pushing Mortimer out of his warm spot he sat down beside me. "Hey! You never know, I might get some of my socks back," he said.

"Don't count your chickens . . . or your socks before it happens," I said.

"How about ducklings?" Geoff laughed.

CHAPTER
FIVE

Boaters Fear Unkindly May,
Gales By Night And
Rain By Day.

Charlie, buried under a pile of clean washing, stared mournfully out of the window. "Is this rain ever going to stop?" she asked.

"I don't know, love." I huffed in exasperation as I found yet *another* DVD that I'd thought I'd lost and had paid to replace.

She looked over as I waved the case and had the good grace to look a little chagrined. "Sorry, Mum, I really didn't know they were all under there."

"Well you might as well keep them now," I said.

With two vehicles packed to the roof and her rats sitting in state on the front seat of Geoff's work van we were finally ready to move child number two out of our lives. I looked up and down her tiny boat; it looked very sad with no clutter to cosy it up.

I was surprised at the house in which she'd chosen to live. Very contemporarily decorated, there was no television, and hardly any electrical gadgets. But it was cosy and warm and the most important thing, as far as

Charlie was concerned, it had a bath. It was all she'd talked about for days.

I did understand. There are days when, if offered the opportunity, I would probably have sold something medically essential just to have an hour-long bath in deep, hot bubbly water. The type of baths that I'd spent at least twenty per cent of my life in before we took to the waterways. A long drink of something a little alcoholic and a really good book. Other people may dream of Ferraris or winning the lottery, I dream of having a nice long bath.

If anyone ever asks I tell them that it's the one major drawback of life afloat. Water, water everywhere but we are doomed to quick showers, ridiculously tiny baths, and hot water cylinders that don't hold enough to fill a bucket. The newer boats are much better equipped, some of them have proper baths but there is something irritating about having to refill your water tank every time you have one.

I peered into the bathroom at Charlie's new home and I had to admit I was a little jealous. Just for a moment, I considered asking if I could borrow the bath while the owners were out of the house. I didn't, I felt that it was possibly a little inappropriate.

Geoff staggered in with the rats' unwieldy cage and placed it carefully on the floor. "That's the last of it," he said.

Charlie nodded and looking around at all her worldly goods boxed and labelled, she appeared a little glum.

Geoff gave her a hug. "Call us if you need us," he said. "You know you can always come home. No questions asked. We'll miss you and your boat's just going to be waiting for you."

Well, that was a bare-faced lie. He'd spent the previous evening gleefully drawing up plans to turn it into a floating shed and workshop. Obviously, even when afloat, a man without a shed is a man missing something important.

Charlie looked up at him and gave him a big smile, she obviously wasn't fooled for an instant. "So you won't be putting anything in it while I'm away then," she said.

Geoff laughed. "I might store a couple of things."

Charlie rolled her eyes at him and, after giving him a hug, pushed him out of the door.

When we had put all her stuff away in a room that seemed to be only a third the size of her boat, I dragged her down to the supermarket and bought a week's worth of food for her. "This should keep you going for a while," I said as we staggered back, both with bags over each arm. Hmm . . . walking to a supermarket, well that was an interesting experience. I could see how this "living in town thing" might have its benefits.

I stopped when we got to her front door and placed everything on her front step. I gave her a hug. "You know you can come home at any time, right?" I seemed to have a lump in my throat and it was difficult to get the words out.

Charlie seemed to have the same problem. "Mum, I'll be fine, good grief I'm only twenty miles from home." She coughed and wiped her eyes with the back of her hand. "Go away." She gave me a big grin to take the edge from her harsh words.

I nodded and, with a last hug, walked back to my car leaving her waving forlornly on the pavement. The rain seemed to be getting heavier. It was a little difficult to see as I drove away.

The rest of that week the weather matched my mood. Heavy grey skies and cold winds made all of us grumpy and short-tempered.

"This is ridiculous," Geoff said. He rested his head on the window. "I've got so much to do to the outside of the boat. All that rust needs to come off. She needs priming and painting. We need to get her out of the water. I can't really do anything on the inside either because we need to paint and in this weather it just won't dry." He banged his head gently on the window and I winced as with each gentle bump there was a cold splatter of icy condensation that wet his hair.

I shrugged, there wasn't really anything I could say and to be quite honest I wasn't feeling that positive either. The rain filled the front deck and although we had drainage holes to empty any overflow into the river, the water was coming in faster than it could escape. Cascading down over the front step in three or four little rivulets, it had soaked through the towel I had put there to catch it and was rapidly soaking the floor. The other irritation was that the smell was back. I couldn't trace it, it was like some intermittent ghost that only seemed to haunt me when I was alone.

As Geoff walked back into the boat I grabbed his arm. "Please tell me you can smell it now," I said.

"I can't smell anything." Geoff sniffed the air for the tenth time that day and shrugged.

"Well it's not there *now*." I was beginning to become exasperated with the fleeting whiffs of awful sweet corruption that would disappear as soon as I'd been in the boat for more than ten minutes. I'd become so paranoid about it that I'd taken to burning incense almost continually and was living in a permanent sweet-smelling fog.

"I think you are losing the plot somewhat." Geoff waved a piece of paper at me. "Anyway, never mind that for a moment, have you seen this?"

I looked up at the ubiquitous white envelope that he was holding. I could see that "Mr and Mrs Browne" had been scrawled on the front. My stomach did a slow turn that was nothing to do with the intermittent stench.

I sighed. "Let me guess, they're putting the mooring fees up yet again."

Geoff shook his head. "No," he said, "it's worse than that, it's a completely ridiculous demand to get all the moorings cleared."

I flopped down onto the sofa and grabbed Mortimer for a cuddle. He was used to this sort of behaviour and obligingly turned himself upside down so that I could work out my woes with a tummy scratch. "Well, we did know this was coming, we'd been warned. When does she want it all sorted out by?"

"There is evidently a big clear-up scheduled for this weekend." Geoff scratched his head as he took a closer look at the letter. "Oh no," he said.

"What?" I didn't like the look on his face at all.

"They want *everything* moved," he said.

I shrugged. "Well I suppose the bikes can go in storage and the lawnmower as well . . ." I tried to think of something else that we have lying about.

Geoff carefully folded the paper and handed it to me. "They want *everything* moved," he said again. "*Everything.*"

I opened the letter and had a look. It didn't take very long for the words to sink in. "But if we move the log store all the lizards are going to be homeless. Where are we supposed to put all the wood and coal and what are we supposed to do with the fence?" I scrunched the letter into a ball and viciously kicked it down the boat. "We can't do all that over one weekend, especially a weekend that's going to spend most of its time raining on us."

Geoff stared vacantly at me, I could tell he was thinking and not really paying attention to anything I was whining about.

"Hmm . . . I'll be back in a bit." Geoff headed out of the boat leaving me fuming in his wake.

He was gone for about an hour and I started to worry that he'd gone to beard the "Owners" in their den and they'd buried him in wet concrete or something even more Hollywood. Eventually he stepped back through the door.

136

"Well," he said, "it seems that everyone feels pretty much the same way. It's not what we are being asked to do that's causing a lot of the rants. It's the time that we're being given to do it in." He paused for a moment. "And the threats aren't going down very well either," he said.

"Threats?" I retrieved the scrunched up letter and smoothed it open. "What threats?"

"Bottom line." Geoff peered over my shoulder and stabbed at the relevant sentence with a finger. "If we don't move all our stuff, they'll do it for us and charge us for the privilege."

I spluttered for a while. "So what are we going to do, just get on with doing what we're told?"

"I don't think so." Geoff gave me a rather evil grin. Let's see exactly how many people are irritated about this, shall we?"

I often say to people that as a couple Geoff and I fit together perfectly. I am fiery and impetuous and on the whole I'm usually my own worst enemy. Geoff, on the other hand, considers a situation from all angles and takes the road that leads to definite but boring compromise. This might sound a little dull but he gets the job done. I'm the one that wades in if we need a little madness in our lives; he's the one I follow when we need to "take a stand".

Another hour and he was waving his own piece of paper at me. "What do you think of this?" He grinned as he passed it over. "I think I've covered all the bases there."

I sat down to read. I was only halfway down the page when I began to chuckle. "Yes, honey," I said, "I think you've covered everything."

The letter he had concocted was obviously meant to include signatures from those in our boating community who were going to be affected by the latest list of demands. The letter started out with an assurance that we would always endeavour to cooperate with their programme of works. It then went on to state that the amount of notice we'd been given to complete these works was inadequate and, further, for them then to try and impose a charge when we could not possibly comply was beyond unreasonable.

He also pointed out that they had changed the rules yet again and were now asking us to move things that had been specifically classed as acceptable in a previous letter. He gave all the reasons why we have what we have outside our boats and gave very good reasons why the coal, the wood, and the fences need to stay. He quoted the marina rules and the date that they'd been set. In a *pièce de résistance* he then went on to outline the breeding season and habits of the common or Viviparous Lizard and warned that Mr and Mrs Owner were in danger of contravening the Wildlife and Countryside Act of 1981.

His very last paragraph asked for revision, consultation, and adequate notice of changes. It was all beautifully written and sounded more than reasonable. I knew that it was going to be a thorn in the paw of the lion.

By the end of the evening we had every signature except one. That one was understandable, the people in question worked for the marina. I could understand that, if they took part in this, the danger to their income was probably going to be considerable.

The very next morning he dropped the letter into the office and I sat back with some trepidation to await the outcome.

There is a very real danger to being the one that sticks your head above the parapet when trying to take a stand. You are the one that gets shot at. So, when Mr and Mrs Owner could be seen wandering along the top of the flood defences, I knew exactly where they were headed.

"Geoff, GEOFF!" I shook him awake and waited, hopping from one foot to the other in anxiety, as he slowly came to. He opened his eyes and sat up from where he was having a quiet nap on the sofa.

"Wha . . . ?" he said.

I pointed out of the window at the approaching pair. "I'm not getting involved in this," I said. "I know me, I'll lose my temper and just make things worse."

Geoff nodded and grinned. "That's fine, you chicken." He yawned hugely and stretched, humming "Ride of the Valkyries" by Wagner. "I know how much you love this type of situation." He stepped out to meet our nemesis.

I have to admit, I hid. Sitting myself down at the computer I drew the curtains. I told myself that the sun was shining on the screen and made it impossible to see what I was doing. From where I was sitting I could hear the sound of two raised voices occasionally punctuated by Geoff's much more measured and even tones. I felt terrible, I should be out there supporting him, but I was already in a major panic and as usual I would merely add another layer of aggro to the whole situation. He was wrong, I'm not a chicken, I'm a full blown coward.

Eventually all became quiet and Geoff wandered back into the boat with a grin.

I leaped up to put the kettle on for him. "So . . . how did it go?" I asked.

"You are such a wuss-bucket." Geoff flopped back down onto the sofa with a sigh. "We've been given two weeks to clear everything and the log pile gets to stay."

"I'm sorry, I just do angst so badly. I always make things so much worse." I did feel bad, but it was true, confrontations make me very uncomfortable.

Geoff glanced up at me. "It wasn't really a confrontation, pet," he said. "They weren't angry, they just wanted to make sure that we knew what was going on."

"It *would* have been a confrontation if I'd been out there," I said.

Geoff settled back onto the sofa, groaned as Mortimer climbed onto his chest and then closed his eyes again. "Just remember," he said. "Calm blue ocean, find a happy place."

I watched him as his breathing deepened and his hands relaxed.

"But I have found a happy place," I muttered, "it's here and they're threatening to mess it up."

Geoff just snored.

As May progressed the swans, coots, and grebes all built nests over the other side of the river and we watched with great amusement as "Battle of the Builders" moved from outright fights to hit and run skirmishes and quick-fire terrorism.

For the most part, the swans ignored the screaming squawking low-lifes that were the coots. Mr Swan was far more interested in attacking the odd group of canoeists that occasionally paddled past. Braving the terrible weather and paddling grimly toward a welcome pint at the next pub down, they were never even aware he was there. He would wait until they were level with the nest and then, screaming and hissing, he would try to climb into the cockpit of one of the canoes. We could always tell when he was trying to sink one of them as the screams and loud splashing from just outside our boat would be enough to wilt cabbage.

Despite the big swan's terrorist tactics it was the coots that caused most of the disputes between the various nesting families. For a small bird they were certainly the most aggressive and vocal. Eventually, the coots' constant raids on his wife's nest drove Mr Swan to begin SWAT tactics. He would hide in the reeds, lying quietly in wait until Mr Coot was almost at the nest and Mrs Swan was having mild hysterics. At the very last moment he would leap at full wingspread out from undercover and race, hissing and flapping at the surprised little vandal. Mr Coot, chirping and screaming in alarm, would perform a smart about-face and shoot off like a little arrow down the river back towards his own stacked and untidy nest. Mrs Coot, standing guard over her own clutch of eggs, would watch his approach with a certain long-suffering attitude. She would then stand up and scream abuse at the huge white swan. This abuse would continue long after Mr Swan had gone back to lurk amongst the reeds once more.

While all this was going on the grebes were pretending to be Switzerland. They maintained a haughty indifference to the warring factions on either side. Taking turns on the nest they would make sure that they gave each other time away from the tedious job of egg warming and would always take the time to have a brief cosset as they swapped over. They were incredibly sweet and managed to maintain this aloof indifference in the very midst of the loud, wet avian battles that were going on around them.

Until one fateful day.

Running screaming from the latest defending assault Mr Coot, shooting back down the river and away from the pursuing swan, caught sight of a small boat with two wet fishermen inside. Panic stricken and disorientated he obviously decided that the nest to the right of him was his and without even a peep hopped out of the water and into the nest right on top of Mrs Grebe (or it could have been Mr Grebe, it's difficult to tell), who was happily having a bit of a nap.

All I can say is that hell broke loose that day. Mrs Grebe's outraged screams obviously brought back-up. Unlike with the swans, there was no fancy splashing and honking, in fact we didn't see Mr Grebe arrive at all. Now back in the water after having been knocked off the nest by Mrs Grebe, Mr Coot was swimming in agitated circles and screaming abuse at the elegant looking bird above him. As we watched he went momentarily silent and I could have sworn his eyes widened and there was a definite "oh shit" moment. Mr Grebe had obviously arrived as silently as the nautilus and had come up beneath the small black bird. That sharp, pointed beak was used to devastating effect on Mr Coot's tender nether regions and he erupted out of the water like a dolphin leaping for a flaming ring. He took off up the river flapping, screeching, and screaming. We could only assume that Mr Grebe was shadowing the panicked coot underwater as every so often Mr Coot would leap out of the water and attempt to swim in mid-air for a couple of seconds. We had no idea how far he was chased but about half an hour later Mr Grebe arrived home looking very sleek and contented. Mr Coot arrived back about an hour later; he was rather wild around the eyes and looked very much as though he'd been put through a washing machine, his feathers and his demeanour were massively tousled. Mrs Coot was not impressed and, for the rest of the afternoon, there was loud screaming and peeping coming from the tall and untidy stack the coots called their home. Home sweet home? I think not.

After this the grebes were far less inclined to take such a laid-back view of the nest invaders. Every time that Messrs Coot and Swan started their little battles, Mr Grebe would dive silently below the grey green waters and as Mr Coot headed back towards his nest, beaten once again by the great white birds, Mr Grebe would help him on his way. He never missed and, by the end of the month, Mr Coot had developed a noticeably nervous twitch and would swim with his head on one side so that he could keep one eye on the water below his feet.

For the next two months we watched the birds and marvelled at their dedication. Despite the appalling weather, despite the hit and run raids by the coots, despite the mould that was growing on every nest, they just sat and hoped. The coots managed to hatch half of their eggs and paraded up and down the river with their tiny balls of peeping black fluff in tow. The great crested grebe eggs never hatched and eventually Mr Grebe got bored and wandered off. Mrs Grebe sat on the nest for another two days but, in the end, she too decided the weather and the incessant cold had obviously damaged her eggs and there would be no offspring.

The swans on the other hand refused to give up. Day after day Mrs Swan sat on the nest, her once sleek plumage becoming scraggy, scruffy, and positively grey. Mr Swan was obviously at his wits' end and had taken to swimming away from the nest and calling for her. She would climb down from the sodden pile of sticks and reeds they called home and would set off after him. She'd always manage about twenty foot before she would stop, hover in the middle of the river, dithering for about ten minutes and then she would head back to the nest and her beloved eggs that were obviously cold and lifeless. It was heart-breaking.

144

Eventually it was the coots that ended the sad saga. While Mrs Swan was having one of her moments of indecision, Mr Coot snuck up to the nest, climbed aboard and before she came back had rolled the eggs into the river and had destroyed the pile of reeds and grasses that the swan family had been hoping to call home.

Mrs Swan was visibly distraught and I had to physically stop Sam from throwing rocks at the coot. The sad and thwarted would-be mother stayed around for another twenty-four hours poking sadly at what was left of her nest. Eventually Mr Swan firmly collected her and together they swam away. We didn't see them again that summer.

We didn't really see much of anything else that summer. This, I put down to two reasons: one, it was raining so hard and so consistently that we were hard pressed to actually get out of the boat, and two, the windows were almost permanently steamed up.

Geoff, who was bored and becoming more dangerous by the day had decided to go through the paperwork. It was more for something to do in the dry than actually a job that needed doing.

Handing him a cup of tea I peered over his shoulder. "What's that?" I poked at the bit of paper he was holding.

He turned around with a frown. "This," he said, shaking the grubby paper, "is our boat safety certificate."

I lost interest. "Oh right. You haven't found anything like unpaid insurance claims or a couple of shares we didn't know we had then?"

"This is better," he said.

Obviously cabin fever had robbed him of whatever sanity he once possessed. "And, why exactly is that better than finding lost shares?"

Geoff jumped to his feet. "This is about to run out." He placed it carefully on the side and grabbed his boots. "We have to get another one at the end of this month."

I was very confused. "Well we just get an inspector in to give us a new one don't we?"

Geoff nodded. "But I've changed loads of stuff since the last one." He stood up and pulled his coat on. "If you want me I'll be in the engine room. It's about time I got that engine running."

With that he was up and out of the door. I groaned at the small personal weir of rain that cascaded over the front step in his wake and then looked around at the paperwork devastation. Great, that lot had to be cleared up, it looked as though I suddenly had a job as well.

A couple of hours later he reappeared. Sam and I were cooking and we jumped as he banged through the door.

"You do not look like a happy man," I said and put the kettle on.

Geoff dropped his wet coat into the space between the sofa and the wall with a heavy sigh and then set about making tea. I picked the soggy garment up and hung it up in our little coat space placing it carefully above an old towel that acted as a drip catcher. As I moved the other coats out of the way a waft of stink hit me. "That smell's back again," I called down the boat.

I grabbed a torch and peered into the darkness below the coats, the smell was definitely present but I couldn't see where it was coming from.

I wandered back down the boat to tell Geoff.

"That smell's back again," I said again.

He gave me a particularly haunted look. "I can't find my oil filter."

Not a response I was expecting so I just blinked at him. Eventually I realised I wasn't going to get any more information unless I pushed for it. "What oil filter?" I said.

"Well, that's just it, there isn't one." Geoff frowned into the depths of his tea. "I'm fairly sure there should be an oil filter on a boat engine; it's a big diesel engine. All engines have an oil filter, don't they?"

I gave him a completely blank look. "Honey, I have absolutely no idea."

"Well, where could it have gone?" He looked completely befuddled by the whole thing. "I know I deal with electrics and not mechanics but I'm fairly sure I'd recognise it if it was there."

I shrugged. "Can you see where it fell off?"

"That's the other odd thing," he said. "I can't even see the place where it ought to attach to. It just seems as though it never had one. But I think it should."

Our engine is an air-cooled Lister ST3. We have no idea how old it is but it's certainly a replacement engine for whatever was originally installed. If you look carefully you can see where a big square had been cut out of the roof for the purpose of winching said engine into place.

It's very big, very smoky, and sounds like a set of vintage motorcycles revving up whenever Geoff works out how to make the whole thing go.

Squatting like some sulphurous toad in its own pool of diesel, oil, and water in the very centre of the engine room, I am convinced that it laughs whenever I go near it. For that reason alone I try to have as little to do with it as possible.

"Is there anyone you can ask?" I winced and waited for the response; I know he'd rather just get on and fix things. He hates being "taught". Nobody goes at the right speed for Geoff's learning abilities and he gets bored and zones out.

"Nope, but I can probably buy a book," he said.

About an hour later there was a triumphant "Aha!" from over by the computer.

"So is it supposed to have an oil filter?"

"I have no idea, but I've found someone who is reprinting all the old vintage engine manuals. It's going to cost us a fiver."

I shrugged; I could live with that.

A couple of days later Geoff was blown through the doors with a blue book in his hand. He settled down to read, almost immediately making all sorts of little noises that meant he was learning vast amounts in a very short time. Later, while he was out of the room, I picked it up and had a flick through it.

Now, I don't consider myself a complete dunce when it comes to engines. I know enough to be able to check the oil, I know what the spark plugs, the HT leads, the coil, and the alternator do. I know how the basic engine works so I can usually hold my own in a conversation in Halfords and can occasionally fix my own car. This book was like reading something from Rudolf Diesel's original drawings, there were words in there that I'd never even heard of.

The first page I stopped at was talking about Sterngear. Well, that was OK, I knew about the stern gland and the stern tube but what on earth were plummer blocks? A couple of pages further on and the book was explaining the workings of the Listatex Anti-Vibration mounting and how to top up the Manometer reservoir, (the what?) Further on and the author became quite excited, extolling the virtues of a good oil feed to the Jabsco pump. There was a section on the Raised Hand Starting Assembly, the Cyclopac air cleaner, the coupled decompressors and the *piéce de résistance*, the Agglomerator.

Completely baffled I placed the book carefully back where Geoff had left it. I knew his cunning plan, he wasn't fixing the engine at all he was building a warp drive and he just didn't want to tell me about it.

The book obviously gave my husband the information he needed because he became quite blasé about the whole thing. I heard him discussing different viscosities of oil with Drew one Saturday.

"What on earth do you need specialist oil for?" Drew looked completely baffled. I knew how he felt.

"We don't have an oil filter." Geoff was much happier now that he had all the information. I'm happy to live my life in a permanent state of bafflement, my husband is not.

"You don't have an oil filter?" Drew winced as he rotated his shoulders, the casts on his wrists were still there and he was having a huge amount of difficulty with pain relief. No one had seen Drew laugh for weeks.

I stepped out of the boat with one coffee and one tea. Drew took his awkwardly with both solid hands and gave me a half smile before staring mournfully into his mug.

"Don't even think about it." I gave him a long look. "There's no way you're getting pirate coffee until you've finished taking those tablets of yours," I said.

As I left them to it I could hear Geoff explaining that the filter was an optional extra on our engine. They wandered off to have a look at this marvel of elderly engineering. I left them to it, at least they weren't underfoot.

"Drew's given me the name of his boat safety examiner." Geoff stepped back inside about an hour later. He was covered in oil and stank as badly as if he'd been swimming in a diesel reservoir.

I crinkled my nose. "Yuck," I said. "Dump those clothes and have a shower, you smell as bad as that engine of yours."

He handed me a piece of paper with a scrawled telephone number on and tried to give me a kiss as he went past.

I shrieked and, lips thwarted, he ran an oily hand down my face then, giggling, ran off down the boat.

"I think I might start her up tomorrow and see what happens." He obviously didn't need an answer as I could hear the water running in the shower.

Later, clean, fed, and generally warm and cosy he dragged out a scruffy bit of paper covered in lines of writing.

"Another list?" I glanced up from where I was sanding down the top of the new bedding box. The weather was driving me mad, the box needed priming and painting but everything was so wet it would take days to dry.

Geoff nodded. "We're never going to pass an inspection as we are at the moment," he said.

"So what's got to change?" I watched with a certain amount of consternation as drips of water appeared on my newly sanded wood. Looking up I could see that the rain was leaking through our roof hatch. Well that was just one more thing that needed fixing. If it carried on like this we would be more tarpaulin than boat. We had tarps over both side doors and over the cratch support at the front. At some point we intended to get a cratch cover but at nearly £700 it was just "on a list" and now we were going to have to throw one over the roof as well. This flaming boat was falling apart around us.

"Well, we need to get the gas installation certified," he said.

"But you put that gas in last year," I said.

He nodded and shrugged. "Yes I did, and I should have had it certified months ago."

I nodded. Like most things in life, there was always tomorrow.

Geoff continued. "I need to finish the engine repairs, I need to remove the diesel feed from the old heating system, the electrics around the battery bank need tidying up, we need to put ventilation into the bathroom, and the old favourite, sort out some fire extinguishers and a fire blanket for the kitchen." He frowned and stopped to draw breath. "I think that's about it."

"Oh, just trivial bits and pieces then," I said. "Hang on, we've got loads of fire extinguishers."

Geoff nodded. "And they're all wrong," he said. "That one there . . ." he pointed to the one nestled beneath the kitchen shelf ". . . is three times the size it needs to be. It has a higher fire rating than is needed for two boats."

I was confused. "That's a good thing isn't it?"

He shook his head. "No, it's just wrong so it's a fail and the other two are wrong as well."

I was still very confused. "So wouldn't they work?"

"Oh yes, they'd work but they're not right, they're wrong. So they'd fail." He gave me a happy grin. "Don't you just love regulations?"

"No, not really." I stared around at the fire extinguishers. "So have we got to replace them? They're very expensive."

Geoff shook his head again. "No, Blackadder, I have a cunning plan."

"Do I want to know about it?" Sometimes Geoff's "cunning plans" make me wince a little.

"Probably not." He gave me an innocent smile.

"Right," I said. "I'm going to wander off down this way with my fingers in my ears, OK?"

"You do that," he said.

The day before boat inspection day is always a trial. I spent my day rushing about cleaning, tidying, and making sure that there was tea and a new packet of biscuits. I'm sure that safety inspectors wouldn't take bribery well but there was no harm in extreme hospitality.

About half an hour before the inspector was due to show Geoff suddenly leapt to his feet with a yelp.

"What?" I was worried by the stricken look on his face.

"I need to chain the cooker down," he said. His voice wafted back to me as he made a bolt for the door.

Watching him rush past the windows as he headed toward the back of the boat I stared at the cooker. It looked back at me with obviously well feigned innocence. "Now why on earth would we have to chain you down?" I asked it.

Sam gave me a quizzical look. "Why are you talking to the cooker, Mum?" he said.

"Because evidently it's dangerous and needs to be in chains," I said.

"Huh?" He shook his head and went back to the model he was building.

Geoff jumped back through the door with two small lengths of chain and some screws.

"What are you actually doing?" I watched as he began screwing the chain to the box that the cooker sat in.

"It's part of the safety inspection." He explained as he used pliers to place the chain through two little rings on the side of our cooker.

I'd always wondered what those little rings were for and even when shown I still couldn't see what the chains were supposed to accomplish.

"But why?" I gave the chains a rattle. "What on earth is the point of these things?"

Geoff shrugged. "Stops it sliding off if we hit choppy water I suppose."

I looked out of the window at the mirror surface of the water outside. "Like that happens a lot to narrow boats does it?"

Geoff huffed. "How about we just do what needs to be done, and we'll discuss the idiocies afterward, shall we?"

I wandered off; I can take a hint, especially from a man with a hammer in his hand.

The inspector looked as though he was the same age as Amelia and I did my best to keep out of his way. There is something about a dour-looking man with a clipboard that makes me very nervous.

After the inspector had gone, Geoff threw himself onto the sofa with a sigh of relief. "Well, that's over for another four years."

"Did we pass?" I handed him a cup of tea.

"Barely," he said. "We've got some advisories and he did take a hard look at the extinguishers."

154

"Oh yeah, I'd forgotten about those," I said. "So what exactly was your nefarious scheme?"

Geoff laughed. "There are three extinguishers here that exactly fit what is required for the safety certificate."

"Here?" I wasn't sure I understood what he was trying to say. "Where here?"

"Down the line," he said. He took a sip of tea and then dunked a biscuit into what was left. "All that happens is that we all have inspections on different days, and we swap these three extinguishers about so that we pass."

"Oh good grief," I said. "Isn't that a bit immoral?"

"The whole thing is stupid anyway," he said. "I have this certificate in my hand and with it I can get my river licence." He raised his eyebrows at me, making sure I understood what he was saying.

"Right . . ." I shrugged.

"Well, if I waved that guy off and then ripped out the entire inside of my boat and replaced it with open fires and made petrol cans into furniture I still have a boat safety certificate," he shrugged. "They really are a complete farce, very expensive and unnecessary." He frowned. "And, of course, it doesn't help that we have to have two of them."

Well that brought me up short. Each inspection was a hundred and thirty pounds. "What? Why on earth do we have to have two, for pity's sake?"

Geoff looked at me as if I'd gone made. "We have two boats you know."

"Charlie's isn't a flaming boat, it's a metal box. There's no running water, no toilet, no gas, no diesel, and it's only twenty-seven foot long. What the hell is he going to inspect in there, the decorations?"

Geoff shrugged. "It's a boat, it needs a safety certificate," he said. "He is going to knock twenty quid off that one though."

"Oh well, big flaming deal," I said.

"I take it you don't care what I do with the fire extinguishers then?" Geoff laughed.

"No I don't, tie the inspector to them and drop them in the river for all I care." I sighed. "Two hundred and forty quid. That's a flaming rip-off. That could be used to tax the car."

Geoff nodded. "Ah well, at least it doesn't have to be done for another four years."

Well, that was the end of that. A lot of people seem to be under the impression that living on a boat is a cheap alternative to a house. It isn't really; we just have different bills to pay.

At the end of May I received the expected telephone call, "Hi Mum."

Aha! Middle daughter, what a surprise.

"Hello, chucky egg," I said. "What can I do for you? I assume you're calling for help?"

Charlie gave a nervous laugh. "Sort of."

"Money, groceries, clothes?" I chuckled. "What have you run out of?"

"How much stuff has Geoff put in my boat?" she asked.

"Nothing permanent, why?" I knew why, but after the fuss she made about being able to move out there was no way I was going to pave the way back again.

"Can I come home please?" she said.

I laughed. "Of course you can," I said. "Why?"

"Thankyou, thankyou . . ." Charlie gave a huge sigh of relief. "Why is everything so bloody expensive? I can't afford to live on my wages, this is ridiculous."

I thought back to the hours I'd spent trying to explain the cost of living to her. My figures had been "pooh poohed" as being wildly inaccurate, she had been positive I'd been making up the prices just to keep her at home for another year.

"Really, I never would have known," I said.

Charlie sighed again. "Yes, you were right . . . again. Can you come and get me at the weekend please?" she asked.

"We'll be there on Saturday morning, all right? Can you survive till then?" She was the skinniest person I'd ever seen before going on a budget-induced diet, I dreaded to think what she'd been eating.

"Thanks, Mum," she said and hung up.

I stared at my silent phone for a moment before deciding to collect purse and shopping bags. If Madam was coming home, the cupboards had better be full.

"But . . . but . . . but what about my shed?" Geoff grumbled when I told him we were just about to become a family of four again.

"It's not a shed, it's a boat, and she needs to live in it again," I said.

157

"Oh for goodness' sake." Geoff sulked off to take out all the wood and "useful" stuff he'd been happily squirreling away in the depths of the little boat.

I had to laugh. It is always assumed that our life is so different from "normal" people, it isn't. Kids leave, they come home, they're always hungry, and there are never any socks. It doesn't seem to matter where or how you live. There are constants to parenting that run right across the board. Happy or sad, rich or poor, mansion or a hole in the ground, some things affect us all.

CHAPTER
SIX

Rain And Wind And Yet More Rain. Frustrating Trip In The Slow Lane.

With Charlie happily ensconced back in her tiny boat, eating me out of house and home and generally contented with her lot once more, it was obviously time for daughter number one to have her moment in the sun.

On Friday the 1st of June at a very respectable eight o'clock in the morning I had the phone call that we'd all been waiting for. It was from Chris, Amelia's husband. I'd expected him to sound excited or panic-stricken but no, he was perfectly calm and as organised as ever.

"Hi there mother-in-law," he said as I picked up the phone.

I laughed for a moment and then stopped as I realised what the phone call was going to be about.

"Better get your skates on," he said. "We're just going to the hospital now but I don't think there's any major rush."

"Oh, oh, oh my goodness, right." I babbled at him. "Um . . . I'll leave in the next ten minutes and I should be there in about four hours, tell her to hang on."

159

"I don't think I can do that, Marie," he said with a laugh.

"Right, no of course you can't. I'll be there as soon as possible."

"OK, no panic," he said. Then he rang off.

Geoff had been listening and had already handed me the last half of my early-morning tea, made me a sandwich, and was looking for my bag. "I take it you're heading for Cardiff, are you?" he said.

I nodded and spilled my tea. "Oh, it's Sam's birthday tomorrow," I said. "If I'm not back you know where his presents are don't you . . . ?"

Geoff nodded.

"And, there's a meal already made in the fridge."

Geoff nodded.

"And Charlie needs to be taken to the train station."

Geoff stopped nodding and just looked at me. "I can cope with all of it, now go away."

"Right, yes, I'm going, I'm going, and I'll ring you later, OK?"

Geoff nodded and, taking my empty mug, hoisted me out of the door. "It'll be fine, just go."

Three hours later and I had just managed to make it to Birmingham. It occurred to me that Amelia had picked the very worst weekend to decide to have a baby. With the extra bank holiday for the Queen's Diamond Jubilee, the roads were packed to capacity with people making the most of a long weekend. It seemed that most of them were heading for Wales.

Stopping for petrol after driving very slowly for at least five hours I had taken the opportunity to call Chris and explain why I was taking so long.

"I'm so sorry, the traffic is horrible," I'd said.

"Don't worry about it," he'd said. "Things are going really slowly, we're having a wander around outside to get things moving."

"How's Amelia doing?"

"Oh, hang on, you can talk to her," he'd said.

A strained voice reached my ears. "I don't want to talk to anyone." Amelia finished that sentence with a long drawn out groan. "Yes I do, give her here."

"Uh oh."

"Where the hell are you?" she screeched down the phone.

"The traffic's bad . . ." I was going to tell her what was going but she cut me off.

"Well just put your foot down and stop lollygagging about. I don't want to talk. Go away." There was a rustle as the phone was obviously handed back to Chris.

"Did you get that?" he laughed.

"Yes, and I'm not going to do any more lollygagging and I'm going to put my foot down," I said.

Chris laughed and I heard Amelia's voice again. "Chris stop talking to my mother and ow, ow, ow, ow, ow . . . OW !!"

"I think I'd better go," he said.

I laughed "Yes we've both got our orders." I'd hit the off button and headed back to the car.

I finally pulled into the Cardiff hospital no less than ten hours after I'd set off. I wasn't sure how Amelia was holding up but I was a frazzled mess.

Walking through the hospital, well, sort of jogging really, I was struck by how hospitals were all alike. There is a definite smell that is all pervasive. Like all others this one was a complete rabbit warren and, by the time I'd finished following the directions I'd been given, I was on the wrong floor and at the wrong end of the hospital. Very good.

Eventually I found the maternity unit and, after taking a moment to catch my breath, the door clicked and I pushed it open. The midwife on the desk looked up with a smile. "Can I help you?" she said.

I explained who I was and she knew immediately who my daughter was which made me a little nervous. "Ah," she said, "Amelia, oh she's doing really well."

Uh oh.

I cautiously opened the door and peered into the room. Amelia, although sitting on a huge ball and clasping the gas and air mask to her face was obviously floating somewhere near the ceiling.

"Hello?" I waited for the fury of a woman in pain to fall on me.

Chris gave me a big smile. "Ah, there you are, did you manage to park OK?"

I nodded while I studied my oldest daughter — she seemed to have developed cross-eyes.

"Is she OK?" I asked Chris.

He laughed. "Lots and lots of drugs."

"Oh, right." I walked around so that Amelia could see me. "Hello, you," I said. "How's it all going?"

Amelia managed to focus and gave me a very airy grin. "Is all goinso kay at the mo," she slurred around the nozzle that she had clamped between her teeth. "Hellooo Mummy," she said and then winced as the baby made another bid for freedom.

I winced right along with her.

As the day stretched into evening and the evening into night Amelia became more airy and the midwives more agitated. Her temperature kept rising and the staff's professional smiles were becoming rather fixed. Eventually a well-dressed woman strode in through the door.

"This isn't going well, I'm afraid," she said.

Amelia managed to uncross her eyes for just a moment before sinking back onto the bed. The spinal block that she'd demanded had given her a very positive view of the whole procedure. "It isn't?" she said.

The consultant shook her head and decided to talk to Chris. "Her temperature is very high, we're worried about the baby, and I think we need him out *now*."

Chris swallowed and glanced over at his wife who was currently examining her fingers very carefully. He nodded slowly.

"We're going to have to go for an emergency C-Section." The consultant wasn't going to give him the chance to say no. "She's just stopped and the baby's getting distressed."

Chris nodded more firmly and moved over to discuss it with Amelia who obviously wasn't as airy as she appeared. She managed to get all her ducks in a line long enough to tell everyone in the room, very firmly, that a Caesarean was a fantastic idea and the sooner the better.

Within seconds the room was full of staff. Surgeon; anaesthetist; various midwives, all bustled about getting Amelia ready to move. I felt like a spare wheel and shuffled myself into a corner so that I wouldn't get in the way.

I held her hand as we were whisked down the corridor. They were moving so fast that I was hard-pressed to keep up with the porter as he trotted along pushing Amelia's bed. As we got to the doors of the theatre a midwife laid a gentle hand on my arm. "She can only have one person with her," she said.

I was confused for a moment, I was her mother, of course it would be me. I looked over to the bed where Chris was gently pushing Amelia's hair out of her eyes, they both looked terrified but they were still smiling at each other. No, it wasn't going to be me. She had someone of her own to rely on now. I took a deep breath and grinned at the midwife. "Where would you like me to wait?" I asked.

She gave me a big smile and pointed to a bed in a ward of four. "She'll go in there when she comes back." I nodded and waved Amelia and Chris through the doors of the theatre and into the brightly and terrifyingly lit room beyond. The door swung gently closed and clicked with a quite hideous finality.

I sat in the hard chair next to the empty bed for about half an hour. There wasn't really anything to do and I tried hard not to think about what was going on next door.

In the quiet of the darkened room I remembered my own times in hospital wards very similar to this one. Each birth was different and each birth should have given me an idea of what the child was going to be like. Amelia had been early and then, at the last minute, changed her mind. She'd decided that the outside world was too fearful a place in which to venture. She was dragged, kicking and screaming into the light, looked around, decided that she liked it, and thrived from that moment on. Charlotte, as always, was in a rush. She shot out at speed only to be caught and stopped by a rather deft midwife. She had spent the first two hours of her life screaming in anger; nothing had changed. Sam, on the other hand, was late. He had to be encouraged and cosseted through the birth process. Even after all the intervention, he was so determined to stay attached to the warm safe haven in which he'd brewed for the previous nine months that he eventually had to be lifted out through an exit created by surgery. I had the feeling that getting him out of the house and forcing him to use his own wings might yet prove to be met with the same reticence.

I was just wondering if I'd have time to get a cup of coffee when alarms went off and flashing lights lit the corridor outside. The sound of running feet brought me to mine.

I stuck my head out of the door and asked the nearest midwife what was going on. I didn't like the look of the flashing alarm light above the theatre door. Looking down the corridor I could see two nurses racing toward me with what I recognised as a crash cart. My whole insides turned cold.

From the colours on her uniform the midwife I'd asked was way up in the scheme of things and she turned to me with a look that I'm sure had been withering trainees for about twenty years. "Nothing that you can help with, keep out of the way!"

Cowed by the tone I nodded and backed into the ward. When I felt my chair hit me on the back of the knees I sat down. Five minutes later she was back. "What are you doing in here?" she demanded.

Well, I hadn't broken in, that was for sure and her tone was beginning to irritate. "I'm where I was told to go," I said. "How's Amelia, how's the baby, is everything all right?"

She pulled herself up to a full five foot one and snapped "I don't know, I'm not in there I'm out here dealing with you."

Oooo, get you, lady. I didn't ask to be "dealt with".

"I do know that you are not supposed to be in here, you can wait in there." She stabbed a finger toward a door across the corridor. "Go on, off you go. Take a seat and someone will let you know what's going on as soon as they can."

With a sigh, I grabbed my bag and trotted across the corridor. There was no point arguing with her, I worked in the same sort of place, I knew it wouldn't do any

166

good. Through the door was a tiny waiting room which, obviously due to a lack of space, was also being utilised as a store room for maternity supplies that were waiting to be unpacked. The room was white, bright, and completely featureless, I felt as if I'd been shoved into a cupboard. I'd been tidied.

A nervous hour later and a young midwife finally stuck her head around the door. "Oh, there you are," she said. "We've been looking for you, Amelia was getting worried you'd gone home."

I opened my mouth to tell her exactly how I'd managed to get here but then thought better of it. What would be the point? "Is everybody OK?" I asked.

She nodded with a big smile. "Everyone is fine," she said. Trotting ahead of me she led me back to the ward. "Look," she said. "there they are."

With a swift pat on my hand she whisked away. I wandered over to the bedside. Amelia was lying on the pillows, she looked tired and very pale. "Where were you?" she said.

"I got tidied into a cupboard, don't ask." I gave her a long look. "How are you feeling?"

"Like I've been run over by a truck," she said. She waved a languid hand toward a clear Perspex crib that had been wheeled to the side of the bed. "But look what we made." She gave me a huge smile.

Chris reached into the fish tank and gently picked up the little red person inside. He gave his son a smile and said to him, "This is Grandma, you'll get used to her, she's a bit mad but you learn to live with it." He handed him to me and after a long look at my new grandson I came over all odd and tearful and had to sit down so that I could study him.

"So," Amelia demanded, "what do you think?"

I stared down at him again. What could I say? It's not like I was commenting on a new pair of shoes.

The baby fluttered his long eyelashes and gazed blankly over my shoulder with that big blue stare of all new-borns. He scrunched his little face up and then relaxed again, his little fingers curling and uncurling. "He's absolutely beautiful," I said. Suddenly I didn't mind being a grandma at all.

Amelia gave a huge yawn. "I can't believe how tired I am, I've been lying in bed all day as well."

Chris laughed. "Well, you have been a little busy even though you have been flat on your back."

I shook myself away from staring into those big blue eyes. "So what happened? What was with all the alarms and running and shouting?"

Chris glanced at Amelia and they both looked more than a little haunted. "He wasn't breathing when he came out and it took them a little while to get him up and running."

Amelia swallowed hard and sniffed a little as Chris took her hand.

"The surgery team didn't realise, so when he came out they told me to go and have a look. When I tried to see him the baby team told me to go away again. All I caught was just a quick glimpse, he was a really odd blue colour." Chris let go of his wife and rubbed his hands together. I could see he was itching to take the baby back just to make sure he was all right. I didn't want to give him up but I could well understand that if I'd seen one of my children blue and lifeless I'd want exactly the same thing. I handed him over with a smile and Chris gave a huge sigh of relief.

"Oh, what time was he born?" I didn't really have a clear idea of what the time was now, I was so bone-tired it could have been the next day for all I knew.

"Eleven fifty-two." Chris read Finley's tiny plastic bracelet.

"Well, he got his own birthday then," I said. When both of them gave me a quizzical look I laughed. "Eight more minutes and he'd have been sharing one with his Uncle Sam."

Amelia groaned. "Sam's birthday, oh I forgot."

"I think, under the circumstances, he'll forgive you," I said.

As it was so very late, the hospital only gave us another ten minutes before throwing us all out again. I gave Chris a ride home.

"Where are you staying?" he said.

"I hadn't considered staying," I said. "It's Sam's birthday tomorrow or um . . . today."

Chris nodded. "You could stay at ours, you know."

I thought about it for a moment and studied him, he was nearly as pale as Amelia had been. "I don't think you need to be worrying about a house guest," I said.

He nodded gratefully.

"Look, how many people are coming down tomorrow?" I navigated around one of the seemingly hundreds of tiny roundabouts that make up modern Cardiff.

169

Chris yawned hugely as he tried to calculate. "Erm, my mum and step-dad and your mum and dad."

That was a lot of people trying to hug a new baby. I thought back to my first born. All I'd wanted was for everyone to go away so that I could study my new arrival and take in every detail. "I think that's enough for one visit don't you?" I said.

Chris nodded, he really was seconds away from falling fast asleep.

"I think I'm going to head for home," I said. "The roads will be very quiet and I can make it by . . ." I checked the clock glowing in the dashboard, oh dear, it was later than I'd thought, ". . . dawn. We'll all come down next weekend. That will give you a chance to get both of them home and settle down a bit."

Chris didn't respond. Turning to look at him I could see that his head had fallen against the window, his mouth had dropped open and as I grinned at him he gave a gentle snore.

After dropping Chris at home I headed for the motorway. I kept yawning and it did occur to me that this was probably a really stupid idea. I decided I'd drive until I couldn't drive any more then I would pull over and take a nap in the car.

Another stupid idea, that evening nearly had one generation arriving and one leaving. Driving down the empty M50 towards Tewkesbury I fell asleep and it was only providence that woke me just before I hit the central barriers. Shaking and filled with adrenaline I pulled off the road at the next services, killed the engine and lights and, after dropping my seat back, was asleep within seconds.

When I awoke, dry-mouthed, gluey-eyed, and completely disoriented it was just after eight o'clock, so much for making it home by dawn. I called Geoff and then wandered into the services in the hope of finding a decent coffee. I staggered into the toilets and caught sight of myself in the mirrors. My hair looked as though someone had back-combed half a beehive and then lost interest. There were bags beneath my eyes that any big supermarket would have been proud of and, just to put the cherry on the top of the cake, where I'd been sleeping against the seat, the piping had driven deep grooves into my cheeks and forehead. With my smeared make-up and crumpled clothes I looked crazed; it was no wonder that I'd been getting some funny looks.

After five minutes communion with a cold tap and some paper towels I felt awake and looked almost human again. I treated myself to one of those weird chewy toothbrush thingies that they have in the machines in the toilets and with a large coffee in hand, I found a place to sit and enjoy waking up.

By the bottom of the cup I was feeling quite fantastic. I decided that I was completely fine and could easily manage the rest of the drive home. I stood up and stretched, yes I was one hundred per cent again.

I was just about to head back to the car when I felt a hesitant tap on my shoulder. I turned to face a young lady who was looking at me with concern.

"Erm are you all right?" she asked with a smile.

"Yes?" The word emerged, drawn out and slightly questioning.

"Are you sure?" she said. Taking my arm she gently pulled me back down onto the seat, I was so confused I didn't bother to resist.

"Yes." The word was still drawn out but I tried to inject some positivity into it.

"We have a first aider on site if you'd like to see him."

Great, the only time I get decent customer service and it's for something I don't want, typical.

She didn't say anything more, just gave me a look that said, "I think you look like cack and I don't want you having a heart attack on my nice polished floor."

I managed to get my wits about me. "Thank you," I said. "I had a very late night and I had a sleep in the car I don't think I've quite woken up yet."

She straightened up obviously relieved to find that I could actually speak in full sentences. "Oh, I'm so sorry," she said. "You just looked really pale and unwell."

"No, no really it's fine." I stood up again. "I always look like this, even in summer I only manage to attain a dirty white colour. See me in a cold winter and I am actually pale blue." I clamped my teeth together; it seemed the only way to stop myself from babbling like a complete loony.

She laughed and then looked embarrassed. "I'm really very sorry."

Oh it's awful when you try to do something nice for someone and they don't need help, it makes you feel a

172

right fool. It's like asking a chubby woman when her baby's due (I've done that) or offering your seat to someone who takes the whole thing as an insult (I've done that too). I decided to throw her a line.

"Really, I do appreciate it, I know I look half dead at the moment and it was incredibly sweet of you to check up on me."

She nodded, gave me a slightly sickly smile and, cheeks flaming, walked away.

I watched her go and felt guilty. For a moment I wondered if I could bring on a faint or something just to make her feel better. Looking around I realised that one of those "non crowds" had started to grow. People weren't exactly gathered but they were definitely looking and listening. It was time to go.

I finally staggered back into the boat at about eleven o'clock and after wrapping myself in a quilt, collapsed face first on to the sofa with a groan.

Handing my phone to Geoff and Sam so that they could see the pictures of the new family member, I didn't see the world again until about three o'clock in the afternoon.

I awoke to Charlie's face, very close to mine. I pulled back with a little yelp.

"Hi, Momma Bear," she said, "I brought you a cup of tea.

Telling myself that it was just a nice gesture and I was NOT to immediately assume the worst about my middle child. I took it with a smile. "Bleugh, good morning."

She hovered, watching me drink the tea. "Well, it's good afternoon really," she said. "How was the baby, was it all terrible? I'm never going to have one."

The tea was the perfect temperature and I gulped it down. I stared sadly into my empty cup and, deciding to push my luck slightly, I held it out to her in the hope that she might refill it.

She took the mug with a big smile and said, "Another?"

I nodded. Maybe I should have listened to those little alarm bells that were beginning to ring in my head. I didn't, I was obviously still too full of the memories, both good and bad, of my grandson's birth. "It was ..." I hesitated; I didn't want to put her off completely, she already had enough negative views about pregnancy, "... complicated. Amelia was running a very high temperature and in the end they had to intervene."

Charlie shuddered. "Did they have to ... you know, cut ...?"

I nodded. "Better out than in really applies in this case."

She handed me my new mug of tea. "I saw the pictures," she said. "He looks quite cute, for a baby."

I laughed, Charlie has never been and would never be the hearts and flowers pink child. She's never dreamed of a big white wedding and has never been interested in home-making. Even talking about this baby was making her squirm.

"Well," I said, "I think humans have probably the least cute babies on the planet."

174

Charlie shook her head. "No, birds have the ugliest babies."

I had to agree with that. "I think it's the lack of fur that makes them a little odd looking but they soon become cute, at six months he'll be totally adorable."

"Kittens are cuter," she said.

I nodded. "But they grow up into great damn cats. I'm not keen on anything that grows up to be a murdering psycho."

"But kittens are so cute." Charlie pushed.

There were those alarm bells again.

"So are puppies," I said.

Charlie waved a blasé hand. "Kittens are much cuter than puppies."

Alarm bells getting louder.

"We're not getting a kitten," I said.

"No, we don't need to get a kitten," she laughed.

"I should think not, it would be mayhem in here, Mortimer would eat it and it would just be a flaming nightmare . . ." I was going to go on and list all the reasons why having a kitten would be just plain stupid when she cut across me.

"Cos we've already got one." Charlie gave me a great big smile and dropped a rather surprised looking handful of black fur onto my chest. "Hoorah!"

Well, the little ball of fluff wasn't nearly as surprised as I was and with a yelp I grabbed it and deposited it rather suddenly onto the sofa beside me. At least, I tried to. As my hand gently closed around the tiny body the kitten panicked and dug every claw and most of its teeth into my hand.

I screamed.

The kitten gave a squeaky hiss and bit down harder.

Charlie screamed.

Gritting my teeth, I tried to lever the fuzzy little pin cushion from my fingers. All I managed to do was transfer it to my other hand.

To this day, I have no idea why I did what I did next. I can only assume that I managed to confuse kittens with parrots. I decided that, to calm everything down, I would stick my kitten covered hand under the quilt in the hope that sudden darkness would calm it down.

It didn't.

Plunged into a warm darkness I can only assume that the little fur-ball thought that it was being eaten and, letting go of my hand, it attached itself to my naked thigh and then proceeded to claw and bite its way up my bare leg heading for my stomach.

Well, that was MUCH more painful than my hand so, with another scream, I leapt out from beneath the cover and proceeded to do the "shake" this attached furry thing off my stomach and out from under my T-shirt dance.

I didn't want to slap it away but I was certainly getting close to doing so. The kitten was making squeaky little growling noises, the poor thing was obviously terrified. Weighing in at what looked about three ounces, this cat was a fighter and it wasn't going to be eaten by this big pink thing without giving as good as it got.

"WILL YOU STAND STILL!" Charlie grabbed the kitten as I lifted my T shirt.

"Getitoff getitoff GETITOFF!" I bellowed at her.

"I'm trying to," she shouted back at me.

The screaming and shouting had obviously roused Mortimer from where he had been happily chomping on a bone outside. He burst through the front doors of the boat and promptly leapt up Charlie's leg attempting to get at the growling ball of fluff in her hands.

Knocked over by the force of the jump Charlie dropped the kitten.

Wide-eyed, spitting, growling and screaming, all claws outstretched I watched the poor thing fall straight towards Mortimer's open mouth.

"Oh my GOD!" I screamed and made a valiant grab for the falling cat.

I missed.

Charlie, flat on her back on the sofa watched the kitten's descent and covered her eyes.

The kitten had had enough. With a beautiful natural elegance it turned in mid-air and landed paws first on Mortimer's face. Claws and teeth were immediately attached and all I managed to see was Mortimer's big golden eyes widen in pain.

The dog screamed and took off down the boat with the kitten impaled on his nose and eyebrows. He looked as though he'd just been attacked by that face-hugging thing from the film *Alien*.

As he ran, the dog attempted to wipe the kitten off on the wall, he failed. Eventually he stopped and beat his face against the floor in an attempt to knock it off. When this also failed he spun in circles. However, the more frenzied the dog became the harder the kitten held on.

Charlie got to him first; I was only half a step behind.

She grabbed the kitten and I grabbed the dog. Holding his head still I managed to give her enough time to detach the frantic little animal from his face. She took the spitting, swearing kitten to the other end of the boat and attempted to calm it down. I was left trying to stem the flow of blood from the multiple punctures around poor Mort's eyes and nose.

Eventually peace was restored, although it took a very long time to calm everybody down.

Mortimer, sore and punctured, took himself off to sulk in Sam's bedroom. He didn't even come out for food.

"What the hell possessed you to get a damn cat?" I cornered Charlie in her boat after dinner.

"I didn't *get* him, he was given to me," she said.

The kitten looked up at me from where it had been asleep on her lap. Narrowing its eyes it hissed and slowly stretched, fluffing itself up to twice its size. It was still very small and fluffy but the vehemence with which it yowled surprised me and I took a step back. This had not been the best start to a human/animal relationship. "Who gave him to you?" I watched as the little ball of fluff yawned showing me its long teeth and then stretched, all claws out. Yep, this animal definitely did not like me. I can't say I blamed it.

"There was some woman with a box of them on Christ's Piece," she said. "She was giving them away to anybody."

178

"Well that's just damn irresponsible." I sighed. "I'm sorry, you can't keep him. You're going to have to find another home for him. It's not fair to keep him in your tiny boat and he can't come in ours because of the dog."

"I had to take him, Mum," she said. "He could have gone to someone horrible and he was the last one left, no one wanted him."

"I don't want him either," I said.

"But if I hadn't taken him she might have done something awful like just dropped him in the river or something."

"So, instead he comes here and you terrify him by dropping him on me and then he gets attacked by a great big dog." I shook my head. "I'm sure that wasn't what he was hoping for out of life."

"I promise I'll take care of him," she said.

"You can't." I decided that, for once, I was going to spell it out for her. "You work full time, you go out at nights, you're never here, and you don't have any money."

"I'll stay home more," she said. "It'll be fine; look, I've already got everything I need for him."

I looked around and sure enough there was cat food and bowls and a tray with kitty litter in it. Her boat already had a slightly funky smell to it but that could have been the piles of socks that were littered across the floor.

"All right," I said. "I can see how this is going to play out, so here are the rules: I am not looking after him, this is NOT an animal that is going to be palmed off on me." I held my hand out and the kitten immediately hissed and raised a paw. "And you can see why. You feed him, you spend time with him, you clean up after him, and he's your responsibility. You're a big girl now and I'd like to see you take care of something. He's not coming in our boat."

"But . . ."

I held up my hand to stop her. "No, you got him without my permission so he's yours."

Charlie looked mutinous.

"And here's the other thing." I leant forward to make sure she was listening. "The minute I decide that he's not being taken care of properly or you ask me to look after him or he isn't fed, that will be the day that I find him a new home, one that can take care of him, OK?"

Charlie nodded. "Fine," she muttered.

I managed to stick to my rules for about a week before I felt so sorry for the poor little thing stuck all alone in her boat that I relaxed the rules about him coming into ours.

It was, as I expected, complete mayhem.

Mortimer had quite a good memory but, like most Staffordshire bull terriers, was forever hopeful of finding a new friend. The kitten would sit on the sofa and Mort, wary and still scabby from their last encounter, would place his head on the sofa next to Zeus. The aptly named kitten would crack open one eye and watch the dog edging closer. When the animals were about six inches apart the low growling would begin. Mortimer, in an attempt to placate would try to lick the snarling little creature. At the first touch of a

180

big wet tongue the cat would leap in the air and go straight for the dog's eyes.

Every time these encounters would end with the dog being put outside or the cat being put back in Charlie's boat. Charlie of course, with work and her social life was never around to see it.

By the end of June I'd had enough.

"I'm sorry, love, we need to find him a new home," I said. I waited for the explosion. Surprisingly it didn't come.

"Yes, yes, you were right," she said.

"Well I don't really take any pleasure in it," I said.

"I did want to take care of him," she said. "I just never seem to have any time."

"I know. They take a lot more looking after than people think. You can't just put food down and that's it, they need play time and cleaning up after and stimulation," I said. "I wouldn't have Mortimer if I wasn't at home so much."

"My boat smells of cat poo." Charlie studied her fingers. "When I come home I'm really exhausted and just want to sleep. Zeus is wide awake and wants to play. He's widdled in my clothes and eaten through the wires on my new skull candy headphones and the wires to my stereo, he's used my guitar as a scratching post and I feel just awful that I can't look after him."

"So, can I find him a new home?"

Charlie nodded. "No more kittens."

"No more animals of any kind." I agreed.

Zeus went to a lovely family whose older cat had just passed away. They had no other animals and mum, who was very much a cat person, was at home all day while the kids were at school. It was perfect and, as I waved them off with kitten and all his possessions, I was satisfied that he'd be looked after beautifully.

It took Charlie a whole weekend to get her boat straight but she never did manage to get her stereo working again.

CHAPTER
SEVEN

In July The Sun Is Hot, Is It Shining? No It's No .... Well, Actually Yes It Is ... Amazing!

"Your dog needs a bath." Drew stepped into the boat and wrinkled his nose at the smell. "What on earth has he been rolling in?"

Mortimer looked slightly affronted as I rolled over on the sofa and sniffed his back.

"Mort doesn't smell," I said. "It's the boat that smells and if you'd like to explain to Geoff that it smells I'd be very grateful. I don't think he believes me, he thinks I have olfactory psychosis."

Geoff looked up from the book he was reading. "Oh all right," he said. "The next time we go to pump out I'll look for the source of the smell."

"Thank you," I said. "I can tell you where it's coming from if you like."

Geoff sighed. "I know where it's coming from, I just don't want the job of fixing it."

I was slightly miffed. "You've been telling me that you couldn't smell anything."

He coloured slightly. "Well, I only get whiff's of it now and again."

"But . . . but . . . you made me think I was imagining it." I was quite grumpy about the whole thing.

Geoff stuck his head back in his book.

I carried on glaring at him and eventually he looked up at me.

Closing the book he shrugged and gave me a slightly embarrassed smile. "I was clearing out our grot cupboard at the other end of the boat," he said. "When I took all the coats and other bits and pieces out I got a really strong snort of it." He sighed. "One of the pump-out tubes is in there and I'm fairly sure that one is completely blocked up." He shrugged. "It's a horrible job to replace it though. I was sort of hoping the smell would just go away all by itself."

Well, I could understand that. The one thing that all boaters and boats have in common is the age old problem of what to do with waste. Some of us have big tanks that have to be emptied once a month or so. Some have cassettes that they drag over the flood defences in wheelbarrows and know that they are going to be avoided while they empty them into an Elsan point and then wash them out with hoses. Some have sea toilets which whizz everything up and then dump it straight into the river. Thankfully, these are actually prohibited on a lot of waterways and unless they are coupled with a black water tank can restrict the boats movements quite extensively.

We were quite lucky in some ways. Because *Minerva* had been a commercial boat before we purchased her, we had two huge holding tanks. They took up quite a lot of space and had massively restricted the size of the bathroom we could build. It did mean, however, that we didn't have to pump out as often as a lot of other people.

The tanks are connected beneath the floor by a large cylindrical pipe and we have pump out points on each side of the boat. One of these had never worked and, even after owning the boat for over two years, fixing this problem was still sunk way down the list of urgent jobs.

Like the contents of the tanks, the problem was rapidly rising to the surface.

"Well, I'm sorry about your smell problem," Drew said. He held out a white envelope with our names scrawled on the front. "But I think we have a bigger problem. Here, this is for you, I picked it up at the office when I was up there."

Geoff and I looked at it, neither of us felt the urge to say anything. We'd seen these white envelopes before, they never contained good news. Eventually Geoff took it and opened it.

"What do they flaming well want this time?" I knew it was going to have to do with money.

Geoff sighed. "They're putting a service charge in place."

"But they've only just put the price of moorings up again," I said. "How much do they want this time?"

Geoff frowned as he read the letter. "Starting in 2013 they want another £550 per year."

"So . . . what exactly are we paying for?" I had to scratch around in my brain to find out exactly what would be considered a service. I could see rubbish removal could be classed as a service but other than that . . .

"Erm . . . hang on," Geoff read through the letter again. "Water, refuse removal and sewage removal."

"But we don't use the sewage removal," I said.

Geoff shrugged and then frowned again. "That's not good."

I peered over his shoulder and he pointed at an underlined point in the letter — it said: Without the introduction of a service charge, residential moorings at the marina would not be viable.

We looked at each other and Geoff shook his head. Every time we had a letter from them it seemed that this was the threat they held over us. If we didn't do as we were told, they would have to get rid of the live-aboard moorings.

"This is ridiculous," I said. "I take it I don't have to find five hundred and fifty quid between now and Christmas, do I?"

Geoff shook his head. "No; ten pound in September, twenty in October, thirty in November and forty in December. The full charge will come into effect next year."

"So, if the surcharge is for . . ." I peered over his shoulder again and quoted, " 'The sewage and the water and the . . .' " I spotted another line and read it with a frown: "To cover the shortfall in funds which has to be rectified," it said. I snorted a laugh. "It appears that all the changes they've put in place have cost more than they expected. I think they may have overspent

186

their budget and now we have to cover their mistakes." I shrugged, "So, if the new surcharge covers all this, what exactly does our mooring fee cover?"

Geoff dropped the letter onto the sofa with a sigh. "I'm fed up with this," he said. "Every month the price of things just goes up and up and the whole place doesn't get better. Everything just gets moved around, nothing new turns up."

"What are you going to do?" Drew pulled his own letter from his pocket.

Geoff shrugged again. "There's nothing we can do, is there? We've got nowhere else to go, we're going to have to pay them."

That weekend we pulled into the pump-out station and, as usual, we pumped out on the port side. (The left). After we'd finished, Geoff put everything away and we turned the boat around to have an attempt to pump out on the starboard side. Nothing happened; you could hear the hiss and gulp of the big pump as it pulled air from inside the tank. The smell was quite incredible. Eventually, after two fishermen had made loud gagging noises and, leaving their equipment on the bank, had gone for a walk, Geoff stopped and shook his head.

"Either that is blocked solid, or it's got a crack in it and we're pulling air from inside the boat," he said.

I wandered over to stand beside him, dragging the water hose with me. I was attempting to beat the wretched thing into submission and get it rolled up neatly again. It was resisting me vigorously and I felt as though I was trying to stuff an octopus into a string bag, I'd just manage to get one loop settled when all the others would erupt out into a cat's cradle of green plastic. I was getting quite miffed with the whole thing.

"So what do we do about it?" Having a sudden bright idea, I grabbed the beginning of the hose and, turning slowly in a circle, began to wind it around my hips. At the end I merely stepped out of it and it lay in a neat pile of loops. "Ha! Take that." I muttered at it. I looked up to find Geoff giving me one of "those" looks. "What?"

He shook his head. "We're going to have to get some more tube," he said, "and I'm going to have to replace all the tubes."

"Ack." I couldn't really think of anything else to say. Each tank had one large-bore pump-out point and two vent tubes. It wasn't going to be an easy or cheap job.

We moored *Minerva* up and, leaving Sam and Mort playing ball on the green, we wandered up to the chandlers. We were lucky that there was one so close to the waterfront in Ely, it made carrying things a lot easier.

The assistant was very helpful and they actually had enough stock of pipe to hand.

"This is good stuff," he said. He held up a length of white tube. "It's been specially treated inside so that nothing sticks, not even the smell." He gave us a big smile. "Of course it's a bit more expensive than the normal green that people usually use.

Of course it was more expensive. Geoff and I glanced at each other, neither of us were surprised.

With a bank account now a distressing number of pounds lighter, Geoff and I wandered back toward the boat. The only way to carry the unruly material was to wind it around our shoulders. If we'd also purchased a couple of funnels we'd look like we were playing tubas.

Back at the boat I dug everything out of our grot cupboard. The smell was horrendous and I had trouble keeping my lunch under control. Eventually, I stepped out of the way as Geoff came past with some of the cut white pipe and a couple of Jubilee clips.

"Do you want a hand?" Holding my breath made it very difficult to talk.

Geoff laughed. "I think this might be a job for a man with no sense of smell, don't you?"

I nodded gratefully and backed away down the boat.

About an hour later and Geoff was, once again, making up new swear words.

"What's up?" I handed him a cup of tea.

"This flaming pipe is just a little smaller than the tube coming out of the pump-out tank." Geoff glared at the offending piece of tube.

"Yes."

"Well, the pipe's so slippery and runs so close to the side of the boat that I can't get a good enough grip to force the two together."

I must have given him a blank look because he continued, "If I can't get it pushed on properly then there won't be enough of a seal to stop the contents leaking into the boat."

"Oh yuck, that would be bad wouldn't it?" I'm not any sort of engineer but I can see the potential for disaster when I concentrate.

Geoff nodded. "Very bad." Geoff held up a finger to make sure he had my full attention. "The bigger danger is that the pipes separate and the next time we try to pump out on the other side the back pressure will push the contents of the tank out and into the boat." He gave me an evil smile. "You moan about the smell now? Just imagine what a couple of gallons of effluent cascading over the bathroom floor is going to smell like."

I could imagine it and, feeling just a little sick, I held up a hand to stop him from labouring the point further.

"I just need to attach the new pipe to something solid so that I can push it down." He studied the Jubilee clips in his hand and then his face brightened. "Do you know what, I think I have just the thing." Handing me his mug he dashed off, coming back moments later with a short length of grey plastic tube.

Slipping the flexible pipe inside the rigid one, he added a Jubilee clip and forced the entire contraption on to the pump-out tube. Grinning triumphantly he then repeated the process to connect the pipe to the outlet. It looked a little odd, as the length of grey tube was left halfway up the white pipe, but I could see that he felt that the fix would hold. "There," he said, "Captain Bodgejob saves the day yet again."

"I promise I will get you a celebratory T-shirt," I said. "Or would you like pink spandex? Captain Bodgejob, Righter of Wrongs."

190

Geoff laughed. "Hey," he said. "If it works let's not look too closely at the *way* it works shall we?" He reached down and gave the new pipe a wiggle. It stayed nice and firm. "Heath Robinson, this one's for you," he said.

"Did you find any reason for the smell?" I gave an experimental sniff. The aroma was still there but it seemed to have dramatically reduced.

Geoff nodded. "The pipe had a split in it."

"I wonder how long that had been there." I didn't really want to rub it in that I had actually been aware of something intermittently horrible for a couple of months. "Hang on though, why did the smell keep coming and going?"

"Ah, well, as far as I could tell, the pipe was right at the back of the cupboard so the more stuff we piled in there the less we could smell it." He gave me a big smile. "I didn't really need to fix this at all, we just needed to pile more grot up."

I gave him a strained smile. "So is that it, it's fixed?"

Geoff nodded.

"So we actually didn't need to buy all that pipe, we only needed one short length?"

Geoff nodded and then shrugged. "I should really replace all the other pipes so we will need it. It's getting late so I'm not going to do any more today," he said. "I'll store the rest of the pipe and do the others when I get time."

"Ha, that job's back on the list then."

Geoff just grinned.

We weren't the only ones doing some frantic work on our surroundings. Mr and Mrs Owner had decided that the toilet block not only needed to be moved but needed to be locked up as well.

We watched as the unit was mobilised down the hill and into the car park. It was now stuck in a dark place in the middle of the comings and goings of cars. I was glad we had a shower on board. At least I only needed to use the washing machine and that I could do in the daylight.

When it was all installed we'd all been given the code to get in and out. We amused ourselves for a little while attempting to get ourselves locked in but it wasn't much fun. There wasn't much in there to see. The washing machine wasn't working and only one of the showers would actually produce water. Outside, they had decided to put in new drainage, the smell was prohibitive and strongly reminiscent of our own recent problem.

Bill and I were standing in the car park chatting when we noticed that Geoff and Drew had disappeared around the side of the building. We followed them and found them studying the main drain from the shower unit.

"What are we looking at here?" Bill and I were used to strange behaviour.

"The wonderful workmanship on this plumbing." Geoff laughed as he lifted a foot and used it to point at the big pipe that was coming out from under the floor of the Portakabin that acted as our toilet block.

I stepped forward and Geoff grabbed my arm. "I wouldn't get too close if I were you," he said.

"Why?"

"It's the main drain from the toilets and it hasn't been supported properly." He pointed to where the pipe was attached. "Look, that's just hanging there. One knock or a flush too many and that's just going to fall off," he said.

"But doesn't that mean that anything going through would just spill out into the car park?"

Drew grinned "Yep. Up to our ankles in sh —"

Bill cut across him. "Effluent," she said.

"Lovely." I couldn't see the difference the "big plan" was making to our lives here. I couldn't see why we were being asked to pay more. I didn't think it was right to pay for the fun opportunity to be covered in human waste, it was like playing poo roulette. As usual I tried to see something good in all this. "I see they've put lights up though, at least we can see what we're going to be asked to wade through."

Bill snorted. "Shame they put such cheap lights in." She pointed to the steep steps that led from the main marina into the car park. "That light up there manages to illuminate the top two steps, then you stagger in complete darkness down to the bottom where that other light manages to light up the bottom two steps. You then have to walk across the car park in the pitch black before the sensor picks up movement about ten foot away from the toilets and starts up the main lights. It's so badly designed; a couple of quid more and this could have been so much safer. One of the little ones is going to fall down those steps.

"Don't moan," I poked her in the shoulder. "You should be grateful, don't forget we're now getting all the grass outside our boats mowed as well."

"Oh yes, how silly of me." Bill threw her hands up in a gesture of exasperation. "That daft twit comes along at the most inconvenient time and hacks down the grass. We all did a far better job of it when we did our own. But the very best thing is that he just leaves all the grass cuttings lying around. We walk through them, they stick to your boots and then you proceed to drag them right through your boat." Sticking her cold hands into the depths of her pockets she frowned at the offending pipe. "Everything is half-arsed in this place, everything is half-done or just done badly."

By this time we'd moved back up the steps and I could see down into the marina. "Well at least they've still allowed the boats to be craned out and the blacking is still going on."

Bill shrugged. "I wonder how long that will last for."

"Donna's looks a little precarious stuck on the end like that," I said.

Bill and Drew looked at me. "Did you not hear about that?"

Well, obviously not. Donna didn't actually live in her boat, she lived with Steve, our next-door neighbour, and her boat was rented out to a nice man with a little boy. I saw a lot of Donna and Steve but I didn't often see her boat, it was right down the other end of the line.

194

"The stern tube gave out," Bill said. "One minute it was fine and afloat, the next filling with water and heading for the bottom. Her tenant phoned her very early one morning last week and said "I'm sinking, what should I do?" Well everyone piled round there and bailed it out and they managed to effect a sort of bodge repair but it had to come out as quickly as possible and now she's got to get the stern tube replaced and she's got that new engine to put in as well."

"Oh dear," I said. "What happened to her tenant?"

"He had to find somewhere else to live and pretty quickly." Bill looked a bit sick. "Just goes to show, these things can go from placid to panic in an instant. You don't get that with houses."

We wandered back along the flood defences discussing the awful things that can happen on narrow boats.

"Did I hear recently that some bloke got blown up?" I couldn't remember where I'd heard that but I knew it was fairly local. I knew Bill would know, she seems to hear everything that goes on on the local waterways.

She nodded. "He was lucky."

"Lucky?"

"Yeah, he had a fire and his gas canisters blew, luckily he was outside and when they went up the explosion blew him off the boat and into the water . . . Lucky."

Fire is one thing we're all afraid of. I've never seen so many fire alarms and CO_2 alarms as people have on boats. It's sensible, I suppose. We all live in a long tube, lined in nice dry wood. An unchecked fire can obliterate a narrow boat in less than ten minutes; you barely have time to get yourself out before the whole thing becomes one big pyre. If the fire service are called and there's gas on board there's very little they can do except cut the ropes and kick it into mid-stream. If it's going to blow you just want to get the other boats as far away as possible.

It was a strange coincidence that merely one week later the fire service was called to the marina. Luckily it wasn't a fire, it was a cow.

On the far bank the young bullocks wander up and down during the day. Apart from terrorising dog walkers and making a mess of the bank they don't really do anything or cause a problem. That is until one of them decides it wants a drink. Nine times out of ten they manage to get out again but about once a month one gets stuck. The poor fire brigade are called and they have to drag the unhappy and unhelpful animal out of the water.

Of course it wasn't always something as daft as cows that had to be dragged from the water. Only the previous year we'd all been watching the rescue helicopters and the search boats go up and down the river after the tragic deaths of two young men. They hadn't been messing about, they weren't tourists, and they weren't drunk. One young man, a trainee game warden, had been trying to save some geese in distress and had fallen out of a boat. His brother, trying to save him, had tragically died as well. It was a terrible accident and their family must have been devastated. It proved to all of us that even when you know what you're doing the dangers are very real.

July seemed to be the month for disasters and accidents. With the promise of a little good weather for the last weekend of the month, Steve and Donna decided to organise one of their parties.

These were always loud and raucous affairs but none of us minded. Steve would load all the revellers on to his boat and transport them off into the wilderness where they could revel to their hearts content and the rest of us could sleep in peace.

The only time we ever saw the party people was on arrival and at departure. It was quite funny, they would arrive in good spirits, chatting, laughing, and happy and would leave twenty-four hours later, still happy but somewhat subdued, the talking would be much muted and a lot of them fell down the flood defences.

Sunday morning and I'm laughing at the hang-dog expressions at the staggering trail of people that are weaving across the tops. One young man seemed more hang-dog than the rest and, as he reached the top of our steps, he stumbled and had to sit down rather quickly.

Geoff and I looked at each other, he grinned at me,

"Oh all right, I'll go and see if the idiot needs some pain killers or something." I put my boots on and climbed out of the boat.

"Hi," I called. I walked through the gate and stood at the bottom of the steps looking up at him, "Are you all right, can I get you a coffee or something?"

He was very pale and I noticed that his hands were shaking. Oh for goodness' sake, how much had this guy had to drink?

It took him a moment to focus on me and then he gave me a smile. It was a very slow, slightly hazy smile. "Could I have a drink of water please?" he said.

"Sure." Subconscious alarm bells were ringing but I couldn't put my finger on what was bothering me. As I turned to head back to the boat I realised that what I thought was a wet patch on the thigh of his shorts wasn't water, it was blood. As I watched, a thick trickle of dark blood emerged from the leg of his shorts and ran in a steady stream down toward his trainers.

I got him a glass of water and picked up my medical kit, which had been kindly put together for me by my best friend Helen when we bought our first boat. She's a paramedic and she put together an incredible amount of useful stuff.

I handed him the glass of water. "Do you know that you're bleeding rather heavily?"

He looked up and blinked at me. "What?"

"Your leg's bleeding." I pointed to where the blood was pooling on the grass.

He glanced down and looked shocked. "I thought it hurt," was all he managed to say.

"Can I have a look?"

Putting the glass of water on the step beside him, he stood up. "Yes please," he said and promptly dropped his shorts.

I was slightly taken aback. I could easily have just lifted the material or rolled it back but obviously this didn't occur to him. I debated asking him to put them back on but decided I didn't really want him standing up again. He wasn't as stable as I might like, physically or mentally.

Elaine stuck her head out of her boat. "What on earth are you doing to that young man?" she said with a laugh.

"Bleeding." I pointed to his leg.

She pulled a face, "Yeauch! Call me if you need me."

I didn't think she actually meant it.

Taking a couple of capsules of saline solution I snapped the tops off and poured them over the wound. Taking a clean pad I started to clean away the old blood. I was rather unnerved to notice that it wasn't a cut as I'd first suspected. Under the dried blood was a deep puncture. I could see what I hoped was white fat and the dark pink of muscle beneath. There was no doubt this guy needed stitches. I was also a little confused, the deep puncture should have been bleeding freely but it was only when he moved that it welled up. This wound looked as though it hadn't happened any time recently.

He didn't move as I cleaned him up and when I looked at him he was staring off into the distance and humming to himself. "Do you remember how you did this?"

He grinned down at me. "I fell in the river."

"OK, then what happened?" After sluicing as much muck as I could out of the wound, I stopped. He'd started to wince at my ministrations. I could still see bits of dirt and grass in the wound but he really needed some pain killers before anyone went probing around in there. Quite frankly I wasn't convinced of my ability to get any more out, someone more trained than me needed to do that.

The pain had obviously gone some way towards sobering him up and he seemed to realise that he was sitting on the top of a set of wet steps in his underwear with a woman he didn't know dabbing away at his leg. He grabbed his discarded shorts and placed them carefully over his lap. "I'm so sorry," he said.

"Don't worry about it, I used to work at the hospital — you wouldn't believe what I got to see."

He relaxed. "Well that was lucky, to be found by a nurse."

I concentrated on making sure that the covering I was putting over the wound was well stuck down. "Oh I'm not a nurse," I said.

"Doctor?" He sounded hopeful.

I gave his bandage a gentle press and laughed as he winced again. "Television engineer," I said.

He began to look rather sick again.

"So what happened to this?" I began packing my bits and pieces away.

He sighed and frowned. Obviously the evening was rather hazy. "I remember trying to jump off the boat and onto land," he said. "I slipped and went into the water." He shrugged.

"Did you fall between the boat and the side?" I was fairly sure I now knew what had made the big hole in his leg.

He nodded. "I remember the boat hitting my back, it squashed me against those weird grey things. That's when I hurt my leg. I remember someone telling me that I was bleeding, but I couldn't feel it so I didn't bother with it."

The water would have been very cold at night so I could only assume that's why he hadn't been able to feel the pain. All along the side of the river, corrugated sheets of asbestos are held on by big steel bolts. The head of each bolt is about the same size as the hole in his leg. He'd obviously fallen in up to the waist; I could see where his white T shirt had a tide mark. As the boat swung back it had crushed his legs against the side and one of the bolts had punctured the skin. He was lucky he'd only gone in half way, if he'd gone under and the boat had swung back I doubted whether he would have been able to get out and I was fairly sure that none of the other party-goers would have noticed he was missing until it was far too late. Alcohol and boats are a very bad mixture.

"I think we'd better get you to A&E," I said.

He nodded and attempted to stand up. "That really hurts now."

Yeah I just bet it did.

Leaving him sitting with his leg up I scouted around to find someone that could take him to the hospital. No such luck, those that knew him were still mostly drunk or hung over and in no position to drive. I did consider calling an ambulance but after spending a fair amount of time with Helen I knew that calling an ambulance for a non-life threatening situation would have her screeching at me like a banshee.

"Dammit all, I'm going to have to take him." I griped at Geoff as he came out with a coffee for me.

"Why can't one of his friends take him?" It was a reasonable question.

"Look at them," I waved a hand at the staggering, wincing crowd that was now a steady flow across the tops. "They're all heading back to their cars, none of them are going to be able to drive; they're just going to sleep it off." If I did make one of them take him there was every possibility that they wouldn't get to the end of the drive before having an accident.

"Ambulance?" Geoff asked with a hopeful air.

"Helen," I said. "He doesn't need an ambulance; he just needs someone flaming sober."

"Good point," he said.

An hour later and we were sitting in A&E. Rob (I'm fairly sure that's what he said his name was, it was what I called him for four hours anyway, he didn't correct me), was now afflicted with a really painful leg and a headache to match.

"I'm so sorry about this." He'd been saying sorry for about an hour and a half and it was beginning to wear a little thin.

I was pleased when his name was finally called and we went through to see the doctor. Rob lay down on the bed and, this time, merely rolled the leg of his shorts up so that they could see what they needed to see.

202

The doctor obviously wasn't one to mess about and, grabbing one end of my ridiculously well stuck down square of meloline, just ripped it off. It came away hairy and bloody. Rob squeaked.

The doctor laughed. "Whoops," he said, "You've got a bit of a bald patch there now."

I looked away as he poked about in the wound, completely oblivious to Rob's gasps of pain. I don't actually mind dealing with wounds myself but I cannot watch someone else do it. My stomach started to roll.

The doctor stood up. "That'll need cleaning out and some stitches."

I stood up.

"You're not going are you?" Rob grabbed my arm.

"They're going to give you an injection and then they're going to wash that out."

The doctor nodded. "And then we're going to stitch you all back up again."

"If I have to stay and watch that, they're going to be sweeping me up off the floor and I'll just be in the way." I grabbed my coat. "I'll wait outside."

The doctor followed me out.

"We'll make sure we numb that area," he said. He took on a look of concern. "I know it's not easy to watch one of your children in pain, it doesn't matter how old they are."

I wasn't sure whether to be amused or insulted. "Oh, he's not my son," I said. "I'm not even sure I've got his name right."

"Oh, I'm sorry," the doctor obviously was wondering what the relationship was. "Did you find him like this then?"

"Not really, I was just the one lucky enough to be there when he sat down and started bleeding all over my steps," I said. With a big grin at the doctor's obvious confusion, I headed over to the coffee shop and after treating myself to a large, cream-covered mocha, I settled back into the waiting room with my Kindle. Hey, you have to take those "me" moments where you can, I didn't want the day to be a complete bust.

We finally got back to the boats mid-afternoon. Rob thanked me again and again and then crawled off to sleep in his van. I noticed that a lot of the cars had now disappeared. A couple of people that I didn't recognise wandered over and asked me how he was. When I told them that he was sleeping it all off in his van they wandered over to hammer on the sides. I had to laugh. Sometimes, having fun-loving friends can be a double-edged sword.

One surprising revelation that came with my forced trip to the hospital was that I missed it. My redundancy had come into force on Monday the second of July and I'd taken a short temporary contract with a medical drug company. However, after only a couple of weeks spent working in the "real world", I found that I hated it. It didn't take much for me to realise that when the contract ended I was going to make a concerted effort to get back to the rush and stress of the hospital.

I planned to start applying for NHS jobs as soon as possible but, by the end of July, the sun had come out.

It looked as though the school summer holidays were actually going to be rain-free and, as we had a long list of "dry" jobs that had to be done, the importance of getting a job faded with the promise of barbecues and long days in the sunshine.

CHAPTER
EIGHT

Hay Fever, Blue Skies, Barbecues And Lollies; Plus Thieves And Bugs And Runaway Brollies.

"Mum?" Charlie stepped into the boat and dumped her leather jacket and helmet on top of poor Mortimer.

"Uh huh?" I was holding on to Sam's face with one hand, trying to administer his anti-pollen eye drops. This never went well as he always managed to blink at the wrong time and the whole procedure was one big tussle.

"I'm going into town to look for a new job," Charlie said.

"You're what?" I looked up and Sam, now that my attention was no longer on him, squirmed out from under my hand and high-tailed it up the boat. He locked himself in his bedroom and all we could hear was a volley of sneezes that just seemed to go on for ever.

Charlie watched him go with a frown and then shook her head. "He doesn't get any better each year, does he?" she said.

"No," I put the cap back on the eye drops and turned to wash my hands, there always seemed to be more on my hands than in Sam's eyes. "He doesn't." I was sure I'd forgotten something and then it came to me. "What did you say about your job?"

Charlie winced. "I need a new job, a proper job, I can't afford to keep this one, it just doesn't pay enough."

"That's because it's not a job, it's an apprenticeship." I had to keep reminding her of this but every so often she would go off on a major rant.

"Well, it's not fair," she said. "I do just as much at that shop if not more than others that are getting paid twice what I am."

I have to admit I agreed with her, she went in early to open up, she worked through lunch and she often worked six days a week. It wasn't fair. "You haven't quit already, have you?"

She shook her head. "I'm not stupid, Mum."

No, she wasn't, but I had the feeling she was going to be disappointed if she expected another job to just fall out of the blue.

I shrugged. "Well, see what you can find and then think long and hard before you decide to do anything."

She nodded and, grabbing all her gear, disappeared out of the boat.

I watched her go and then picked up the eye drops again. "Sam! Come out of there," I shouted.

All I managed to get in reply was wet sneezing and a general feeling of negativity.

Five minutes later and Charlie was back, she looked worried. "Mum has Geoff moved my bike?"

"I don't think so." I tried to ignore the slow rolling in the pit of my stomach. "You didn't get in until late last night and he was gone by six this morning, I don't think he'd have had time."

We both stared at each other.

Charlie's face fell as she realised what had happened to her beloved bike. "Oh no," she said.

I checked with Drew that he hadn't moved it for a joke. He looked quite affronted by the whole idea. After a moment he laughed and agreed that it was something he would do but on this occasion was completely innocent. I then spent the next two hours dealing with the police and the insurance company. Luckily the bike was well insured and Charlie had locked it up with a big chain and padlock. We knew this because we found the chain, still with its lock in place, lying in the grass. The links had been severed by some very large bolt cutters.

Drew came down to see us as we were scouting around in the grass Nancy Drewing for clues. "Oh damn," he said. "Another one gone?" He looked over toward his own bike still locked up and safe in the car park.

"Another one?" I'd heard that we'd had night visitors but they'd been chased off by security.

He nodded. "So far there's been two cars broken into, two bikes have gone missing, and a couple of batteries and some other boat bits and pieces. We know who's doing it but so far we haven't managed to get hold of them. We've told the police but unless we can give them a registration number there's nothing they can do."

"So who are they?" I knew we'd always been targets for thefts but I hadn't realise it had become so prevalent.

"Two middle-aged blokes in an open-back lorry," Drew said. "There's a sign on the side that says Countrysomething Gardening Services." He shook his head. "We keep seeing them turn up but when anyone approaches them, they jump into the van and leave."

"Well, if they have a name on the side of their truck surely they can be traced through that," I said.

"We've tried and the police have tried and there *is* a company with that name but they're totally legitimate and I should think they'd be quite annoyed that someone was using their name." He stared out over the flood defences and rubbed his wrist. Both wrists and hands were now out of plaster but were still giving him a lot of pain. "Obviously they've painted that on the side of their truck to look as if they're supposed to be here. I'm in no fit state to chase them down," he said.

Drew had been acting as part-time security for the marina for a little while now. He was fully qualified and had previously held a position as a prison officer so he was good at what he did. "And it's only going to get worse," he said.

I looked up from where I was watching Charlie viciously kicking the clumps of grass as she stamped around in an angry circle swearing sulphurously. "Why?"

"I've just been told that security is being done away with here," he said. "They've decided that we don't need it. More cost-cutting I'm afraid."

I waved a hand at the empty space that had once been the proud possessor of Charlie's bike. "Well we obviously flaming well do," I said.

Drew shrugged. "Not my call any more."

I suddenly realised that this meant he had lost his job and subsided. It wasn't his fault and there was never any lights or real security here, he couldn't patrol all night long.

"Well, I'm sorry about your job," I said.

He gave me his normal grin. "I think, when I've healed properly, I'm going to go back to being a mechanic," he said. "At least I'll be able to work for someone that doesn't keep changing their mind, putting up new and petty rules and regulations and actually knows what they're doing."

I nodded. "Sounds like a plan."

The theft of Charlie's motorcycle affected us all. Instead of the lazy mornings I had been enjoying I now had to leap out of bed to take her to the bus. She was furious with the whole thing and her social life was in ruins. The whole situation made her very tetchy and difficult to live with.

Most of August was relaxed and enjoyable. Apart from Sam struggling with hay fever and Charlie moaning about her lack of transport we indulged ourselves in sunbathing, lots of barbecues, and even managed a week by the sea.

As August came to an end and the new school year loomed ever closer, I suddenly realised that this month had been the whole of our summer. We'd been so busy enjoying the warmth that we hadn't actually managed to get any of the jobs on our list completed. I looked at our rusty, tarp-covered wreck of a boat and sighed.

Sitting on the steps with a coffee and a book, I studied *Minerva*. She really was becoming a very sad sight. Although the inside was coming along nicely, the outside made her look like the wreck of the Hesperus.

Rust ran in long lines down the length of the roof where the water pooled and her once deep red paint was now pale and dull. Geoff came to join me, as usual he was carrying a cup of tea.

"I was just looking at our paint job," I said.

He glanced up and then shrugged. "Modern Art."

I snorted.

"I think we will call her *Boat with the Blues*," he said.

"I think it would be more correct to call her '*Boat That Once had the Reds but has Now Faded to Rust and Holes*." I shook my head at him. "She honestly looks terrible."

"We should have painted her while we could, but the summer's sort of slipped away from us, hasn't it?" he said.

I nodded. "In our defence," I said, "we've really only had a few weeks of decent weather and I didn't really want Sam's summer holiday to be spent working on the boat."

We fell silent and stared at her. Apart from the desperate need for a paint job, all the wood needed replacing: The doors, the hatches and the overhead sliding hatch. I told myself that we'd have needed more than six weeks of sunshine to do all that but, in all honesty, I would have been lying to myself. What we actually needed was a better work ethic, there was no one to blame but ourselves.

"I wonder what it would cost if we had her stripped back and re-painted professionally." Geoff was obviously pondering aloud but I decided to find out. For the next hour I hit the net and then made a couple of phone calls.

I didn't come back with good news. "Lowest quote, eight thousand," I said. "Highest quote was ten thousand plus."

Geoff looked gloomy. "Well, we're not going to find that down the back of the sofa, are we?" he said.

"Nope."

Geoff shrugged. "Well I know one job I can do which will make life much better when the winter comes back," he said.

"What's that?"

"I'm finally going to take out all those windows, reseal and reseat them," he said.

Well I couldn't really argue with that. Apart from the one he'd already reseated, every window had been leaking intermittently since we got *Minerva* and I was getting sick of wet beds and soggy clothes. I looked up at the sound of a mower in the distance. "Oh for goodness' sake. You weren't thinking of doing it today were you?"

Geoff nodded with a grin and then his face fell as I pointed out the mower wallowing along the top of the flood defences toward us. "But it's flaming Saturday." It was almost a howl.

The mowing interfered with almost everything. As soon as you started a job, the mower would turn up. Sitting out in the garden underneath an umbrella with a long drink and a book, the mower would turn up. Having a barbecue and lazing about with family, the blasted mower would turn up.

On one spectacular occasion I had been asked to take part in a television programme about changing lives. Just outside the boat was the family, the producer, a camera man, a sound man, the producer's assistant, and the actress comedienne who was introducing the show. Into all this the mower turned up. He took one look at all the people, the huge camera, the vast fluffy boom mike thing and, ignoring it all completely, carried on mowing. Eventually, the camera man, who had muscles on his muscles, put the camera down and had a quiet word. The mower shut down while the gardener made a phone call.

Climbing down from his mower he walked toward me holding out his phone. "Wants a word . . ." he muttered.

"Who does?" I tried to ask him but, after pushing his phone into my hand, he wandered back toward his machine.

I put the phone to my ear. "Hello?"

"What are you doing?" Strident, clipped tones that I knew only too well blasted one of my ear drums across my brain and into the other one.

This was nothing to do with her and I was tired, irritable and fed-up, I hadn't eaten and it was beginning to rain. "Sorry, who is this?" I said.

"It's me," she said.

"Oh hello," I gave Mrs Owner a cheery greeting. "I hope you don't mind but your lawnmower man has been asked if he could start down the other end of the line because he is rather loud."

She ignored me. "He said there was a film crew there," she said. "What are they doing there without my permission?"

"But we did get permission." I was very happy to be able to contradict her. "We informed the office that this was going on and we were told that it was fine."

Silence . . . then: "What are they filming?" She sounded quite worried.

"The boat, the family." I couldn't help myself. "All sorts of things, they want to know what it's like living on a boat and how we all deal with it."

"I should have been told," she repeated.

"We did tell you." I could also repeat myself when necessary.

"You didn't tell *me*." Her voice had gone up a couple of octaves.

"You weren't here when we informed the office." I tried to sound reasonable.

"I should have been told," she snapped down the phone.

214

"Yes, you should." I could only agree with her. "Anyway, we're nearly finished here but I do need to go before it starts to rain, I'll talk to you soon."

There was a long silence and then she said, "Right." At this point the phone went dead. I looked at it as Geoff wandered over to see what the problem was. "How very rude." I couldn't help myself, I smiled a lot for the rest of the day and the mowing was started down the other end.

The owners never spoke to me again. I can't say I was devastated.

The insurance company was alarmingly efficient with the claim for Charlie's bike and before long a nice cheque appeared. Charlie opened it when it arrived and frowned. It was for much more than we'd claimed for, which didn't seem likely at all.

Despite Charlie's desperate desire to grab the cheque, pay it into the bank and keep quiet about any possible mistake they might have made, I decided that I really didn't want them coming back to me and asking for half of it back so I called them.

Evidently the amount was correct. We'd bought the bike from a young man who had used it on his father's farm for just riding around the fields. Drew had helped restore it and it was a rather rare import. The cost of replacing it far outweighed what we had paid for it and the insurance company, after doing their homework, had coughed up enough to replace the bike like for like.

Charlie however, had no such plans and for once came up with an idea that made perfect sense.

"Winter's coming," she said. "I don't want to ride a bike through another winter like last year. I think I'm going to take my driving test with the money."

Well I certainly couldn't argue with that. Living out in the country I always felt that having reliable transport was one of the most important things we could have. Learning to drive was expensive and time consuming but she would only ever have to do it once in her entire life. It didn't matter if she didn't have a car, she could drive mine but once she passed she would never have to take the test again. Well, until she was over seventy and that seemed a long, long way away.

"Well you'd better find yourself a driving instructor then," I said.

She nodded. "How long do you think it will take before I can take my test?" she asked.

I shrugged. "I honestly don't know, but I would think you should be able to take it within six months."

Charlie looked aghast. "SIX MONTHS?" She shook her head. "I'm not going to wait six months," she said.

I had to laugh. "Six months isn't that long," I said. Some people take years to pass a driving test but I wasn't going to tell her that, she'd probably cry.

"Well it's too long for me." She marched into the boat and I could see her starting up the lap top.

I settled down in the sunshine with a book but unfortunately my relaxation time was cut short. It was very irritating, the wind had got up and it was difficult to hold on to the pages.

By the time Charlie came back the wind had really picked up and it was getting cold. The clouds had rolled in and the sun had disappeared. The only good thing about it was that the wind had blown all the insects away. It was a great year for wasps and for the last two weeks, going out in the garden with a sugary drink had become tantamount to suicide. I'd taken to throwing apples along the top of the flood defences in an effort to give the little stingers something else to concentrate on. It hadn't worked. En masse they had made short work of the fruit and had then come looking for something to wash it down with. As Charlie stepped out of the boat I was just trying to lower the sun shade that took pride of place over the picnic table. I wished I'd done it earlier.

"Can you give me a hand with this?" I called her over as the big blue umbrella threatened to lift me off my feet and deposit me in the river.

Looking back I'm really not sure how much help I expected her to be. Standing all of five foot two and sporting less fat than a sparrow's kneecap, Charlie really wasn't in any position to try and take control of a large and cavorting umbrella.

With her holding onto the central pole I fumbled with the catch, desperately trying to unlock it and lower it to a folded and less enthusiastic state. A particularly vicious gust of wind ripped the umbrella upward and I let go as one of the wooden spars snapped and gave me a swift rap across the knuckles. As the umbrella took off, Charlie, showing more than her normal amount of

217

self-preservation instinct, let go as well and we watched as it took off.

Charlie stared up at the floating umbrella. "Mary Poppins lost at sea," she muttered.

Up it went and then, turning over, began a rather hurried descent. It landed with a particularly sickening thud on top of Steve's boat. I winced at the sound and really hoped it hadn't scratched his paintwork.

Charlie and I looked at each other and then hurried over to retrieve it. We dragged the snapped and mangled sun shade back to the garden.

Charlie prodded it with her foot and winced at the damage. "Geoff can fix that?"

"Probably." I had a closer look. Two of the spars had snapped but, apart from that, it seemed OK. "Good job it didn't land in the river," I said. "I stripped off the canvas cover and laid it gently down at my feet.

Mortimer had been lying in the shade of the boat. Being black he didn't like hot days and spent most of his time wandering from shady patch to shady patch and drinking copious amounts of water. I'd taken to filling his water bowl with ice cubes and he would delicately pick one up and hold it in his mouth for a few moments before spitting it out, staring at it, and then holding it in his mouth again.

The drop in temperature had revitalised him and, heaving himself up from his favourite spot, he wandered over to see what we were doing.

Well, we obviously had a very big stick. Grabbing one end of the umbrella he began tugging it down the garden. I yelped and Charlie groaned as we watched his strong teeth close around the fragile spars.

After we had chased the dog around the garden and retrieved the mangled umbrella skeleton, Charlie prodded it again. "Do you think Geoff can still fix that?"

Nearly every spar was now broken, bent or missing. The central pole had a Morse Code line of teeth marks embedded in the soft pine. I dropped it to the ground. "Probably not."

After we had folded the cover and shoved the upright into the log store, Charlie finally remembered what she had been going to tell me before the sun shade debacle.

"I've booked myself one of those intensive driving courses," she said.

"So how does that work?" I'd heard of these. I'd heard they were good but very expensive.

"I managed to get on a course next week. The last space. I drive every day, all day for that week and then at the end of the week I take my theory test," she said.

"OK, what about your actual test?"

"That gets taken as soon as there's a space," she said.

"Have you booked this already?" It sounded like quite a good idea.

Charlie nodded. "I've booked it in Peterborough so I can go in with Geoff."

Well that *was* a good idea. I took a deep breath and asked the question I knew I wouldn't like the answer to. "How much was it?"

Charlie winced. "Eight hundred and eighty-eight pounds."

Yikes! Obviously instant gratification comes with a designer price tag.

Every day for the next week, I waved the van off with Charlie and Geoff inside. She would turn up at the end of the day, tired but happy. It seemed as though she was managing to get to grips with driving just fine. I supposed that two years on a motorcycle had given her that extra level of caution that new, young drivers seem to lack and commented to Geoff that maybe every new driver should have to spend at least a year on a moped. The accident figures would go down and maybe the insurance rates as well.

He'd stared at me for a moment and then commented that yes, perhaps the car accident figures would go down but the bike accident figures would go through the roof. On reflection, I had to agree, I hadn't considered that.

On Friday morning my middle child was, quite frankly, a gibbering wreck.

"What if I fail my theory test?" She was wandering up and down the boat and the rest of the family had taken refuge on the sofa in an effort to get out of her way.

"You'll do fine," I said. She'd spent every night of the previous week reading the highway code and running practise theory tests on the computer. "But if you let your nerves get the better of you that's when you're going to be in trouble."

She nodded and took a couple of deep breaths. "I can do this."

I nodded "Of course you can."

220

"Can you pick me up from the train station at about twelve-ish?" She gave me a big smile. "My test's at ten and after that I've got nothing to do."

I assured her I'd be there to pick her up and then I booted them out of the boat. As the silence descended Sam and I settled down to work out what we were going to do with our morning. We finally decided that we'd go bowling, it kept Sam out of nature's way and the alley was right next to the train station so Charlie could come and find us.

Around midday, after Sam had beaten me seven games to three, we got *the* phone call, I made a cautious face at Sam and put the phone on speaker.

"We're over at the bowling alley." I winced and then asked the question I'd been dreading, Charlie's telephone manner never gave anything away. "So, did you pass?"

"Duh, yeah of course I did, Mum." Charlie's voice was loaded with scorn. "Why, did you think I wouldn't? Huh typical, nobody ever gives me credit for anything."

"That's just not tr . . ." I shut my mouth and looked at the phone, she'd already gone.

Sam looked at me and shook his head. "Nice try, Mum."

I had to sigh.

Charlie was high on success for about a week but as her actual driving test approached she became more and more morose.

"I'm going to fail." She had spent hours on the computer looking up pass statistics and had been listening to horror stories from friends and relatives. "Nobody ever passes first time."

I shrugged. "Well, if you do fail you'll be in good company, won't you?" I said. "You can always book another test." I thought about the whole thing for a moment. "Tell you what, I'll pay for the next one. If you keep in mind that passing first time is unlikely and just look at this as a practice you won't get nervous and make mistakes."

It was the same advice my father had given me thirty years ago when I'd been worried about my own test. I'd failed the first one and he'd been proved right. The second test I passed with flying colours and no nerves at all.

Charlie nodded. "I suppose so," she said. Picking up her bag she checked her watch. "Well, let's get this over with shall we? Can you give me a ride to the train station?"

Searching for shoes, rucksack, and car keys, I really hoped she was going to be one of the few that passed first time.

Later that afternoon Geoff brought her home. He'd called me from the end of the drive to put the kettle on and had deliberately given me no information at all. Sam and I waited with rising trepidation; a failed Charlie was going to be an angry Charlie. Eventually, she stepped through the front doors and I breathed a huge sigh of relief. The big smile on her face told us everything we needed to know; she had passed.

"Oh, well done you!" I said. "So, apart from actually passing how did it go?"

222

"Terrifying," she said.

"Really? Did you get one of those dour examiners with no personality and a desire to make you as uncomfortable as possible?"

"No, not at all," she said. "The examiner was great. But, we were driving down this road and he was saying that we were going to find somewhere quiet to do a three-point turn."

She looked up at me to make sure I was paying attention.

I nodded "Go on."

With a bit of a laugh Charlie cracked a couple of knuckles; she always does this when she's nervous. "Well we turned into this really shabby housing estate but halfway down the road we were blocked by police vans and cars. There was an ambulance there as well." She paused to take a breath.

"Oh dear, not what you want to encounter on your test," I said.

She shook her head. "No," she said, "not really. Anyway, we pulled over because this policeman waved us down and then the doors of the vans opened and all these police in riot gear leapt out and attacked a house over the road."

"What?"

She nodded. "The examiner called the policeman over and told him that we were on a driving test. He asked if we could turn around and the policeman said it was all right. So the examiner had me do a three point turn there and then and go back the way we came."

"Oh good grief, it could only happen to you," I said.

Charlie nodded again. "As we were driving away there were three really big bangs that sounded like gun shots. I put my foot down and I'm fairly sure we were exceeding the speed limit as we went round the corner. But the examiner was looking out of the back window so he didn't notice and I did slow down as soon as we were out of sight." She gave a shaky laugh. "I'm fairly sure that should have been an immediate fail."

"Well, it might not have been a gun," I said. "It might have just been one of those great big ram things they use to bash in a door. I can imagine that would make a fairly big bang."

Charlie shrugged. "I don't know," she said. "I wasn't looking out of the window, I was just looking forward."

I had to laugh. "Ah well, at least you passed."

She nodded. "When he said I'd passed, he said that I'd performed an excellent three-point turn, under pressure and I was very deft." She sat down on the sofa and began to laugh. "I'm fairly sure I could have done a 'U' turn if I'd been given the opportunity."

"Well, however you passed that's it, you've done it!" I reached into the cupboard and brought out a cup cake. "Well done, you never need to do that again."

She thought about it for a moment and then gave me a great big smile. "I really don't, do I?" she said.

I shook my head and watched with a certain amount of trepidation as she ate the cup cake in silence. I could almost see the cogs whirring around in her head. I knew exactly what was coming and sure enough . . .

"So . . ." She wiped the crumbs from her face and grinned at me. "Can I borrow the car tonight?"

224

I handed her the keys. "You break my car, I kill you and hide your body, do I make myself clear?"

Charlie jumped up and gave me a hug. She never took my threats seriously. "Thanks, Momma Bear."

After she'd disappeared I turned to Geoff. "Guns?"

Geoff nodded. "Actually there are quite a few places now that have gun problems. It's not just London, you know," he said.

"Really?" I couldn't believe it, I know that we live in quiet isolation but it was hard to believe such a sleepy town had that sort of a problem.

Geoff nodded again. "There's a problem with real guns, but they have quite a lot of trouble with imitation guns as well." He frowned for a moment. "Well, they used to; I'm not sure how it is now."

"So it *could* actually have been shots fired on Charlie's test today." I was aghast, I'd put it down to her over-active imagination and a desire to make things seem more "exciting".

"Oh, quite easily." Geoff took a sip of his tea. "I like living out here, don't you?"

I nodded slowly. "Wow, the only thing we have to worry about is funny smells and the occasional bit of thievery."

I realised that, in the time we had lived here, real life seemed to have passed me by and I was completely out of touch with what was happening in the world. The thought didn't really upset me. If that was the way society was going I'd be more than happy to stay on the sidelines.

CHAPTER
NINE

September's Weather's Cold And Strange. Looks Like Things Are Going To Change.

September is a bit of an odd time for boaters. It's one of those months that's ignored as we all rush about getting ready for winter. With the first leaf to hit the ground, the first child in a new school uniform, and a decided lack of tourists on the water we all tend to turn into hoarders and spend every waking hour adding to our stockpiles of wood and coal.

"Can you order some coal today?" Geoff had his head in the cupboard trying to reach the last of the teabags.

"No problem." I was hammering on Sam's door. After a long, warm summer holiday he was strangely reticent about getting out of bed and back to the hubbub of school life. "Don't forget I've got my interview today so I'll try to call them when I come back this afternoon."

Geoff emerged from the cupboard and grinned at me. "Good luck for that," he said. "Are you sure you want to go back to the hospital?"

226

I swatted him with a tea towel. He'd had to put up with my constant whining about working in the "normal world", as I'd put it, for most of July. He knew very well that there was no way I was going to work anywhere other than the hospital.

Working the short contract with the big drug company in Cambridge had been a very odd experience, certainly unlike anything I'd ever experienced before. The two ladies I worked with in the Accounts Department had been lovely, welcoming, and just happy that someone was willing to step in for a short time while they found someone full-time.

I'd been there about three hours before I could feel the general malaise setting in.

I stuck out like a sore thumb. The company was progressive, modern and decidedly "young" and those that weren't naturally young worked extremely hard at appearing to be. Although the working environment was intended to be casual and laid back, I found the whole thing extremely stressful.

The "casual" clothing that the staff wore seemed to be well beyond even what I would consider to be my best. Designer labels and stiletto heels, lots of make-up and high-pitched laughter followed the ladies around. The men wore those odd shoes that seemed to be six inches too long for their feet and end in a vicious point. The whole place stank of expensive perfume and aftershave and designer, fair trade, and recyclable fruit boxes littered the pristine canteen.

The longer I worked there the more irritated I became with the whole thing. The windows wouldn't open and the whole building was either freezing cold or boiling hot (obviously "climate controlled" meant the staff not the building. I would have agreed to anything if they'd promised to turn the heat down.) My new boss was ill the entire time I was there but there was no way she was going to take time off to recover. She seemed completely panicked that, if she let go of the reins for even one moment, she would be replaced. So, despite having a chest infection where she was actually coughing up blood, she would drag herself in day after day and stress herself into infinity that she wasn't getting enough work done. At the end of the day she would pack up her laptop and prepare to do at least another two hours at home. It was madness.

Moving some old invoices one afternoon, I was amusing myself by wandering around the huge filing room and opening the sliding shelves to see what was hidden there. Right at the back was an entire shelf filled with costumes and water guns. I pushed the shelves apart, curious to see what else was hidden from sight. Sequined cowboy hats, fairy costumes, cushions, glitter and right at the bottom were eight big bottles of champagne. Not your normal-sized bottles, these were huge, I think at 300cl, they're called Jeroboams and it wasn't a cheap supermarket brand. Oh no, there were three bottles of Moët, four bottles of Bollinger and one, normal sized, bottle of Dom Perignon. Out of curiosity I did a quick price check on the net. Over £1000 worth of champagne just stuck in a cupboard. It seemed to really epitomise the way the company worked. It's no wonder the NHS is struggling, now I know why companies charge so much for drugs.

The contract had ended the day Sam had finished school for the summer holidays. Although I'd miss the two rather put-upon ladies I'd been working with, I knew full well I wouldn't miss the other shallow, money-hungry members of staff at all. I left without one single regret and from then on made sure that getting back to the comfortable, budgetarily constrained, stressful environment of the hospital my number one priority.

Standing back in the hospital that afternoon I was attacked by the nervous stomach butterflies. I had been lucky to get an interview for this job, I wasn't really qualified to be a Physiotherapy Assistant but I could see the benefits of getting such a position.

Surprisingly the interview went very well and even my practical test, which involved a role play of helping someone with an injured leg negotiate stairs on crutches, went well. They went up the stairs and came down the stairs and neither of us ended up in a broken, crying heap at the bottom.

The very next day I got the telephone call I'd been waiting for.

"We'd like to offer you the position."

The poor man on the other end of the phone must have been deafened by my whoops of glee.

"Shall I take that as acceptance of our offer?" He laughed at my ecstatic agreement.

So that was it. Back at the hospital I entered the strange and slightly stressful realm of the physiotherapy teams and it only took about two weeks before I realised these people don't get anywhere near the respect they deserve. Working with the elderly in the trauma ward I spent my entire day overseeing exercises, helping ladies to the toilet, and supporting them in every way after some particularly painful operations such as hip replacements. There was extensive and in-depth training in techniques that I was expected to use immediately and I was teamed up with either a senior assistant or a physiotherapist.

I watched as physiotherapists were slapped, shouted at, pushed away, or just ignored and wondered where on earth they got their incredibly positive attitudes from. I was just an assistant but they had been doing this for years. Each patient got their undivided attention, they changed their tactics to try and get people mobile, did nursing jobs that really weren't in their job description, and generally acted like little rays of sunshine.

It was like working with super beings and although I was incredibly proud to be wearing the dark blue trousers and light blue tunic that was the assistant's uniform, I was never sure I could ever live up to the way they worked. It was amazingly enjoyable and rewarding but totally exhausting and, after the first month, I could see why so many of them opted to only work part-time. The days were filled with small victories which balanced out the occasional sadness but at the end of every day I felt as though I'd been run over by a truck. Working full-time, I began to look forward to January when my hours would change.

As the weather changed once more to the cold and wet that we'd been enjoying before our brief glimpse of summer, I found it even more difficult to drag myself into work. Every night I slept for as many hours as I could possibly fit in and a lot of the time the day-to-day jobs that I'd been able to do before I went full-time were left uncompleted.

Charlie, of course, was the first to notice that things were beginning to fall apart.

"There's no food," she said. She slammed the fridge door and frowned in my general direction. "What's for dinner?"

"I don't know," I looked up at her from under a pile of washing that I'd managed to get into the launderette on the way home. "How about *you* cook something?"

Charlie shook her head and stared at the clock. "It's gone seven o'clock, I have to go to work in ten minutes."

She'd recently taken a second job to get more money. She was slinging pizzas in Cambridge town centre. She was even more exhausted than I.

This was getting ridiculous, I was definitely falling down on the job. Travelling an hour to and from work, a full working day, trying to live a life that was activity-heavy, and dealing with children was just getting to be too much. I could feel myself fraying at the edges, there was just too much to do and no time to do it in.

It didn't take long before my shifts moved around to give me a day off during the week. I'd planned to catch up on the all the jobs that I hadn't managed to complete. My list was almost as long as one of my husband's.

"Did you order the coal?" Geoff asked.

I nodded. "It's coming today," I said. "I ordered twenty bags, that was right, wasn't it?"

Geoff grinned. "Yeah, that'll keep us going for a while."

The delivery was beautifully timed and as I staggered up the flood defences for the third time carrying clean washing and a week's worth of groceries the coal truck appeared in the car park.

I decided that, as I'd already spent a lot of time dragging things about, I might as well move the coal as well. It shouldn't take that long to move the bags up the flood defences and stack them next to our boat. Geoff always did the heavy lifting so I decided that it would be nice if I did it for once.

Sometimes I was really stupid.

Grabbing the trolley from the engine room I began moving the bags three at a time. After the first two trips I couldn't breathe, my legs felt like jelly, and I couldn't feel my arms at all. I decided that maybe more trips with less coal would be the way to go. Three trips with two bags on the trolley and I felt even worse. I could hardly put one foot in front of the other and I wanted to cry as I looked down the hill and counted that there were still eight bags to go.

The remaining bags came up the hill one bag at a time. By the time I was down to the last bag I was completely convinced I was having a heart attack. My chest hurt, my stomach hurt, but there was no way I was going to give up. The last bag was nearly my undoing, it took me nearly ten minutes to drag that one bag over a distance that would normally take less than a minute to walk. I tipped the bag of coal onto the ground and then collapsed, face down, on the grass. That was where Elaine found me.

"Are you all right?" she asked.

My mouth hurt, I couldn't speak so I just lifted one of my jelly arms and managed to give her a thumbs up just to prove I was still alive.

"Did you just move all of that coal yourself?" she looked around at the haphazard pile of bags that littered the top of the defences.

I gave her another thumbs up.

"I was asleep, Jake barking at you walking backwards and forwards woke me up," she said.

"Sorry." I tried to lift my head to look at her but my neck wouldn't work.

"Don't be silly," she said. "I didn't mind being woken up. Why on earth didn't you come and get me? I'd have given you a hand."

In all honesty I hadn't realised she'd got the day off otherwise I might have asked, especially after the first three trips.

I dragged myself to my knees and, spitting out some errant blades of grass, I rolled over to a sitting position. "I wanted to see if I could do it myself," I said. Sometimes I say some really stupid things.

She looked at me as if I was insane.

She was probably right.

"Well done," she said. "You look as though you nearly killed yourself doing it but you succeeded, well done you." She gave me a huge grin. "You're going to need handfuls of pain killers later on, you do know that, don't you?"

I gave her a sad nod. The whole exercise now seemed like a fairly stupid idea. I hoped that Geoff would appreciate the effort but I knew that he'd probably just laugh. He'd have been able to move twice the coal in half the time. I really needed to raise my levels of fitness.

Giving me time to get my breath back and my limbs in working order again, she wandered off to make coffee. I was on my feet when she came back but only because Jake, who obviously considered anything on the floor as fair game, kept dropping his ball onto my head in an effort to entice me to play.

"So what do you think of the latest rumour?" she said handing me a big mug of steaming energy substitute.

Elaine makes the very best coffee so I took a long swallow before answering. "Oh that is good, thank you," I said. "What rumour?"

"The marina is closing and we're all being kicked off," she said.

I nearly choked on my coffee. "Where on earth did you hear that?" I said. "I haven't heard anything like that."

She shrugged. "It seems to be the latest idea coming from quite a few people."

"Is this about that email that got sent out?" I said.

"What email?" Elaine asked.

"You don't have email, do you?" I said. "Damn I forgot, I should have brought it round to show you."

"What did it say?" Elaine looked worried.

"Basically it said that . . ." I stopped. "Hang on a mo and I'll get you a copy."

I went inside and printed out a copy of the latest email. As I was downloading I noticed another had appeared from the same address. I printed a copy of that one as well.

The new email was short and succinct and very bad news.

Once I had managed to claw my way out of the boat, I handed the first email to my next door neighbour and stood quietly by while she read it.

"Oh dear," she said.

I nodded. The tone of the email was petulant to say the least. In part, it read:

"Due to ongoing resistance to the continued investment in marina facilities / infrastructure and to the introduction of a residential service charge, it has been decided that the latter shall <u>no longer</u> be introduced.

We maintain however that investment is vital for the future of the marina and we are therefore looking at alternative ways of continuing the improvements and giving the marina a proper foundation for a viable future."

"We tried to pay the first instalment only last week," I said. "But the lady in the office couldn't take it and would only say that the plans had changed."

Elaine nodded, "We tried to pay it as well," she said. "I wonder why she didn't tell us what was going on, she must have known."

I held out the other email. "I don't think we need to worry about that either."

Elaine took the email and read it. "Oh dear," she said again.

The email was a list of new opening times for the office and to inform us that the man that mowed the grass would now be in charge of electricity cards and mooring fees. On the surface it seemed innocuous enough but when you read beneath the surface it appeared to mean that, for some unknown reason, the cheerful and helpful lady in the office would no longer be available.

"Has there been ongoing resistance to changes in the marina?" Elaine quoted from the email.

I shrugged. I hadn't seen that many changes apart from surface tarting and I really couldn't see why that would cost so much.

"Can I keep these?" Elaine waved the pieces of paper at me.

I nodded.

"I don't think this is the end of this." She looked mournful. "Do you think they'll ask us all to leave?"

I honestly didn't know, I wanted to say "no, of course not" but I just couldn't bring myself to actually say it out loud, it would be a lie. These people didn't appear to care that there had been a boating community here for over twenty years. They didn't appear to care that we had children and jobs and a life here. All they seemed to see was the profit margin and, with that in mind, I was fairly sure that, like the newts and hedgehogs, we were merely an irritant that messed up their "Kew Garden" ideal.

With the loss of our helpful lady in the office, morale on the marina went from bad to worse. Rumours ran riot and small knots of people could be seen gathering together and the talk was always of what was to come.

Donna's boat had all the repairs to the stern tube finished and was ready to go back into the water. She was telling me all about it when I bumped into her in the car park one cold and blustery afternoon.

"Just don't talk to me." That was her opening sentence when I met her. "I'm so angry I may well say something I regret."

"What's up?" I said.

"The boat blacking has been cancelled." Donna was almost spitting feathers.

I must have been having a dim day because I couldn't see the problem. "But yours is already out and fixed and blacked," I said. "What's the problem?"

Donna fixed me with a glare. She was only tiny but I was eminently glad that that glare was obviously someone else's fault even if it was currently directed at me. "If other boats don't come out," she said, "they won't be going back in so mine won't be going back in, will it?"

I held my hand up, there were far too many ins and outs in that sentence. "Hang on, so yours is still out, it didn't go back in with the others last month?"

She nodded and slumped against the bonnet of her little white van. "I kept it out because there was supposed to be another round of blacking and mine was going to go back in with the next batch," she said.

"Oh . . . So what happens now?" Being part of a big batch of boats going in made the crane hire very reasonable. Paying to do it all by yourself was an expensive job.

"Well I'm stuffed on both fronts," Donna said.

"Both fronts?" I was a little confused.

She drew circles in the raindrops on her bonnet. "Hmm, I went and 'had words' and I may have got a little angry and said some things I shouldn't. I've just been fired."

"What?" Well, no job and a boat to put back in, that really was stuffed on both fronts. "When did this happen?"

Donna shrugged. "A couple of days ago," she said. "I've just been told my services are no longer required. They've made up some excuse about cutting staff but I know it's because I may have called her something not exactly complimentary."

"Oh dear." I seemed to be saying that a lot recently. "So what are you going to do?"

Donna gave me a big grin. "Well, I'm going to make sure all the work is done on that boat before she goes back in the water, which means it'll be standing outside the office for a fair while yet." She shrugged. "If it's in her way I'm happy for her to put it back in the water."

I laughed. "Seems fair."

"I don't suppose Geoff could have a look at the electrics for my new engine, could he?" Donna looked hopeful. "I have had someone look at it but they couldn't work it out."

I pointed down the road, I could see Geoff's van approaching, the ladders bouncing as the van dipped in and out of the huge pot holes that we were expected to negotiate. I always wondered where our mooring fees went, it certainly wasn't on anything necessary like safe travel.

Geoff parked his van and climbed out into the rain, he looked a little alarmed as both Donna and I approached him with big smiles. "Uh oh," he said, "this looks like trouble."

He was quite happy to re-wire Donna's engine and, before the next weekend was out, the engine in her boat was happily turning over and ready to go. When I asked him how come the neighbours get such prompt service and I've been waiting for him to put up a blind for six months he happily informed me that sometimes doing something different was as good as a holiday.

At the very end of September the rumour mill took off and once again everybody was worried that the marina was no longer going to be open to live-aboards.

Half the boaters were getting ready to go, the other half were debunking the whole idea. It really wasn't a cordial place to be.

CHAPTER
TEN

Then October Adds A Gale, A Bad Time For Boats Trying To Set Sail.

On the 3rd of October, the question on everyone's lips was answered with gut-wrenching finality:

" . . . ('the company') hereby gives you notice that the licence by which you occupy a mooring space . . . ('the Marina') will be terminated with effect from 4pm on Wednesday 9th January 2013 ('the Termination Date') and requires you to vacate the Marina by no later than the Termination Date."

There was a lot more: Threats of what would happen if we failed to comply, threats of what would happen if we didn't leave and, on the back of the letter, the threats were repeated in legal jargon.

There was a second letter that accompanied the first. In a totally different tone it informed us that due to the works to improve the marina it was going to have to be closed for at least three months while these "essential" works were being done, however, they hoped to open the marina again in April and we would all be welcomed back with open arms.

240

Oh well, I thought that's not too bad. Geoff caught my expression and silently pointed to a line I'd missed. It said: "However, please note that when the Marina reopens NO residential use of boats moored at the Marina will be permitted. This will be a rule which we will enforce strictly, and once it reopens the Marina will be exclusively non-residential."

"I'm not sure I understand." I handed the letter back to Geoff.

He took the letter and handed me a cup of tea. "What don't you understand?" he asked.

"Nobody in their right mind would throw sixty-plus live-aboard boaters, some of whom have children, most of whom have jobs and cars and responsibilities out of their moorings in early January." I couldn't believe what I'd just read. Boaters don't move much in the winter, we live a hand-to-mouth existence as it is and the idea of having no safe haven in the worst months of the year just convinced me that I was right to think how incredibly stupid and ill-informed this woman and her chump husband were.

Geoff slumped onto the sofa. "Well we always suspected that they had absolutely no idea about this lifestyle."

I nodded as the whole thing sank in. "Oh my God! What are we going to do?" While *Minerva* was perfectly capable of moving under her own power, we still depended on having access to an electricity supply and Charlie's little boat didn't have an engine at all. I took a breath and waited for Geoff to be the voice of reason and calm.

There was silence for a couple of moments.

I nudged him . . . "Geoff?"

He stared at the wall for a couple of moments and then he shrugged. "I honestly don't know."

Well that wasn't what I was expecting at all.

We were sitting there in silence when there was a knock on the door. I opened it and Bill climbed in waving the same letter, Drew was no more than a step behind her.

"So, what are you going to do?" Bill looked down at her letter and shook her head. "Three months is nowhere near long enough for people to get ready to go," she said. "Some of these boats don't even have engines, some of the people down here have no other electricity than shore line. These aren't travelling boats, these are boats that are lived on and occasionally taken out for a nice jaunt."

Drew shook his head. "This is bullshit," he said. "Where on the local river will sixty-plus homeless boaters go?" He looked out of the window as the rain dropped like stair rods from the glooming clouds. "This weather is just terrible, how on earth are we supposed to get ready to move in this?"

Bill took over. "And what are we supposed to do with all the stuff in the storage units and where are we supposed to go?"

"Where are we supposed to go? Where are we supposed to go?" Those six words were to become everyone's mantra for the next three months. There were no answers and, as usual, I got up to put the kettle on.

That week things began to look really grim. By Thursday evening groups of angry boaters lined the flood defences and cluttered up the marina car park. People moved from group to group but the conversations were all the same.

A car drew up and a photographer for the local paper got out. "Hello," he gave us a cheery wave. "I'm looking for some pictures of the boaters that are going to have to move."

I knew he was coming, I'd called the paper. I'd had a nice chat with the reporter and given him the bare bones of the story. I was a little confused to see just a photographer though, I'd been expecting the reporter as well. I asked what had happened to him.

"Oh, he's already got the story," the photographer didn't pause from lining us all up on a rickety staging. "He just needs this picture and I have to be quick because it's going in this evening's issue. Now come on, no smiling, you're supposed to be sad about all this."

"We ARE sad about this," I said. "Where did he get the story from?" I had to push because I know I hadn't given him any major details at all.

"I don't know, I just take the photos," he said.

I stared, stony-faced, into the camera and hoped that the reporter had taken the time to talk to another of the boaters.

The next morning Bill stamped into the boat her face flushed with anger and waving a paper. "Have you seen this?" she demanded.

My heart sank, "No, and I'm not sure I want to know who he talked to."

"Who do you think?" Bill snapped.

I picked up the paper and read the piece with a sinking heart. As suspected the "reporter" had gone straight to the owners who'd basically made it look as though we were moaning about being asked to leave (for our own safety) for just three months and then we'd be welcome back in the spring. It looked as though we were just looking for something to gripe about.

"Call himself a reporter?" Bill was fuming. "Those of us that live aboard haven't even been mentioned."

"If he didn't ask the right questions, she won't give him any answers, will she?" I kicked the paper down the boat and watched with a grin as Mortimer tore it to shreds.

There was another knock on the door and I opened it to find Andrew, an older live-aboard from some way down the line holding a copy of the paper. "Have you seen this?" he said.

I sighed. "Yes we have."

"I called the paper," he said.

Oh well that was interesting. "What did they say?" I said.

"That they were very sorry and they'd try to print some sort of balancing piece," he said.

"Try?" Bill huffed in exasperation.

"It's too late, the damage is done." I wandered over to put the kettle on. "This was the first piece and the first time we tried to do something about it and it's failed."

"We can't think like that Marie," Andrew was obviously furious with the whole thing. "I haven't got anywhere to go, I can't just move, my daughters are here, what am I supposed to do?"

"I have a job, Geoff has a job, Sam's at school, Bill has a job, there are other kids here that go to the local schools. What are any of us supposed to do?" My brain had turned to mush.

As I wandered out to see them both off, Elaine from next door waved at me.

"Hey there," I wandered over to their boat. "How are you doing with all this?"

Elaine gave me a relieved smile. "We've found a place at a local marina," she said and handed me a piece of paper with a telephone number scrawled on it. "Dion went out there yesterday to have a look, it's a fair walk to the mooring but I hate the thought of not knowing where I'm going."

I could understand that sentiment.

"Ring them now," she said tapping the piece of paper that she'd put into my hand. "We'll go together, we've been neighbours for so long I'm not sure I want someone new."

Well that was nice; at least we weren't bad neighbours. I grabbed my phone and dialled the number. The lady on the other end was most encouraging; she'd already heard about the debacle at our marina and laughed as she said she was just waiting for the deluge of phone calls. She told me to call back on Tuesday but everything should be fine.

Well, that was easy.

245

Geoff, not being one to hang about decided that our first task was to clear out the storage unit. "We really need to get this done you know," he said. "We should have done it ages ago."

He was right of course and grabbing my coat I followed him down to the unit.

I pushed a bag of old clothes around the gravel with a gentle foot. "You know," I said. "I can't help thinking that kicking families out in January is about as low as you can get. It's going to ruin the run up to Christmas for everyone with the worry. This is my home, my kids have been brought up here, they built swings in those doomed trees, they know all the walks around here and the animals and all sorts of things. Milestones have happened to them while they were here. Hopefully they've got a lot of good memories about the place.

"When Charlie left her dad, here is where she came. When she made her first friends in Cambridge, here is where they came. I'll always remember Jack mincing down that flaming muddy slope, complaining loudly about the country and desperately trying not to let his designer boots touch the common soil, or Scarlett coming up over the flood dressed in huge boots and a tutu, with the light behind her looking like an evil fairy. Sam learnt to ride his bike here; he must have face-planted himself about a hundred times before he got the hang of it, he was just one big bruise for days. He learnt how to climb trees and took part in all the odd things people do here. Like that time that Jo and Nat took him and little Jake to sing Christmas carols down the river in their rowing boat and he sat in the pool of water at the bottom and came home soaked. The terrible set of cars we all have and the mass jump lead sessions in the winter as everyone has trouble getting their vehicles started. Steve's terrible parties and his awful music which nobody minds because he always takes them away. The barbecues, the laughter and the friends, all of this will just dissipate as we're forced to find new places to stay. These sort of things have been going on here for over twenty years. Does she not understand that she's not just closing the place to a couple of boaters, she's breaking up a community. She's like some sort of Victorian landowner, she's a Scrooge. With one badly worded letter and the flick of a pen it all ends because some spoilt brat wants to make more money."

Geoff sighed and opened his mouth to say something but I was still in mid flow and didn't shut up.

"I just want her to know how she has affected our lives so very very badly and I want her to feel ashamed. I want her not to be able to look my kids in the eye. I want . . ." I ran out of steam and stood in the drift of our possessions trying not to cry.

Geoff stared at me for a moment then gave me a hug. He stayed silent for a moment just making sure I'd finally run out of things to say and then, as usual, tried to inject some sanity into my ranting. "But she doesn't know about any of that." He held me at arm's length and gave me a long look. "They're running a business and all she ever gets is grief. All she sees is that we are trouble and everything they try to do we kick against."

"Well maybe if she took the time to get to know us rather than prancing about like the landowner's daughter and making up petty and ridiculous rules she'd see things differently. We kick against what she's doing because a, it's stupid, and b, we were happy the way we were." I bent and picked up an old teddy of Sam's that was laying face down and grubby in the gravel. Shaking it hard I flicked the bits of grit from its little tan paws and polished its eyes on my shirt. "Quite frankly I'd pay her money just to go away and leave us alone. I think we'd all do that."

Geoff nodded and, leaning on each other, we stood for a moment watching the black clouds roll in. Eventually, he became all business again. "What on earth are we going to do with this lot?"

I looked at where he was pointing. Buried under boxes of books and black plastic bags full of old clothes was a fourteenth-century burgundian tent resplendent in blue and yellow and three complete sets of armour and weapons ranging from the middle of the 12th century right up to the Tudors.

"Oh my goodness, I'd forgotten about this lot," I said.

Geoff looked sad. "I'd always hoped we'd finally manage to go back to re-enactment one day."

I picked up my barbute; it was very rusty and a lot heavier than I remembered. "I'm not sure I could still wear all this stuff and fight," I said.

"I'm not sure this would even fit me now." I pulled my steel breast plate from the top of the pile and strapped it on. Armed with sword and buckler I gave

Geoff a couple of experimental pokes just to see if I could prod him out of the dark humour I'd put him in with my rant.

He never could resist a scrap and, after placing his own barbute on his head, he picked up his favourite weapon, an axe.

Once, the fight would have lasted for at least ten minutes, today we could barely manage two before we collapsed in separate heaps, giggling uncontrollably and contemplating calling an ambulance due to the chest pains, nausea, and aching limbs.

"What the hell are you two playing at?" I looked up to see Bill and Drew standing behind us laughing.

"Well, I'm playing at being a dead body and Geoff is playing at being fit and young and the winner," I said.

Drew laughed. We'd done a lot of re-enactment with both him and Bill over the years. "What happened to you, old woman?" he prodded me with his foot. "You used to be evil with that buckler, you used to wait until they were watching your sword and then brain them with that flaming shield. There's more than one man with a crease in his armour due to you."

"I'm old." I staggered to my feet and took my helmet off.

"Well, I'm not." Grabbing my helmet and sword he advanced on Geoff.

"I wouldn't do that if I were you . . ." Geoff laughed and backed away from him.

"Why, are you scared I'll break you . . . Granddad?" Drew began to back Geoff into a corner.

"No . . ." Geoff took his helmet off and tucked it under his arm. "I'm scared that if you do manage to swing that sword, your wrist will break again and then you'll be back where you flaming well started."

"Oh phut!" Bill had obviously forgotten about Drew's newly healed bones. "That could have been awful."

Geoff sighed and threw the axe back into the big basket of weapons. "Let's face it, I'm winded after a couple of minutes and I can't even lift the basket of armour without giving myself a back injury. I used to be able to wear it all and still do cartwheels."

Packing everything back into the basket he dragged it into the storage unit and, with a shove of his foot, slid it along the floor into a far corner. "It's too late to do anything now," he said. "You lot go back, I'll lock up and be up in a minute."

I nodded. "I'll put the kettle on." Geoff was such an easy-going happy person that it was very easy to forget that he had feelings as well, he was always dealing with mine. I wandered over and gave him a hug. He sighed and rested his forehead on my shoulder.

"Aww," I said. "It'll all come out in the wash, we've been worse off than this."

I felt him nod and then, determined to give him some space, shepherded everyone else away.

"He's not a happy boy," Bill looked back, we could just see Geoff against the coming dark leaning against the unit wall and staring up at the sunset. "What's the problem? Loss of home, loss of youth, loss of possessions?"

250

"A bit of all of them I imagine," I couldn't believe we had to go through this again. Luckily this time our home moved with us, and due to my almost obsessive need to keep our possessions down to a minimum we had very little that was actually precious to us.

As we walked along the tops we could hear one of the boaters having an argument with a woman that sounded suspiciously like Mrs Owner.

"But this is our home . . ." It was a male voice, I couldn't see who it was talking. "No," the woman snapped at him. " 'This' is your home." She gave his boat a push with her foot.

Bill's eyebrows disappeared into her heavy fringe.

"This . . ." she tapped her foot on the grass, "isn't."

We looked at each other and as one walked down the flood defences and crossed the field. We stood and watched as the owner stamped away back toward the marina.

"Well . . ." Bill murmured. "I guess that's how she feels about all of us."

After his one little "moment" Geoff became, once more, completely obsessed about getting us all moving. He packed all the re-enactment stuff up and we spent a happy day putting the tent up one final time and taking pictures of all the armour and weapons. The whole lot was put on to a sales site on the net and was sold within the week.

I hadn't realised how much it was all worth and it was a huge relief to finally have a decent slush fund into which we could dip to purchase all the things we needed to take ourselves elsewhere.

Charlie, who, tired of the fast food industry and suitably irritated by working with feet-eating fish, was now working for one of the large supermarkets, had been more than a little worried by our upcoming change of circumstances. One morning she sat us down and said that she wanted a little talk.

"I'm not coming with you when you leave," she said.

I sighed. "We've been through this before, love," I said. "Even with your new job you still don't earn enough to get a place in Cambridge, it's so stupidly expensive here. I'm sorry but I don't see that you have a choice, your job's only temporary till Christmas and after that you could find yourself jobless, homeless, and broke."

"I'm not staying in Cambridge either," she said. "We're moving to Cardiff. I've applied for some jobs there and, if I get one, Tash and I are going to share a flat, they are so much cheaper than here."

Tash spent most of her time with Charlie and at over six foot (with a six-inch multi-coloured Mohican) found living on a boat to be quite a trial. I liked having her around, she unintentionally dusted the ceilings for me and I didn't have to worry about the spiders.

"I have to go, Mum," Charlie shrugged. "I've been trying to do my own thing for ages and I think this might be the push I need."

"What jobs have you applied for?" I hoped they were ridiculous and unrealistic, I didn't want this situation to make her feel as though she was forced out of her home.

252

"There's a big toy store opening in Cardiff," she said.

I couldn't see it, she always said that children should be put in a bin and rolled down a big hill into a lake. "You do realise that 'toy store' will equal vast amounts of screaming kids? What about Tash, what's she going to do?"

Charlie shrugged. "She's lucky, her company will just transfer her to another of their coffee shops."

Geoff, who had been watching the television piped up. "If you're moving to Cardiff you might want to have a look at this," he said.

We all turned to look at the presenter on the news.

"Twelve people have been injured in a series of hit-and-runs in Cardiff which have led to the arrest of a van driver." She sorted out her papers and turned to the camera. "Both children and adults were hurt, and the driver is in custody after a number of apparently deliberate collisions. Eyewitnesses have said pedestrians were deliberately targeted in five or six locations by someone driving a van."

"Wow," Charlie looked a little nervous. "Nothing like that happens in Cambridge."

"I'm glad," I said.

For the next two weeks it was all move round one, just like the mad hatter's tea party.

Amelia's friend Vera was wonderful and, once Charlie had her job, offered to let her crash at her flat until Tash could join them in Cardiff.

Amelia and Chris, deciding that their tiny one-bedroom flat was far too small for a growing family decided to move into a house closer to where Chris worked. Charlie of course moved straight into Amelia's old flat. With us moving and the kids moving there came a point where I wasn't sure where any of us were, it was a very odd experience.

Finley laughed and smiled through the whole experience. Now four months old, he had turned from pudgy baby into a real little person. I began to get pangs that the girls and my grandchild were too far away and, for a while we toyed with moving the boat to Worcester. This would cover all aspects of life. We'd be closer to my mother and father and we'd only be an hour away from Cardiff; close enough to be there quickly if needed, far enough away that we weren't cramping their style.

The day Charlie left was harder than I ever thought it would be. Possessions crammed into Tash's tiny car, she was leaving early so had to wake me to say goodbye.

She shook me awake and gave me a hug. At four thirty in the morning I'm never at my best so I just said goodbye and went back to sleep.

About thirty seconds after the door closed I jerked awake.

"Oh my God!" I screamed at Geoff who jumped and grabbed for his trousers completely convinced that the boat was in imminent danger of hitting the bottom of the river.

"Wha . . . WHA?" He looked at me blearily as I rushed around throwing any clothes on I could find, half of them were his.

"Never mind." I leapt out of our boat and into Charlie's hoping that I hadn't missed her.

I hadn't, she was standing in the middle of her little boat, tears running down her face and just turning helplessly on the spot.

"I'm sorry, I'm sorry," I panted as I grabbed her and gave her a huge hug. "I don't think I was awake."

"I didn't think you cared." Her voice was muffled into my shoulder and I wondered when she'd managed to get so tall.

"Of course I care." I had to sniff hard to try and stop myself from dissolving into tears. Oh well that was the end of that, with two of us trying hard not to cry both failed and we ended up in floods of tears, each making the other cry harder.

Picking up her last box I staggered with her down the flood defences and toward the car. We loaded it into the back seat and then there was a moment of silence. I looked down at her. We'd always had a slightly odd relationship especially as I hadn't managed to get her back until she was nearly eleven. But she was a survivor. I couldn't imagine what life would be like without her. Quieter, that much was certain. If anyone was going to tell me about ridiculous events it was Charlie, if anyone was going to make me laugh it was Charlie. If I was going to have to bail anyone out of trouble it was always going to be Charlie.

I'd always laughed at women who were worried about empty nest syndrome and had said loudly and often that a child leaving home is a sign that the parents have done their job. One thing was certain; her life was just about to get much more exciting, more difficult perhaps but exciting nevertheless. Mine however would be diminished in ways I already realised and, no doubt, in ways I had yet to discover.

I gave her a last hug and handed her physically into the car. "If you don't phone me and tell me that you are alive at least once a week, I will hunt you down and beat you to death with a dirty shoe," I said between tears.

Charlie laughed and gulped and then gave a little sob. "Thanks, Momma Bear," she said. "I love you."

I tried to smile, "I love you too. Please, please take care of yourself and call if you need anything."

Charlie shut the door and wound down the window. "I don't think I want to go," she said.

OK, this had to stop, I wasn't about to make her feel bad. "Go away, have fun, explore a new city, make new friends, and just have a great time," I said.

"But I'm leaving you," she said.

"Good, go away." I laughed. "I'm just jealous and you are so ready to leave and find something new, you've been ready for months. I'm not going to spoil that for you." I put my head through the window and gave her a big wet kiss on the cheek.

"Oh yeauch!" she said.

I looked over her to where Tash was ready to go. "Tash, just drive away, I'll catch up with you later."

The tall girl nodded, her bright green Mohican brushing the plush ceiling of her tiny little car. She pulled slowly away up the drive. I stood and waved until they were out of sight. As the car disappeared over the level crossing my phone gave the little trill that showed I had a text message. It was from Charlie, it said:

Love you, see you soon, I promise I'll keep in touch C xxx

I sent her some kisses back and after closing my phone case cried all the way up the flood defences. Geoff, dressed and with coffee in hand was waiting for me as I came through the door. "She'll be fine," he said.

I had to put the coffee down, there was no way I could drink it with my hand shaking so hard. "I know," I said. "I just wish she hadn't been forced into going by everything that's going on here."

Geoff shrugged. "She's been looking to go for months."

I nodded.

"If it hadn't been the move from here it would have been something else." He gave me a hug and handed me my coffee again. My husband, the most insightful man I know.

I'm not sure if it was Charlie leaving or just the whole situation, but for the next week I just buried my head and completely failed to rise to the challenge of the move. I was driving Geoff insane and although I knew it I couldn't seem to do anything about it. Everything I tried to do either failed or seemed to drop us further into trouble.

The first instance of this was when I phoned the marina that Elaine and Dion were heading for on the Tuesday that that had been specified.

I introduced myself and found that the friendly woman had changed completely. "I'm sorry," she barked down the phone at me as soon as she found out why I was calling. "We're full, there are no spaces here."

"Oh," I said. "But, I spoke to you just before the weekend and you asked me to call again on Tuesday."

"I don't think so," she said. "We've been full for ages and I can't see it changing any time soon." With that the phone went dead.

Confused and wondering what I'd done to deserve such a short brush off I went to find Elaine next door.

"Gah!" she said as she answered the door. "I was going to come and see you."

I assumed she knew what I was there to talk about so didn't bother with any explanations. "What happened?"

Elaine shook her head, she looked furious. "Were you told there's no spaces?"

I nodded.

"We've been told the same thing," she said.

"But you'd been to visit them," I said. "Dion was shown where your mooring was going to be." I just didn't understand what had happened.

My neighbour sighed. "Rumour has it that they came down here and basically held a beauty contest."

"Oh." I looked over at our rusty floating tin can. I could see why, if they were worried about looks, they wouldn't want us. I ran an eye over Elaine and Dion's boat, though not as rusty as ours they had bright orange spots of primer where Dion had been judicious with a paintbrush and sandpaper but hadn't applied any actual colour. "Well, it looks as though we're back to square one then, aren't we?" I said.

Elaine nodded sadly.

There didn't seem to be much to say after that and I wandered back to our boat to tell Geoff the bad news.

He didn't seem surprised.

As the days went on, noticeable gaps started appearing within the marina pond. It was a sad sight. Standing, gazing out over the water one rainy evening I felt a gentle poke at my shoulder and turned to find Drew standing behind me.

We didn't say anything but just stood and looked for a while.

Eventually I had to ask the question that had been buzzing around in my brain for a while. "Where have they all gone?" I said.

Drew shrugged. "It's mainly the holiday boats and the weekenders that have gone," he said. "Most of the live-aboards are still here."

"That's because we've got nowhere to go," I said. I couldn't help feeling a little peeved at the whole thing. "Did you get the latest email from Mrs Owner?" I asked.

Drew shook his head. "I haven't been home yet," he said. "Bill's probably seen it though, what does it say?"

"Well, she's sent us a list of other marinas that would be happy to take our boats," I said. "But I phoned them all today and most of them don't want live-aboards. Those that do are just ridiculously expensive and want either six months or a year up front. Of course we can all afford that sort of money, after all, we're all so well paid."

Drew shook his head. "It's like she's not even taking us into account, there seems to be no idea of what we are or why we do this." He picked up a pebble and tossed it into the water. It fell with a sad "plop". "Loads of people are putting their boats up for brokerage. This is the last straw for them; they just can't find the will to carry on any more. With the terrible weather we've had this year and now this . . ."

I didn't admit to him but selling up had crossed my mind as well. It hadn't taken long for me to kick the idea away but . . . just for a moment . . . it had presented itself as the easy option.

"Hey!" Drew turned to me with a grin. "Have you seen the new security guards?" He gave a deep and meaningful nod to a white van that was parked in the corner of the car park.

Scratching my neck, I stretched and took a surreptitious look. I could just make out a figure in the darkness of the cab of the van.

"What are *they* supposed to be doing?" I was fairly sure that security guards were supposed to walk perimeters and check on buildings, things like that.

"Protecting Madam's interests from irritated and vengeful boaters." Drew choked on a laugh and with each cough winced as the expulsions of air jarred his shoulder.

"And has there been any outraged rioting or group defacings of buildings and gardens?" I didn't really need to ask, it isn't exactly our nature to do that sort of thing. The worst you would get from anybody I knew was a serious moaning at and that would be after drinking too much.

Drew laughed "No!" He coughed again. "Everybody I've spoken to has been very careful to smile and wave and take them cups of tea. It's hilarious to watch her spending her money on employing them. It just goes to show that she has no empathy, she doesn't understand most of us at all." He shrugged and coughed again.

"You don't sound too good," I said.

Drew winced and rotated his one good shoulder. "I feel like I've been run over," he moaned. "Even my hair hurts." Grabbing the zips of his coat he wrapped it around his chest like a blanket. "Maybe I ought to go home. I'm really cold."

I nodded. "I shouldn't think all this rain is doing you any good either," I said. The wet weather had returned with a vengeance and with the river rising and the car parks and flood defences once again resembling swamps it was becoming almost impossible for us all to do what needed to be done.

Drew coughed again. "That's it," he said, "I'm going back to the boat." With a wave, he was gone. I could hear him coughing and spluttering as he walked away.

I stood for a little while longer gazing out over the water, trying to work out how many boats had gone but I now felt uncomfortable. Very aware that a paid set of eyes was watching my every move (I know they were watching me, I was the only moving thing in the whole place), I couldn't enjoy my melancholy any more and decided that before I did something nefarious just to liven up the security firm's night I'd better take myself home as well.

"Are you all right?" Geoff looked up from his list making as I staggered in, wet and windswept.

I told him about the empty pound and the security guard.

He shook his head when I'd finished. "I was talking to one of the families further down the line today," he said.

I nodded.

"They bought their boat for over twenty thousand only five years ago," he said. "Today he had an offer for just over five and he accepted."

I winced, "Ouch. That's a big drop to take."

Geoff nodded. "Well, we really haven't got long left," he said. "We all need to sort ourselves out."

"I know." I handed him a big mug of tea. "I just keep thinking that, if I ignore it, it will all go away. We still don't have anywhere to go. But my biggest problem is that the only places that are really open to us are much further away. I'm going to have to change Sam's school and I'm going to lose my job."

Geoff looked up and then sighed. "Let's not do anything rash until we sort it all out."

That night I couldn't sleep. Despite Geoff's hopes that "something" would crop up I was fairly sure it wouldn't and wasn't looking forward to breaking the news to Sam.

The next day was Sunday and, once again, the sky was grey and overcast but at least it wasn't raining. A

262

cold wind pinned us inside the boat and due to the general miseries, conversation was minimal.

Hiding myself behind the computer stopped me from having the same discussions over and over again. They were conversations that were never going to come out well. What I actually wanted to do was to grab Geoff by the lapels and scream, "what are we going to do?" at him until he came up with an answer. I was fairly sure he wanted to do the same to me. Neither of us even bothered to discuss options, there really weren't that many of them and both of us were avoiding the "maybe we really should sell up" conversation.

I was just wondering if the afternoon was advanced enough for me to put a large shot of rum into my coffee when Geoff stepped into the boat carrying a piece of paper. He stood and read it with a frown. "Marie?" He waved the piece of paper at me. I've just been given this by some bloke who was posting them on all the boats. "What do you think?"

He took one step toward me and then was stopped by a loud knock on the door. Elaine stuck her head through the door. She held an identical piece of paper. "Have you seen this?"

We beckoned her in and Geoff put the kettle on while I read the message:

**UNIQUE OPPORTUNITY
NEW LUXURY RIVERSIDE MOORINGS
WITH ELECTRIC HOOK-UP,
WATER AND CAR PARKING
CLOSE TO TOWN CENTRE**

10 MIN WALK TO LARGE SUPERMARKET
AND TRAIN STATION
FREE WIFI
ONLY FOUR AVAILABLE
INTERESTED? PLEASE CALL . . . . . .

We looked at each other for a moment. Elaine bit her lip. "I've already called him," she said. "I wanted to be one of the first. It sounds good but it's a fair way away. What do you think?"

I honestly didn't know what I thought and looked at Geoff with a shrug. "Geoff, what do you think?"

He stared at the paper for a very long time. Eventually he committed to a comment. "It looks good," he said. "But there's no way Sam would be able to go to his current school. To get there would add another twenty miles to a journey that already takes three quarters of an hour."

"Maybe we ought to go and see it." I always found prevarication a great tool in decision making.

Elaine nodded. "We could go this evening."

Well, that was nowhere near as much prevarication as I would have liked but I nodded.

The rain, that had been sporadic all day, began to fall in earnest as we all trudged out to the cars. By the time we made it to the moorings the roads were awash and it was difficult to see more than about twenty foot ahead.

Eventually, after driving around the small town for about twenty minutes we finally located the tiny dirt track that we'd been looking for.

The car bumped and splashed its way in and out of water-filled potholes and tall trees loomed overhead.

"Hang on a minute." Dion pointed at a hand-painted sign that could be seen glowing in the headlights. "What does that say?"

I pulled the car to a halt and we all peered through the foggy rain smeared windows.

"Private Property, no camping." There was another that said: "Private Property, trespassers will be prosecuted". Then yet another that said: "Trespassers will be shot, those that survive will be shot again". There was a smiley face hand painted on the sign, someone had added an arrow into one of its eyes.

We looked at each other.

"Not happy about casual onlookers then?" I wondered if I'd taken a wrong turn and inadvertently ended up on some sort of base for a religious cult. I was ridiculously glad that we'd phoned ahead.

There was silence in the car and a couple of shrugs. Putting the car into gear I moved gingerly down the track. We all stared out of the windows expecting, at any moment, to see something military loom out of the darkness and open fire. I couldn't help humming the *War of the Worlds* music.

Geoff nudged me. "Will you please stop that?"

Finally the track opened out into a yard that was surrounded by what appeared to be small businesses. There was a shot blasting place and a couple of other unidentifiable buildings and there, lurking in the corners were trucks and other large vehicles. There didn't really seem that much to be so protective about.

The door to a Portakabin opened and a warm yellow light shone across the yard. "Hello?" A man peered into the darkness and pouring rain. "Are you here to look at the moorings?"

Geoff and Dion wandered off to talk to him and Elaine and I hung back, helping ourselves to a good look around the yard. We could see that the edge dropped away to the river and there were already some boats parked alongside the car park.

"What do you think?" Elaine stared out over the yard. "It's a bit close to all these buildings, isn't it?" She stared around at the big trucks that were parked up.

"I don't think anything looks good in this weather." I was trying to keep a positive outlook but the idea of swapping our wonderful rural mooring for this industrial setting wasn't really "floating my boat".

Geoff waved us over and we trudged through the puddles to where they were all standing. "We're going to have a look at where the moorings are going to be," he said.

Through the driving rain, we all trudged out of the yard and on down towards a stand of trees. I looked about as I huddled under my umbrella. Actually, this didn't look bad at all. It wasn't anywhere near the yard and it would be nice and quiet. I glanced over at Elaine who gave me a hopeful and positive nod.

"They aren't built yet." The owner was pointing out bits of the river where he was planning to put the moorings. "But if you need to get here quickly I can probably put you somewhere for now and shuffle things around at a later date." He glared up at the black sky.

266

"This weather isn't making anything easy," he said. "It's like digging in a swamp."

"Do you have any problem with dogs?" I spoke over the thunder and decided that we really ought to get this meeting finished in double-quick time.

He shrugged. "No," he said, "not at all." Shaking rain from his hair he winced as it ran down his collar and under his coat. "As long as they're kept under control."

We all nodded. "So can we fence them in?" I was fed up with poor Mort being on a running line and I was fairly sure that he was fed up with it as well.

"You can do whatever you like," he said.

Elaine and I grinned at each other. Now *that* was exactly what we wanted to hear.

There really wasn't much to look at and, feeling slightly waterlogged, we all took refuge in the Portakabin that served as his office. I was very aware that we were all dripping and turning the floor beneath each of us into a small puddle.

There was a moment's silent communication where we all looked at each other and nodded before we handed over the deposit.

Geoff was trying to get the time frames worked out. "We don't need to leave where we are until early December."

The owner nodded. "That would be good," he said, "it'll give me time to get the moorings finished here for you."

We spent another couple of minutes chatting about the vagaries of boating and then all piled back into the car. It was great knowing we had somewhere to go, now all we had to do was get the boats ready to do a major move and we'd be on our way. There was a definite party atmosphere in the car on the way home. So much so that I had to tell Dion and Sam to stop poking each other otherwise I'd leave them on the side of the road.

The good mood lasted throughout the rest of October and even the seemingly constant rain and terrible weather did little to irritate us. Geoff rushed about, putting in new lights and installing a new battery bank, we'd been on a land line so long we hadn't realised how dilapidated our batteries had become.

"What do you think about this?" Geoff's question roused me from my reading late one evening.

"About what?" Heaving myself off the sofa I wandered down the boat to where he was sitting at the computer. There on the screen were some fairly major pieces of machinery. "What is that thing?"

"Diesel generator," Geoff studied the specs that had come up on the screen, "this one should be enough to give us all the power we need and, unlike a petrol generator, I can install this inside the engine room." He huffed at the screen and shook his head. "They're pretty expensive though," he said.

I looked at the price and winced. £500 was a pretty penny to lose from our rapidly diminishing slush fund. Well, some things are important enough that you have to take the hit and just bite your tongue. "If you're positive that's what we need," I said.

Geoff nodded. "I will have to find some way to box it in to make it quieter and some way of making sure that

268

the fumes go outside." He looked up at me with a grin. "But I've got a plan how I can do that."

"Oh yes?" I tried not to wince. Geoff could get a little over-inventive when he put his mind to it.

"I'm going to need about eight foot of ducting, an electric fan, a chimney, and a switch." He gave me a great big smile.

"That sounds a little Heath Robinson," I said.

"He's my hero," Geoff laughed. "But I promise there won't be any pulleys or strings and it will do what it's supposed to even if it does look a little insane."

"Oh good." I wandered away to put the kettle on. "As long as it looks insane that will be all right, can you make it hiss and rattle as well?"

"I don't think I'm going to have to 'make' it hiss and rattle," Geoff said, "It's going to do that all by itself and smoke as well I should think." He rifled through my bag until he came up with a debit card. He waved it at me over the top of the partition. "So, shall I buy this?"

I nodded and tried not to calculate how much we had left in the bank. "We can't go without it," I said. "Exactly how much have we spent so far?"

Geoff pointed to a spread-sheet illuminated on the screen.

I had to swallow hard: Batteries — £600, inverter — £380, battery charger — £410, new lights — £130 and the cable and connectors and other bits and pieces added another £130. Add £500 to that list and it had cost us a cool £2,110. This was not a cheap transformation, I made a sort of strangled "blarg" noise. All that money, we were supposed to be sprucing the outside this year; that money would have gone a long way towards a new paint job.

Geoff grinned and, studying the screen, began the process of spending another chunk of money. "Look on the bright side," he said, "at least we will never actually 'need' a landline again."

"This thing better be a pretty colour." I sniffed. "And it better have flashing blue lights and look really good."

"Don't worry, my love." Geoff gave me a happy smile. "If it makes you feel better I'll paint it red and white candy stripes if you want me to."

As it turned out he didn't need to. A huge box was delivered within a couple of days and, all excited about his new toy, he called me down to the car park to have a look at it and to help him carry it. Well, there was no way you could miss the thing, it was huge. Squatting on the gravel it stood at least half a metre high and was the same width and length.

"Erm, Geoff?" I stared at the bright red shiny object. It looked very confusing; there were lots of levers and switches. "Are you going to be able to fit that in the engine room? It's really much bigger than I expected it was going to be."

Geoff frowned at it. "It's really heavy as well."

"Is it?" I stepped over a puddle and tried to lift one end. "Oh good grief," I said, "What does this thing actually weigh?"

Geoff shrugged. "Eighty-odd kilos."

We were going to need a lot more help to get this up the steep hill between us and the boat.

270

Leaving him staring at his new toy I went and began the process of rallying our son. He was particularly unhappy to be kicked out of the boat and asked to go out into the rain to drag a heavy machine up a hill. Consequently he spent a long time telling me exactly why he shouldn't have to do it.

Grabbing the wheel barrow I followed the whining and moaning down the hill. Geoff looked up as I approached and frowned at my hopeful conveyance. "I'm not sure that's strong enough to take the weight," he said.

"It's all we've got," I said. "There's no way it would fit on the sack truck so we're just going to have to hope."

Geoff looked unconvinced.

"Well, you come up with an idea then." I knew I sounded more than a little terse but the freezing rain was running down my neck and my feet were rapidly turning into little blocks of ice. My love for the great outdoors, never that huge, was rapidly dissipating.

Geoff shrugged. "I thought we'd just carry it up."

I stared at him until he turned away, busying himself with straps and clips.

It took all three of us to load the generator onto the wheelbarrow and I winced, holding my breath as the front tyre flattened and bulged with the weight. Luckily the wheelbarrow was vaguely box shaped and, with Sam and I taking a side each and Geoff on the handles we made our sloppy, soggy, and slippy way up the hill.

It was a slow job and I began to feel as though we were taking two steps forward and one step back. The rain, which had eased as we were getting the generator loaded, now returned with a vengeance. Sam's yelps of wet indignation could just be heard over the suddenly gusting winds. I didn't blame him, I wanted to bail on this little job as well. Near the top of the hill the incline became steeper and Geoff decided that we should swap jobs. If I held the handles of the wheelbarrow then he could use his greater strength to pull the whole thing up and over the pits and troughs that the continuous rain had created over the last two months.

I was too wet and cold to argue. Easing up the handles on the wheelbarrow I waited for the signal and we all began to move forward again. "One big push," Geoff yelled over the rain. "We've got a bit of a lip here."

I nodded and clamped my lips together in an effort to stop my teeth chattering. Pushing hard I felt the front of the barrow rise as it crested the edge of the little dip and then I was pulled forward as the wheelbarrow rolled away from me. As the wheel reached the bottom of the dip two things happened simultaneously. One, the barrow tipped towards Sam who, being well versed in the art of self-preservation, didn't hold on to it, he just got out of the way. Two, the tyre, already under extreme and unsafe amounts of pressure, merely gave up the ghost and exploded with a loud bang.

Convinced that the generator was falling, Sam leaped clear. In the dark he fell straight over the edge of the steep path and disappeared into the wet gloom with a yelp. Head over heels he rolled down the bank back toward the car park. Luckily the thick bushes and undergrowth stopped him from falling very far. Unluckily, the dense nettles that were hiding in that undergrowth were the first plants he encountered as he tumbled head first into the soaking greenery.

For a moment there was silence. Then, from the wet darkness came the voice of a young teen making up swear words because he knew he wasn't allowed to use real ones. There was a huge amount of "fooping nettles" and "flubbing gyp this really hurts".

Geoff and I looked at each other. "You OK, Sam?" I called into the dark.

"No I'm really, really not." There was the sound of crunching and a few more yelps as our youngest staggered about in the rather aggressive and painful foliage. "Where are you?" he called.

I finally had the presence of mind to use the torch on my phone. I shone the light down the slope and found Sam almost up to his waist in nettles, hemlock, thistles, cow parsley, and long grass. He had the slightly flat-lipped look of a young man at the end of his tether. He would have looked a lot angrier if his face hadn't already started to swell. It's obviously difficult to look appropriately furious when you resemble an overfed hamster.

Ignoring the wheelbarrow for a moment, Geoff and I teetered on the edge of the slope. We managed to reach Sam's outstretched hands and, between us, pulled our irritated and itchy son back to the path. I experienced that moment of severe indecision when you really want to laugh at someone but you just know that if you give in to that need you are NEVER going to hear the last of it. I sucked my teeth in an effort to keep my face straight. Sam, who knows me far too well, just stared at me and waited for my façade to crack. Luckily I was saved by Geoff who was asking for help to lift the generator.

Giving up on the broken wheelbarrow, it took us another half an hour and at least another ten gallons of water down respective necks to get the heavy monstrosity back to the boat. Geoff, although he kept his cool and was very patient with us, must have wished three times over for someone with actual working muscles to be on the other end of the heavy machine.

As we dragged it on to some paving slabs and covered it with a tarpaulin, Sam made a break for the boat. I could hear his wails as he caught sight of himself in a mirror. "I think I'll just stay out here," I said to Geoff.

He laughed, "Come on coward."

Sam was a horrible sight. Most of his face was covered in nettle rash, and the bits that the nettles had missed had been stabbed by thistles. As we walked into the boat he was picking bits of hostile greenery out of his skin and complaining loudly at every thorn and itch.

"Nature hates me," he said.

"No it doesn't." It sounded hollow trying to reassure someone who spent from March to October hiding from all types of pollen.

"Yes it does." He rubbed at his face with hands that were also swollen and red. "When I leave home I'm going to live at the highest point of the largest city I can find. I'm never going to have pot plants, not even plastic ones because, knowing my luck, I'll probably be allergic to them as well."

I hustled him down toward the bathroom. "Take a shower; make it cool and just let the water run over your face."

He glared at me for a moment before shaking his head in exasperation. "Mother," he said, "I've just spent the last half an hour standing in the rain. I think I've had enough of cold water running over my face."

"Then go and have a warm shower," I said. "At least you'll end up dry and clean and we can assess the damage properly."

Sam rolled his eyes but stamped off to have a shower.

Geoff dumped all his wet clothes into the hamper and staggered about in a set of towels. "Is a shower going to actually make any difference to him?" He shivered and rubbed at his soaked hair. "That thing was heavier than expected," he said.

"No, a shower isn't going to make any difference at all." I started dumping my own soaking clothing. "The only thing it will do is warm him up. It probably wouldn't have been so bad if you'd found someone that could actually use their arms. Sam and I, even together, don't really make up a strong person."

Geoff grinned, "Mother and Son," he said. "Matching marshmallow people. Never mind, it's here now."

I nodded and stuck my head in the fridge looking for something to make for dinner. "I didn't expect it to be that big," I said.

"Neither did I." The words were muttered very quietly from over by the computer. I decided not to comment.

"Have you seen the latest email?" Geoff looked up from the laptop as I was busy skinning salmon filets. Mortimer was enjoying the skins as he always does. I swear it was the fish oil that made him so shiny and fit.

I groaned. "Nope." I wasn't even sure I wanted to know what it contained but decided that I might as well have all the bad things in one evening. "What is it 'this' time?"

Geoff laughed. "Evidently, due to an act of 'apparent vandalism' the shower block is out of commission for the foreseeable future.

Maybe I'd been wrong, maybe some of the boaters had taken out their righteous ire on one of the buildings. Try as I might, I just couldn't see it. However, I'd been wrong before so I accepted the email at face value. "Oh dear, I wonder who decided to attack the toilets."

Geoff looked up at me. "I don't think anyone did."

"But . . ."

"Do you remember that day we were looking at that pipe that comes out from the toilets, the main soil pipe?" He grinned at me.

"Yes, I think so; you and Drew were saying what a horrible shoddy job they'd been fobbed off with with with." I laughed at the poorly remembered quote from a Flanders and Swan song.

"Well it looks as though it finally fell off," he said. "Drew was telling me about it and as he said, 'What self-respecting boater is going to get themselves covered in human poo just to irritate 'her'? We spend most of our lives trying to avoid that sort of thing."

This should have made me laugh but it didn't. "So she's just immediately gone for vandalism by one of us instead of actually investigating what happened?"

Geoff shrugged. "I could be wrong," he said. "But it certainly looks that way."

"Wow," I watched Mortimer wipe his fishy whiskers on his bed, oh great, now I was going to have to wash that as well as all our soaked clothes. "She really doesn't think highly of us at all, does she?"

"I suppose I can see her point." Geoff was always the one to see both sides of an argument.

Luckily, before I could say something mean Sam emerged from the shower. Geoff and I both fell silent as we stared at him. His face was swollen and his eyes half closed. I winced and the conversation finished as I went to look for the calamine lotion.

CHAPTER
ELEVEN

Rain, Wind, Mud, And Hail. All Well Thought Out Plans Now Fail.

Geoff handed me a cup of coffee before staring out at the sleet. "This is ridiculous," he said.

"Umph." I felt terrible. Dizzy, heart pounding and nauseated, I put the coffee onto the kitchen worktop. "Phew, I really don't think I can drink that," I said.

Geoff frowned in my direction. "Are you feeling all right?" He wandered over and peered at me. "Frankly you look a bit green."

"Oh, thank you," I said and flopped onto the sofa. "I didn't sleep very well last night. Maybe I'm just feeling the pinch."

"Maybe." Geoff grabbed a pillow and putting it onto the arm of the chair patted it. "Why don't you just collapse here for a bit? The weather is foul and you might as well just take a day for yourself."

A wave of nausea rolled over me followed swiftly by a wave of guilt. "But we've got to sort out the engine room and get that damn great generator installed. I know there's no room for both of us in there, but if you're doing that I ought to, at least, be doing something useful."

Geoff sidled about, fidgeting with the cushion and patting the dog, he seemed to have something on his mind. Finally he looked up and frowned. "How are you feeling about a bit more bad news?" He gave me a cheesy and hopeful grin.

Taking advantage of the cushion I keeled over sideways and closed my eyes, waiting for the rolling waves of nausea to subside. "Hit me with it," I said, "I'm too sick to make much of a fuss, this might be the best chance you've got of me just taking it on the chin."

"Well," Geoff studied me for a moment and then handed me a bucket. "You really look terrible, do you think you're actually going to be sick?"

I shook my head and then wished I hadn't. "No, I don't think so, I just feel really odd. It's like I'm fizzing on the inside." I tried to describe what was making me feel quite so bad and that was the best I could come up with.

"OK . . ." Geoff studied his fingers for a moment. "I called the lock-keeper at Salters Lode yesterday."

"Hmm mmm?" I closed my eyes and watched the pretty display of lights that were being splashed across the inside of my eyelids.

"There's a good chance that we won't make it through until spring." Geoff clipped the sentence off short and stood back obviously waiting for the explosion.

There was a moment of utter panic and then my brain shut down, I couldn't be bothered. "Bummer," I said.

279

There was a long silence from my husband and I cracked open an eyelid to find him studying me.

"Bummer? Really, that's all you can think of to say?" he said.

I shrugged. "What am I supposed to say?" I could feel little sparklers going off in my chest and everything had begun to ache, even my hair hurt. "I'm sorry, do you think we could stop talking now and could you close all the curtains, the light hurts."

Geoff peered at me again. "You don't have any rashes anywhere, do you?" He rolled the leg of my pyjama trousers up and studied my leg and then looked at my stomach. "Does your neck hurt?"

"Geoff, everything hurts, I don't have meningitis, I really love you but please, please go away."

Geoff leaned over and kissed my cheek. "OK."

I heard him get up from where he'd been kneeling beside me and wander off down the boat. "Sam!" He shouted at our youngest who was still lolling around in bed. "I need you to check on your mother every half an hour, she's not well. Wake her up, make sure she talks to you. If there is anything even a little odd you come and get me immediately, OK?"

I heard Sam mumble an agreement and listened to them setting multiple alarms. They managed to get into an involved discussion about what constituted *odd* and they even managed to get into an argument over what exactly half an hour meant. I didn't hear who won, I slipped off into sleep.

Sam took his duties as overseer very seriously and every half an hour, on the dot, I was woken up and

280

"peered" at. This carried on until I threatened to throw him into the river and he grudgingly allowed me a whole hour of uninterrupted sleep. I felt a little better after lunch and was allowed to sit up on the sofa and watch DVDs. Sam decided that I really wasn't capable of watching anything taxing so I was treated to *Pokémon: The Movie* and *Monster House*. Not what I would have chosen but he was right, it certainly wasn't taxing.

For dinner that evening, my two main men decided that neither of them really wanted to eat what the other could cook so Geoff was sent out for a Chinese takeaway. This was an unusual treat for Sam and, after stealing half my quilt he proceeded to inform me that this was one of the best days ever and could I stay sick? It took him about a minute to realise what he'd said and he was still trying to dig himself out of his verbal hole when his dad stepped back into the boat.

Later, when Sam had gone to bed, Geoff tried to get to the bottom of my malaise. "Sore throat?" he asked.

"Erm no."

"Coughing?"

"No."

"Sneezing?"

"No." I shrugged. "I just feel really tired, I ache all over, I feel as though I'm looking up at the world through water and I have this sort of fizzing sensation in my chest and neck. I don't have a temperature. Sam had taken great delight in checking this earlier, he loves gadgets and the ear thermometer definitely classed as a thing to be played with.

Geoff shook his head. "Time to go to the quack's, maybe?"

"Probably not." I really hate going to the doctor's, I always feel such a fraud. Seventy per cent of my ailments all seem to disappear as soon as I walk through the door and it's almost guaranteed that two or three days after any visit I end up with some sort of cold or sickness bug. "Let me sleep on it and we'll just see how I am in the morning, a good night's sleep and it will probably all just go away."

I slept for twelve hours that night and even Mortimer trampling me in an effort to get into the bed didn't wake me up. Geoff told me the next day that he'd woken up to find Mort lying on my chest and staring intently into my face. I was actually quite glad I hadn't woken up and seen that, I'd have probably had a heart attack.

I was a little confused when I woke up the next morning and, thinking over the day before, ran through that sort of body check some people do. Arms and legs all in working order? Check. Headache? No. Ha I was right, I was fine.

I was reminded that I'd avoided food the previous day by a good deep rumble from a rather sad and empty stomach. Feeling the need for tea I jumped out of bed intending to head for the kettle.

As soon as I gained my feet the world tilted sideways. It was an odd sensation, I felt as though someone had made one of my legs shorter than the other and staggering around like a haggis on a flat surface I bounced, first off the bed, then off the wall, I hit my forehead on the wet window and ended up sitting back on the bed. Looking up I could see where my forehead had made a neat oval mark in the condensation.

I ran through my internal checks again. Well this was very odd, there really didn't seem to be anything wrong at all. Deciding that I must have just tripped I got to my feet again. I actually managed to take two whole steps before the world tilted once more and I found myself face down on the kitchen floor.

The crash woke Geoff and Mortimer. The dog jumped off the bed and stood over me, his ears pricked and making soft growly noises in the back of his throat, for once he didn't trample me but he did keep poking me as he gently snuffled around my neck. I rolled over on to my back and, grabbing his collar managed to get myself into a sitting position. Sometimes it's useful to have a dog that has the shape and consistency of a sturdy log.

"Marie?" Geoff hopped over the end of the bed and helped me back to my feet. I managed to stand up and then sagged again. "Whoa!" he said as I slithered down his leg and ended up sitting on the floor again. "What's the matter?"

I giggled. I really couldn't help myself. I felt as though I'd had a bottle of vodka for breakfast. "I can't stand up," I said.

"Hmm." Geoff studied me for a moment. "Let's get you off the floor shall we?"

I nodded happily. I wasn't really worried by all this but all the tilting and turning was beginning to make me feel a little sick and I had a new headache brewing behind my left eye.

I grabbed the end of the bed and, with Geoff's help, managed to hoist myself back onto the bed. As soon as I was flat again everything settled down.

"I think I'm going to take the day off today," Geoff picked up his phone. "We really need to get you to the doctor's. We'll drop Sam off at school on the way."

The car journey wasn't pleasant and, by the time we arrived at the surgery, all I wanted to do was lie down again. The doctor was a little confused and you know there's likely to be trouble when they slip out for a moment and come back with someone older and wiser.

They walked me around the office, made me do odd exercises with my fingers, shone lights into my eyes, and made me look in all directions, all the time talking in hushed tones and ticking things off on a sheet. Eventually the older doctor sat down in front of me and gave me a big bright smile.

Uh oh, I thought, doctors rarely smile unless they have bad news. The rule of thumb goes: the bigger the smile the more awful the news.

"Now then, Marie," he said.

Oh yes. This was definitely not looking good.

"We need to make some telephone calls and we're going to try to get you up to the hospital for an MRI. Nothing to worry about but we just need to make sure that there's nothing sinister going on." He gave me another big smile.

I leant back in the chair. It was a lot easier than trying to hold myself upright. "You think I've got a brain tumour, don't you?" I said. I'd worked at the hospital for long enough that I knew why they were worried.

The smile fell away and he nodded. "It's a possibility," he said. "At the very least we need a neurologist to check you over."

Well, this on top of everything else that was going on was just ducky. "Are you sure it's not just an inner ear thing or stress? We do have some problems at the moment."

"Well that's what we want to find out. What do you do for a job?"

"I'm a Physiotherapy Assistant up at Addenbrookes," I said.

"Which ward?" He pulled a pad of paper across the desk and began ticking things off.

I went blank, I really couldn't remember which ward I worked in. "Hip replacements and the elderly that have fallen over." I sounded like a confused ten year old.

He scribbled a signature on a piece of paper and handed it to me. "Well with you staggering around like that, I think the patients would have to hold you up don't you think? Anyway, you can't drive until you've been cleared so, whatever the outcome, this will sign you off for at least two weeks."

Oh, well that was an unexpected bonus. But then the reality crashed down. I couldn't drive? How on earth was I supposed to get Sam to school? There certainly wasn't any public transport where we were. I couldn't do the shopping, I wouldn't be able to do any washing.

I looked at Geoff for support, living where we did this was going to cause some real problems for us.

"Take a seat in the waiting room and we'll phone the hospital, we'll pull some strings and see if we can get you seen immediately." The doctor gave me another encouraging smile and patted me on the knee.

Geoff and a very capable nurse helped me stagger out to where I could sit in comfort. I didn't feel giggly any more and, sitting out in the waiting room I indulged in a full-on panic attack. Luckily Geoff was there to sort it all out. As I started on my usual long line of "what ifs" he held up a hand and stopped me mid-sentence. "Facts first, decisions and worries afterward," he said.

I nodded but the "what ifs" hadn't gone away. I could feel them, lurking, just beyond my thin veneer of calm.

About twenty minutes later the doctor re-appeared. He looked harassed and began apologising from about ten feet away. "I'm so sorry," he said.

Geoff and I looked up at him. I quashed the very real need to say "What's up, doc?" I could feel slightly hysterical giggling bubbling just below my throat, I either needed to laugh or scream.

"They are completely booked solid, there's absolutely no way they can fit you in for an MRI until Friday," he said.

Actually, that made me feel a lot better; I'm still not sure why.

He handed me a card with a name, a room number, and an appointment time written on it and, after apologising again, scuttled away.

Back at the boat Geoff settled me onto the sofa, he made me a cup of tea and then, making sure I was mostly upright he wandered off to carry on sorting out the electrics. He wanted to stay and keep me company but I was fairly sure I didn't want any so I gently sent him off to his engine room.

After I'd drunk my tea, I hauled myself to my feet and made my unsteady way down the boat toward the computer. I kept giggling, my hilarity had very little to do with genuine humour and much more to do with brewing hysteria. The physical feeling was very similar to that time we'd gone to France on the ferry. The sea had been rather dynamic that day and we'd found out, rather explosively that I suffered from sea sickness. Looking out of the window at the flat water in which *Minerva* quietly wallowed, there wasn't any way I could fool myself that this was the fault of any outside activity.

Turning on the laptop I proceeded to search out everything I could about my symptoms. The doctors were wrong, I was sure of it. They were just being careful; I didn't have time to indulge in something so potentially serious as a tumour. Life really couldn't be that unfair.

Life can be that unfair, but, luckily for all of us, mine wasn't. Over the next four days the nausea and the weaving subsided and, by the time I was due at the hospital, the symptoms had all but faded away. As usual I was going to have to see a doctor and feel a complete fraud.

The neurologist was stick-thin and severe-looking, quite terrifying. If I hadn't been so sure I was fine he would have had me quaking in my boots. However, I was so happy that everything was mostly back to normal I would have faced down Giant Haystacks himself. My protestations of severe good health cut no mustard with the dour little man at all. He listened patiently to all I had to say and then waved me into a chair. It took another hour to run through all the tests and, when he had finished, he finally cracked a smile. It was actually more of a twitch than a smile, lasting only a fleeting second before he returned to his obviously normal blank expression.

"You seem fine, a little wobbly but it seemed to have been more of an inner ear problem than anything else," he said.

"A little wobbly?" I'd thought that the tests would have shown that I was back in perfect health.

He nodded. "There's that one test with your left hand that obviously gives you trouble."

I knew the one he was talking about. You hold out your right hand, palm up and flat. You then place the palm of your left hand ninety degrees palm to palm on top of the right. Turning your left hand over, you then place the back of your hand against the palm of your right and then you alternate, getting faster and faster, swapping from back to front. Almost like buttering bread. I can bat my right hand back and forth across my left but I seem to have a lot of trouble doing it the other way around.

He stared at me for a moment. "But it's not a problem really." He had a laconic, toneless way of speaking. "A lot of people are less dextrous with one hand."

I decided to push the issue. "So I don't have a brain tumour?"

He studied me further, his expression one of extreme sadness. I felt as though I was a pet dog that was going to have to be put down. "Well I would never say that someone definitely didn't have that sort of an issue," he said. "But I would say that its more likely than not that you don't."

I worked my way through all the double negatives and vagaries in that sentence. "So I might?"

"Every single one of us 'might'," he gave a glum shrug as though it was inevitable that every member of the population harboured a lurking, time-delayed parasite deep within our psyche. "But you don't show any signs of having one, but there might be one, hidden away somewhere."

Well, that was cheerful. "Do you think I need to go for this MRI scan?"

He looked disconsolately down at his desk and, after a deep sigh, slowly shook his head. "You can if you want to," he said. "But sometimes it shows things that then need to be investigated that then just turn out to be nothing."

Good grief, this man answered questions like a politician. "If you were me, would you go for a scan?" This was almost beginning to seem like some sort of game. Get a straight answer . . . ten points.

The neurologist shook his head slowly and gave a little shrug. He looked completely dejected. "Probably not," he said.

I subsided. That was obviously the best I was going to get. I thanked him for his time and, after grabbing my coat, stood up. As I headed for the door a thought occurred to me. "So, I can drive now?" I was completely fed up with having no transport, I'd been bouncing off the walls all week.

He nodded. "But it's better if you don't."

I was confused by the difference between his body language and what he'd actually said.

"Why?"

"Cars are dangerous." He sighed and placing the top back on his pen he placed it slowly and carefully back into the red plastic stationery tidy that sat on his desk. "Those things really will kill you."

I was very confused. "But legally I'm OK to drive?"

He nodded again. "If you must."

What? Just . . . What?

Back at home I finally relaxed and immediately started thinking about our looming move. There's a difference between being sure in your own mind that there is nothing wrong with you and having a medical professional, however morose, confirm your suspicions. Now that the immediate problem of possible brain surgery was removed I could concentrate on more pressing issues. With a big sigh I called the local school and made arrangements to visit with Sam. I couldn't ignore the facts any longer; changes were going to have to be made.

When Geoff came home that evening I gave him the good news and after a celebratory packet of biscuits he also turned his mind to our next problem. "So," he said, "what on earth are we going to do between being chucked out of here and being able to get through Denver and out to our new mooring?"

I had no answers for him. Any visitor mooring that was likely to be able to accommodate us was going to make parking the cars very difficult. There was no way that Geoff could empty his van of all the tools and bits and bobs he carried around. If he left the van parked overnight in some remote spot and left everything in it we could almost guarantee that it would be battered and empty by first light.

November was fast running out and with the weather being so very foul it was looking as though we couldn't get anywhere even if we wanted to. Floods covered East Anglia and pretty much every other part of England. Those boaters that had managed to find themselves moorings at Huntingdon and beyond found themselves stuck around Earith. Rivers broke their banks and the surrounding fields began to look like huge pools. Roads were closed, diversions were set in place and still the rain fell in an almost continual stream.

Feelings were running very high about the weather. Walking through Ely one afternoon I stood behind an elderly gentleman while waiting to cross the road at a pedestrian crossing. A car, obviously moving a little faster than it should, hit a puddle and covered the gentleman in muddy water. He spluttered in massive indignation and stamped his feet to shake the water from his raincoat. Turning to me his mouth moved but no sound came out, he was obviously beyond angry. Eventually he managed to get himself under control. Pulling himself up to his full height he sniffed once and settled his hat more firmly on his head. He studied me for a moment and then nodded and leant forward to speak.

I held my breath and wondered what on earth he was going to say. I hoped he didn't think it was my fault he'd been soaked, I took a step back.

He stared at me, eye to eye and then shook his head. "Drought my arse," he said. He swallowed convulsively for a moment and then nodded as though we were privy to some sort of government conspiracy. He raised his finger and shook it at the sky, when he spoke again his voice rose in a shout. "Drought my sodding ARSE."

At this point the lights changed and, at the frenzied beeping from the crossing machine, he whirled and stamped away through the puddles. I'd hovered about and let the lights change back to red. I felt that one more soaking might unhinge him completely and I really didn't want to be behind him when he exploded.

The river running past our boat, wind-whipped into white horses, washed boats, trees, and other flotsam past at a breathless pace. Nobody in their right mind wanted to go out in that. Even if you could battle the side winds long enough to get mid-stream, there was no way you had any real chance of getting where you wanted to go. Most people only went out if they were heading in the same direction as the river. I just hoped that they didn't want to stop or were happy to just run

292

into the bank because trying to pull in gently was just going to be an exercise in futility.

Most of the boaters viewed the conditions with a certain amount of trepidation but we knew that there was to be no stay of execution. Those that had dared to ask had been met with very terse and negative replies. Even Geoff, normally gentle and good humoured, had become quite militant about the whole thing. "I don't care what she does." He stared out of the window and waved as another intrepid boater swished past at a rate of knots. "There's no way we're taking *Minerva* out in this, especially if we're going to have to tow Charlie's boat. We wouldn't even make it to the next moorings."

My heart sank, I'd completely forgotten the other boat. Dragging that was going to put some serious strain on *Minerva*'s vintage engine.

One morning in late November we finally woke to silence and for a moment couldn't work out what had happened. Geoff cautiously peered out of the window. Grey, quiet, and dry, the world stared back at him. "It's actually stopped raining." He sounded surprised. "I need to make a phone call."

I nodded, handed him my phone and watched as he wandered off up the bank with it. Eventually the conversation finished and he trudged back down to the boat. He shuddered as the warmth from the fire met him as he came through the door. The wind may have died down and the rain may have stopped but the temperature was dropping rapidly.

"What was all that about?" I asked.

"I think I may have found a temporary solution," he said. "Grab your coat, we need to go and look at a mooring."

We finally found the moorings after about half an hour of exploring the country roads beyond Littleport. Pulling into an area that was part car park, part boat park, and what appeared to be a large outdoor workshop we searched for the owner. Eventually a tall, thin man, in a check flannel shirt and black woolly hat appeared from behind what appeared to be an old railway carriage. I shivered on his behalf, he didn't appear to have nearly enough clothes on for the weather.

"Did you phone earlier about the mooring?" He grinned at us. "Come on, this way. Hope you're feeling fit, it's a fair walk."

He wasn't exaggerating and, as we trotted along another set of flood defences, our heads tucked into the collars of our coats, he explained how it all worked.

"You can park down in the car park," he said. "It's quite safe and obviously, as there's quite a walk, we supply a trolley for you to drag stuff about. If you have a lot of stuff like coal and shopping, just let us know and we can arrange to bring it over to your boat by lawn mower."

The mooring he showed us was almost perfect. No electricity, but we had our shiny red generator so that shouldn't be a problem and it was only six miles away from Sam's new school so that would cut the school run right down. I recognised a couple of boats from the marina. Bill and Jenny were just over the river and we were to be parked right next to Janis the upholsterer. I laughed, it was like home from home and I felt that, apart from the walk which could prove more than a little irritating if I had a lot of stuff to carry, it would suit us beautifully.

Geoff, however, wasn't that enamoured.

"I'm going to have to get up so early to get to work," he said as we drove back to the boat.

I felt guilty, I hadn't considered that. Geoff already leaves at seven o'clock to make him get up even earlier was a bit much to ask.

"Do we have a choice?" I really wanted to say that we wouldn't bother, we'd find something closer to his work but I knew there was just nowhere, well, nowhere within our budget and nowhere that didn't involve getting through Denver.

Geoff didn't answer but pulled into the car park of a small supermarket just outside Littleport. He rested his head on the steering wheel and then gently banged his head on the leather cover.

The reality of living on a boat, although you appear to have a vast amount of freedom, is that unless you have ability to just travel and you don't need to go to work or get kids to school you are incredibly limited. If you're buying or renting a house and you don't like the first one you visit you know there are always other options. We don't have that luxury and, counting hard, I worked out we had exactly three options: One: sell up. Two: take the mooring we'd just visited, Three: float around, hopping on and off visitor moorings, overstay the allotted time, and just hope that the Environment

Agency were feeling charitable enough to turn a blind eye. With Denver being closed, escaping the system around Cambridge was impossible and under normal circumstances we should have had a big triangle in which to try and lose ourselves along with all the other boaters that had already left the marina. However, the floods and the river closures were rapidly closing that triangle down.

With the hardest, coldest time of the year rapidly approaching and with the seriously inclement weather showing no signs of letting up we had to make some decisions that, obviously, neither of us were comfortable making.

"I just don't know." Geoff lifted his head from the steering wheel and stared, unseeing, at the front doors of the supermarket. "I want to be somewhere safe for Christmas. Ideally I want to be gone by the beginning of December. If we wait it out until the very last moment we could be into ice and snow and if the river freezes again like it did last year we're going to be in big trouble."

"Well, if the river freezes again, there won't be anything we can do," I said. "We just won't be going anywhere."

Geoff shook his head and sighed again. "Can you cope with getting the shopping and all the coal, gas, and diesel to the boat from where the car's going to be parked if we take that mooring?"

I nodded. "I'm going to have to; the nights are just going to get darker. I've already handed my notice in because there's no way I'll be able to get to work and pick up Sam from school. You'll be out for at least another hour a day with the extra travelling." I trailed off and then shrugged. "We have no choices. Until they manage to get the lock open and all of us waiting here can get off the system and out into the Middle Levels here we're all going to have to stay." I gave him a nudge. "It can't keep raining and it seems to have stopped for now. Hopefully the river levels will drop and we'll finally be able to get through."

Geoff turned to look at me. "It's not the river levels that are the problem now."

Oh great, something else had obviously happened; something that I was blissfully unaware of. "Go on," I said, "What's stopping us now?"

"All the rain and the flood water has moved a huge bank of silt right into the lock." He grabbed my phone and tapped at it for a couple of minutes frowning in concentration. "Here, look."

I took my phone and stared at the picture that he'd found. "What exactly am I looking at here?" It looked like a portion of wet sand stuck between two fence rails.

"That's Salters Lode," he said.

I finally worked out that the lock pound was supposed to be between the two rails I was studying. "Oh good grief, that's not going to wash away, is it." The silt had completely filled the lock, rendering it completely useless.

Geoff shook his head. "No, they're going to have to dig that lock out before boats can get through," he said, "and I can't see them doing it until they're sure the weather has improved. That could mean that any one waiting to get through just sits wherever they are for the next four months."

"Four months?" I couldn't imagine having to keep moving for four months.

Geoff rubbed his forehead. "As the man of this household I'm making a decision," he announced.

I snorted a laugh. "Yes, dear?"

"We . . ." he reached over and, grabbing me by the shoulders, pulled me into his arm pit. ". . . are going to do whatever you want to."

"Oh great, thanks," I said.

Geoff laughed and climbed out of the car. "Come on you."

"Where are we going?" I clambered out and then immediately wished I hadn't, the raw wind took my breath away.

"In search of cake." Geoff locked the car and, head down against the wind that had sprung up, strode off across the car park.

I scurried in his wake.

Once inside the supermarket we managed to draw breath again and wandered off arm in arm around the shelves picking up nice but nutritionally valueless comfort foods.

"We don't have a choice about that mooring really, do we?" Geoff piled cheese and olives, crackers and salami into the basket.

I shook my head. "Not really, but the only person that suffers is you."

Geoff shrugged. "Well it's going to be a lot of extra work for you as well because you're going to have to pick up the slack."

"Hey!" I poked him in the ribs.

He laughed. "I didn't mean it like that and you know it," he said. "I just meant that you're going to have to do all the heavy lifting, sort out those big gas bottles, run that generator, make sure all the electrics are working, get coal, water, and diesel, and just do all the things that we haven't had to do up till now."

I nodded. I hadn't really realised how cosseted we'd been on our mooring. Electricity on tap, coal delivered. This was going to be an exercise in really living on a boat, not just playing at it. This was definitely one step into the wilds.

For just a moment I had a sudden weird "I wish I lived in a house" moment. But after being supplanted by images of the dreaded postman and those terrifying piles of bills the moment passed and my resolve was given a firm talking to.

I picked up a bottle of rum and edged it gently into the basket. "We'll survive," I said.

The next weekend was one of goodbyes. Bill and Drew, packed and itching to go, pulled away from the moorings with a lot of waving and shouting of insults (mainly from Drew). They weren't going very far but felt that they just wanted to be away. Bill had, unfortunately, been made redundant and I could understand that they wanted to hang on to as much of their savings as possible, especially with Christmas just around the corner. Spending money on mooring fees when they didn't need to was just another unnecessary expense. I didn't blame them in the slightest but I was still reluctant to leave. Seven years on and off we'd been at this very mooring, the idea of having to leave and never come back made me a little sad.

After waving Bill and Drew on their way, Geoff retired back into his engine room. He'd decided that this weekend was his last chance to service the engine and make sure that everything was ready to go. He set about it with a grim determination.

With our destination now set, I decided to sit Sam down and make sure he was all right about going to his new school. We'd been to visit the previous week and, while far more aesthetically challenged than his old school, the teachers were positive and the atmosphere had seemed excellent.

I had been waiting all week for the final realisation and subsequent meltdown from Sam and, when it didn't materialise, I'd decided to push some buttons and see what came out of that fuzzy mass he calls a brain.

It worked out that he was really looking forward to it. He already had friends there at an out-of-school drama club that he attended and, due to a birthday party he'd been invited to, he now knew many of his new peers. He didn't seem worried in the slightest and I came away from the conversation wondering if it was me that had a fuzzy mass and not him. Well, there were always first-day blues to look forward to but, as that wouldn't happen until January there really wasn't anything I could stress about.

If I had to be honest, the change, if there had to be one, couldn't really have come at a better time. Half way through year nine he was old enough to understand why he had to change and see the advantages. He hadn't started his GCSEs and his options were to be decided at the end of this year and would be done at the new school. It could have been so much worse.

His plan to become an accountant hadn't changed and with the new school specialising in Business and Enterprise, rather than the science and languages that he was used to, he was excited and keen to change. I was definitely the one dragging my heels.

"Mother, you're fussing," he said.

I remembered the bullying he'd taken when, in his first year of high school, his classmates had found out that he lived on a boat. The comments had ranged from speculations about his cleanliness to the possibility that his family were a bunch of thieves and scroungers. It had taken the full and furious might of the entire year staff to put a stop to it. Unlike his sister who put a stop to all comments in her own furious way, Sam was a much more gentle soul and took the comments very much to heart.

I watched him walk away down the boat. Older now, he slouched along, baggy jeans trailing along the floor, oversized hoody with skulls and roses emblazoned on the front and long hair that, hanging way beyond his shoulders filled the hood and fell over his face. He might be able to take the new school in his stride but I had to wonder how the new school would cope with him. He certainly didn't fit in with the general masses, he looked like some rock and roll dropout. His uncanny ability to work through any maths problem with an air of ease and enjoyment only added another layer of oddness to the child.

As I was contemplating all this his father stepped through the door and I had to smile. Sam was almost exactly like his dad had been in his younger days, right down to the hair and the love of maths. I grinned and relaxed, being a little "odd" had never done his father any harm. Slow to anger, friendly, helpful, and meticulous almost to the point of having obsessive compulsive disorder. Both of them dealt with life quite well even if they did sometimes appear to be studying it from the outside. Geoff, feeling me grinning at him looked up with a frown.

He put on a worried look. "What have I done now?"

"Nothing at all," I said and put my worries about Sam's future aside. "Tea?"

CHAPTER
TWELVE

With Boat All Poised And Farewells Said, The Only Way To Go's Ahead.

December the 6th and with no excuses left we finally made the decision to go. The boat had been ready for at least a week. The engine had been serviced, all the electrics were ready, and even Geoff's mad smoke removal device seemed to be finally working as he planned.

We'd meant to leave the previous weekend but unfortunately the first test of our diesel generator had not gone well at all.

With baited breath we'd stood in the rain and watched as Geoff brought the big generator to life. It had coughed and spluttered for a couple of seconds and then settled down to a deep and even tone.

"Well, that works well." Geoff grinned at the big engine as it vibrated gently on a specially created plinth above our big boat engine.

I coughed and waved a hand back and forth. "Smells evil," I said. "Aren't those exhaust fumes supposed to be outside the boat?"

"Aha!" Geoff's grin stretched wider and he pointed to a small white switch set high amidst the silver ducting that now ran from the generator to a hole that he'd cut in the roof. "This is test number two." He reached up and, with a firm finger, flicked the switch on.

Nothing happened. Geoff frowned and peered into the ducting. "Dammit all," he muttered.

"So, back to the drawing board then, yes?" I coughed and decided that fresh air was rapidly becoming a necessity.

My husband ignored me and, flicking the generator off, he began taking things apart.

I left him to it. I have found that standing around and asking questions tends to make him a little testy. The best thing I could do to help was to go and put the kettle on.

As I stepped inside the boat, the smell of exhaust fumes was really quite revolting and despite the sub-zero temperatures I opened every window and door. Sam and Mortimer decided that they'd be safer playing ball and wandered off to run themselves into warmer oblivion.

Geoff came in about an hour later. "I've found the problem." He sat down and studied the fire which was blazing away quite merrily. "It's really cold in here," he said.

I peered at him from under a blanket. I'd also got on three jumpers, two pairs of socks and I'd stolen a pair of his thermal long johns. "I had to open all the windows because the boat was full of diesel smoke when I came back in," I said.

"Oh." Geoff looked a little crestfallen. "Well, I think I've fixed it now."

"Are you sure?"

Geoff opened his mouth but didn't say anything. He stayed that way for a moment and then gave a brief nod. "Ninety per cent," he said.

"So we have a ten per cent chance of dying of carbon monoxide poisoning, do we?" My teeth were chattering.

Geoff nodded. "I don't think I want to trust this system without replacing our carbon monoxide detectors."

So that had ended the possibility of leaving that day.

A week later and the boat was finally declared ready to go. The little boat was tied firmly alongside and all that we had was either in a new storage unit or crammed in or on top of the boat. I felt a sad sense of déjà vu. We'd done this before when we'd sold our last boat. We'd said goodbye to everyone and puttered away, but even then I had the hope of coming back one day and, sure enough, return we had. This time there was no chance of coming back and, even if we could, the community that made the life so good was now scattered up and down several different waterways.

Elaine and Dion had decided to stay until the very end and they waved us off as we pulled away from our mooring for what would be the very last time. There were lots of shouts of "see you in a couple of weeks" but it didn't really matter, we knew that change had been thrust upon us once more and, like the last time, we either rolled with the punches or we went down because of them.

At least the problem of dying by slow asphyxiation had been abated. My clever husband had installed a fan (stolen from a defunct fan heater!) inside a long piece of ducting which, when turned on, pulled all the smoke away from the generator exhaust and out of the chimney that he'd created. It was a little Heath Robinson but it worked very well and the shiny new carbon monoxide detectors that I'd installed at both the front and the back of the boat gave us happy green flashing lights even with the generator under full load. He might be a bit vague at times but you have to love a man that smiles every time he watches puffs of smoke appear from a chimney.

I'd never run two boats together before and was surprised at how easy it was. I'd been imagining that *Minerva* would pull to the left or would be difficult to steer. She *was* a little heavier on the steering but she coped very well and with the ropes untied we pushed her and her cling-on away from the bank and headed out toward the river.

As we travelled past I noticed that the marina was a sad sight. Most of the boats had now left and the odd boat still moored along the river looked like a retired street fighter's remaining teeth. There were no cars in the car park and, with winter making everything look sad and unloved, the whole place was just desolate. It looked so gloomy and forsaken that I had to work quite hard not to think bad thoughts at the people that had brought this change about.

My gloomy introspection stayed with me until I discovered that standing with one foot on *Minerva's* gunwales and one foot on *Hedgepig's* was like very safe surfing. I had great fun watching the water whoosh below my feet as the two boats meandered along side by side. Ah, it's the little things that make life worthwhile. Sam came and joined me and Geoff laughed as we decided that singing Wipe-out by the Beach Boys was definitely the way to go.

It took us five hours to get to the turning down the little river that was to be our home for the next four months. The journey was grey and uneventful. It shouldn't really have taken that long at all but with the swollen river running against us and poor *Minerva* dragging a recalcitrant butty it made the going far slower than it should have. There were no locks and no thrills. The river beyond Ely isn't the most exciting place in the world and the landscape mirrored both the sky and our mood. Flat, grey, and decidedly soggy.

Eventually we slowed to make the right turn into the creek. I peered up at the bridge by The Ship Inn, it looked very low. Turning back to Geoff who was standing on the plate I pointed up at the bridge. "Bit low, isn't it?" I had to shout over the sound of the engine, the water and the wind that had picked up over the last half hour.

Geoff grinned and nodded.

Well, either he knew that we'd have the clearance we needed or he hadn't heard me and was just smiling and agreeing in the same way he used to when we had a motorbike.

He slowed further and I peered up at the underside of the bridge. It really was far closer than I was comfortable with. I tried to ignore its looming presence. Geoff never left these details to chance, he would have checked the height, I hoped he had. Having to buy a new chimney (again) was never going to be high on my list of fun things to do.

There was no problem with the chimney — Geoff had already removed the stack. The bridge cleared the little collar by at least twelve inches. It was a real shame, however, that the television aerial was at least eighteen inches higher than anything else. It wouldn't have been so bad if the aerial had hit the edge of the bridge, bent, and collapsed on top of the boat but it didn't. Being of fairly springy metal, it hit the edge of the bridge and was dragged along the horizontal concrete support, shedding little metal tines as it went. I winced, not because of the rain of metal that was bouncing all around me but because of the noise. Like someone with very long nails attacking a blackboard, it slowly scraped, screeched, and screamed its way across the concrete support at the near side of the bridge.

I breathed a sigh of relief and tried to get my teeth unclenched as the concrete ended and there was a gap. The aerial sprang into the gap and then hit the next support (steel) with a loud shuddering "Boi.oi.oi.oi.ng!" that sent the pigeons roosting in the darkness of the uprights bolting, panicked and screaming, into the air. A rain of pigeon poo spattered the front deck along with a few more bits of metal. "Boi.oi.oi.oi.ng!" the aerial hit the next support and "Boi.oi.oi.oi.ng!", the next and the next and the next, still occasionally shedding the little bent tines that were supposed to pick up the television signal. Eventually there was only the other horizontal concrete support to go and sure enough it scraped and wailed its way across that, ending with another happy "Boi.oi.oi.oi.ng!" as it sprang out from under the bridge and into the open air again.

I looked up at it and sighed. The aerial resembled nothing more than a demented steel Christmas tree, one that had been left up until about February. Bent and naked, all it needed was some frayed tinsel and a couple of broken baubles and it would have been perfect. I looked back at Geoff.

"Whoops," he shouted. "I forgot about that."

No kidding? The neighbours in front of us, when we met them, seemed nice but due to the weather nobody really wanted to hang around and chat. The neighbour behind us, I'd already met and quite frankly she was terrifying.

Janis is what I would class as a "real boater". Standing about five foot ten, she dresses for the weather and pays not even lip service to the idea of "fashion". Her naturally curly grey hair is usually caught up in a ponytail from which it spends its days trying to escape. You can always hear her coming due to the very serviceable and heavy boots she favours. Slightly older than myself, she takes no nonsense from anyone and in no way suffers from my vagueness and my psychotic need to worry and fret. If I needed help she would be high on my list of "capable people". Since the sad death of her husband several years previously, Janis has been running two boats, completely alone. One boat, the larger of the two, is her living accommodation and the other, an overflowing workshop is where she creates elegant soft furnishings and cratch covers for boaters up and down the system. Highly trained and very professional, it's no wonder she has a waiting list for the work she does. I have to admit to being a little in awe of her. She's totally independent, the very idea of needing help is complete anathema to her and she is everything I like to think I could be but know full well that I would never even have the guts to do half of what she does.

We'd been moored for about a week when she came stamping around to "sort out a problem". I'd been expecting her. The moorings were so close together that when our two boats were parked in front of her two boats she couldn't get out. Unfortunately there wasn't really much we could do about it and, rather than have Janis angry at me I'd resolved to ask the landowner if we could move further down and get out of her way.

When I suggested this to her she looked at me as if I was insane.

"Well, I don't want you to do that," she said. Standing on top of the decking, with her grey hair once more creating a windswept halo around her head, she glared down at me.

I felt as if I'd suggested a ridiculous project to a headmistress and had to get a firm grip on myself. "Well I'm not sure what we can do," I winced and waited for her to beat me to death with her barge pole.

"How about if we move *Hedgepig* further alongside *Minerva*? If we tie her to the front of our boat rather than at that back you'd be able to see around both boats and you'd have far more room to manoeuvre."

Janis flattened her lips and stared at me. "Yes OK," she gave me a huge and genuine smile. "That's a great compromise, thanks."

"Oh." I was just about to start explaining myself again when I realised that she'd agreed. "Great," I said. "I'll move her now."

"No you won't," she said. "Move it later, coffee?"

My mouth and my brain tripped over each other and I found myself nodding. "That would be lovely." I managed to stammer out.

Trying to describe her to Geoff later I was definitely failing to find the right adjectives. "Imagine the outcome if Camilla Fritton . . ."

"Who?" Geoff looked completely nonplussed.

"The headmistress of St Trinian's."

Geoff sniggered and nodded.

". . . and Attila the Hun got together and had a child, I'm fairly sure the outcome would be Janis or someone very like her."

Geoff leaned back on the sofa. "Jolly hockey sticks with an axe?" He shook his head and howled with laughter.

As I got to know Janis better I found out that my initial thoughts about her personality had been way off base. Yes, she had a "can do" attitude and yes, not much scared her but she had a sense of humour second to none and a wry view of the world that was both refreshing and catching. I was very pleased that we'd managed to end up with her as a neighbour. She seemed to put up with us as well, she also learnt to deal with Mortimer's over-affectionate nature and he, like the rest of us, would rapidly subside when she turned her steely gaze in his direction.

Being out on a "wild" mooring was quite new to me and it certainly took a little time for me to get myself in gear and sort myself out. There were so many things to do to keep the boat running and, due to Geoff's increased travel time and decreased daylight as the year drew to a close, I found myself trying to juggle all of them.

Bags of coal were no longer delivered but had to be collected and then manhandled (or in this case woman-handled) up a flight of steps and then along a quarter mile stretch of bank to the boat. Gas and diesel also had to be collected. Luckily there was water but as the weather became colder we just knew that the water would freeze and we'd be left with nothing.

One Saturday afternoon I was staring out at the horrible weather. Horizontal sleet carried on strong winds battered the boat and I really didn't want to go outside. I'd been putting off turning on the generator all morning but I knew that any minute now the batteries would run out and I'd be forced out into the cold.

Of course, almost as soon as I'd had this thought the television clicked off and the fridge, humming away to itself under the sink, shuddered into silence.

"Mum, the electricity's gone." Sam looked up from where he was working on a piece of homework about the Great Fire of London.

"Thank you, Sam." I heaved myself to my feet and began looking for gloves, hat, scarf, and anything else I could layer on to keep the wind from stripping the flesh from my bones. "I think I noticed that."

Sam grinned and went back to writing his screenplay. The laptop, with its own battery, would run for at least another half an hour, long enough for me to get the generator running.

I clambered out of the boat and, pulling my hat firmly down over my eyes and ears, battled my way to the back of the boat. I climbed down into the back cabin and glared at the generator, squatting big and red just above the engine. Checking the fuel levels I noticed that the red fuel indicator was nowhere to be seen. I groaned and lifted the jerry can of diesel just to make sure there was some still there. We had loads, the can was so heavy and full it was difficult to lift. "Oh that's just great," I whined to myself. Heaving the can to the step, I positioned it so that I could just tip it and grabbing the plastic jug that I used to fill the generator I carefully held it beneath the can and began to pour. When the jug was full I carefully carried it through to the engine room, climbed the step that I had to use to be able to reach the top and poured the diesel into the reservoir. Three trips like this and the tank was full, job one done. Once the generator had fuel there was a checklist of things to do: turn off the inverter, there's no point leaving the inverter on as the batteries don't charge nearly as quickly as they do when it's off. Walk back around the generator, making sure to duck under all the cables and other bits of engine. Once in position run through the start-up checks: generator on, check. Lever one moved to run, check. Lever marked decompression pulled down, check. Cut-off switches in the up position, check. Turn the key, check.

The generator coughed loudly into life and I waited for the engine note to settle into its normal steady chug while I climbed around to the other side of the engine. Change switch from battery to generator, check. Turn on exhaust fan system, check. I stood and watched as the battery charger illuminated and then, confident that this would run for a couple of hours, backed out of the cramped engine room and into the open air. I waved to Janis who was sitting hunched at her sewing machine and then made a bolt back into the warm; I put the kettle on and then went back to watching my interrupted film.

About half an hour later, Sam and I looked up from what we were doing at exactly the same moment. The engine note from the generator had changed. One minute it would be humming along and then it would dip as though disappearing over a hill and then come back loudly for a moment.

Sam voiced my thoughts. "That doesn't sound good."

I shook my head and without even bothering to dress for the cold hopped out of the boat.

Black and grey smoke billowed in huge clouds from both rear doors. I only hesitated a moment before running at full pelt down the length of the boat. I swung in through the back doors in a mad rush to get to the generator.

I could hardly see a thing. Thick smoke filled both the engine room and the back cabin. Feeling my way around the boat engine I grabbed the emergency cut off switch and pushed it upward. The generator whined and shuddered into silence and the smoke began to clear.

"Are you all right?" Janis stuck her head into the back cabin and was almost pushed overboard as I barrelled out into the open air coughing and spluttering, my eyes streaming tears. "What happened?"

I couldn't answer her for a couple of seconds, I was coughing so hard. "I have no idea," I finally managed to get some words out.

While I indulged in another bout of coughing, Janis went to make coffee and we stood staring at the back of my boat as the last wisps of black smoke escaped from the engine room.

"What are you going to do?" Janis shook her head and gathered up the cups. "I'm not sure that's fixable."

"I honestly don't know." I reached into one of the little drawers in the back cabin and pulled out the user's manual. "I can't wait until Geoff comes home, he might not be back until late. I'm going to have to try and work out what happened."

Janis and I looked at each other. Really, there was no need to say anything at all, we both knew how likely that was going to be.

"Let me know if you need any help," she said.

I nodded, thanked her and then began to study the manual. It didn't make any sense at all, most of it seemed to be in Chinese.

Opening the side hatches gave me a good view of the generator and, in an effort to find some sort of inspiration, I squatted down and stared at the infernal machine. I knew I was going to have to take the damn thing apart but I really wasn't sure what I could do with the bits after that.

Leaning forward I peered into the wooden box that Geoff had made in an attempt to make the generator quieter. A particularly vicious gust of wind blew and after a stumble I fell forward into the engine room. I didn't hit the floor. My reaching hand had found a spar to hold on to. But, from my slightly prone position I noticed something a little odd and, reaching down with one hand I wiped my fingers across the floor. Black oil dripped from each digit back into the dark pool beneath the generator. "I'm sure that wasn't there yesterday." I muttered. Pushing myself back onto dry land I reversed and slid through the hatch to stand on top of the battery box. Using my phone as a torch I shone a light into the generator box. The bottom was slick with oil; the metal feet of the generator were completely submerged in a little pool of the stuff.

A spider dropped down from the ceiling and before it could touch the oil I grabbed its strand of web and deposited it into the back cabin as I was gathering screwdrivers and other implements of destruction. "I'd stay out of the way if I were you," I told it. "I have absolutely no idea what I'm doing here." The spider eyed me balefully and then scuttled off into a corner. "Good choice," I muttered at it.

Armed with every tool I felt that I could possibly use, some that I hoped I wouldn't have to, and some that I wasn't even sure what their function was, I made my way back to the generator and started to disassemble the case. Oil trickled everywhere, making holding the tools very difficult. Eventually I managed to get the sides of the case off and I could see the machine. A small yellow plastic prong thing lay half submerged in the oil. I picked it up and wiped it off. It looked very familiar. I looked up and spotted the same spider watching me from the top of the door. "That's the damn dip-stick for the oil," I told it, it didn't care.

Climbing over the mess I'd made and around to the other side of the generator I triumphantly went to put the dipstick back in its place. I couldn't, there was one already in there. "Is this a spare?" The spider, obviously fed up with being addressed by some eminently confused and oil-stained human completely ignored me and amused itself by dangling from one of the lights, waving its legs around to cast Poe-like shadows on the wall.

I placed the yellow stick into my pocket and began to search through the exploded diagrams shown in the manual. I was really hoping to find out if this was something important or something Geoff had just left in the bottom of the box for want of a better place to put it. Eventually, on a small diagram, uncoloured and unlabeled I saw that there were indeed supposed to be two. Placing my hand beneath the generator I felt around for a wet, cold hole. It was difficult, the sun was setting and the temperature had hit minus three. My fingers felt numb and my teeth had begun to chatter. Eventually I found what I was looking for and after only a couple of swear words managed to get the wretched thing back in place.

It turned out that both yellow sticks had the same use just in two different places. They both kept the oil in the sump. One, however, was used as a dip stick and the other would be the only way to change the oil. I could only assume that, with the vibrations of the generator, it had worked its way loose and had fallen out, thus dumping the entire contents of the sump out of the machine and onto the floor.

I tightened the stick as hard as I could and set about cleaning up the spilled oil. This took longer than the repair and by the time I'd finished I had more on me than the floor. The sun had set and I was working by dim 12-volt light. I refilled the generator with oil and went through all the normal checks. I decided I had two chances, either I was going to be lucky and the gods of heavy machinery would smile on me and the thing would work, or the head gasket had vaporised and I was going to be smoked out like a wasps' nest in an attic. The engine turned over and I held my breath. Apart from the normal wisps of exhaust smoke there didn't seem to be a problem. Unwilling to trust my luck I tucked myself on to the step and sat, listening to the generator for a good five minutes. At the end of this time, the generator was still running perfectly but I was

318

sure I was hovering on the edge of hypothermia. I decided enough was enough and climbed out of the boat.

Two hours later and the generator was still running. Geoff stepped through the door and was greeted by Sam yelling, "The generator blew up but Mum fixed it. Dad! DAD, Mum fixed something."

Geoff looked a little surprised. "What happened?"

I told him about my day and, when I'd finished, he got up and made tea. "I know I said you were going to have to pick up slack," he said. "But I think this goes well above and beyond the call of duty, you know."

"Once I got over the panic it was actually a fairly simple problem." I had to admit I was feeling quite good but I did have to also admit this hadn't been the mechanical nightmare that it might have been. "I didn't actually have to take the generator apart, I just found something that had dropped off."

"Did you find out what was wrong?" Geoff said.

"Well, yes."

"Did you put it back together after fixing it?" He grinned at me.

"Well, yes but . . ."

"Did you recognise what the yellow thing was?" He raised his eyebrows.

"Yeah, but it was just a . . ."

"Shut up," Geoff handed me a cup of tea. "It broke, you fixed it, you get cake." He waved a box of chocolate éclairs at me. "If you carry on being modest you don't get one."

I gave him my best smile. "I fixed it, I get cake."

"So you do," he said.

In all honesty, although it had appeared scary and smoky the repair hadn't been that difficult and over the next two weeks I took on a lot more of those little jobs that previously I would have avoided as if they'd been snakes in grass. By the time Christmas arrived and it was time to go and visit my parents, I'd become a regular handy person and was finding the benefits of living out in the wilds quite extensive, all I needed now was a hat made out of bear skin and I would have been sorted.

After the trials and tribulations of the past five months Christmas was a welcome break. Unlike other years where it was all a bit of a trial, this year I was positively looking forward to the whole thing. Charlie was coming down from Cardiff and my sister and her brood were also making an appearance. My mother was in a whirlwind of excitement and preparation and my father had taken to hiding in the attic with his train set.

The four days sped by and soon it was time to return to our weird little crop of land in the middle of nowhere. My mother, however, was less than convinced by the whole thing.

"So, let me get this straight," she said, peering at me over the top of a large cup of coffee, "You are now living where there are no services at all?"

I nodded and shrugged. "Well, there's no electricity, but there is water."

"And you have to park half a mile away?"

I nodded again. "It's probably not that far but it is a bit of a walk."

320

"So you have to carry everything you need to the boat over half a mile of wind and rain and outsideness."

"Well, when you put it like that of course it's going to sound bad," I said.

She threw her hands up in the air. "It doesn't *sound* bad, it *is* bad," she said. "Honestly I thought your last place was bad enough. I can't even begin to imagine somewhere even more basic than *that*."

"Well, it certainly gives a sense of that pioneering spirit." I gave her a big grin. She wasn't fooled for a moment.

"Don't you ever want to be normal?" She did try to make the question less than accusatory; she failed.

I had to laugh at her pained expression. "Not really no, and when Sam leaves to go to uni or whatever he does then we're hoping to set off into the real wilds."

Getting to her feet, Mum sniffed. "I have no idea where you get this attitude from," she said. "I blame your father."

I looked over at my dad, feet up, big toe sticking out of a hole in his sock, covered in dried paint, fast asleep, and snoring fit to shake the rafters, he looked very comfortable in his own skin. I had to smile; Mum was probably right, there did seem to be a family leaning toward the scruffy and anti-social.

CHAPTER
THIRTEEN

Freezing, Wet, And Windswept Then ... Bloody January Again.

"Mum!"

I jumped and peered at Sam who was currently enticing Mortimer to sit on my stomach. Rolling over, I tried desperately to keep my eyes open as I stared at the clock. It was 5.30 on a Thursday morning. "Wha's the matter?" I yawned again and, grabbing the well-loved and padded oversized checked shirt that acted as my dressing gown these days, dragged myself into a semi-slumped upright position.

"Snow! SNOW!"

"Oh is that all?" Wrapping my shirt around me against the cold in the boat I gently toppled over and landed on top of Geoff who groaned from beneath the covers.

It was no good, once I was awake no amount of pretending I wasn't was going to actually get me back to sleep. I staggered out of bed wincing as the frigid air bit into any part of me that wasn't aggressively covered. I pulled open the door to the log burner and cleared out all of last night's ashes. Grouping the little coven of red coals into a small huddle in the middle of the firebed I carefully applied slivers of wood and then grinned in satisfaction as tiny flickers of light appeared. It doesn't matter how often I did that particular job it was always a happy moment when the flames started licking at the new wood.

I took a couple of minutes more to pile on ever larger pieces of wood and then a layer of coal. I shut the door and then opened the vent as far as it would go. It really wouldn't take long for all that to catch. Wandering down the boat, still half-ignoring Sam who, after checking his school's web site, was ecstatic that it was closed and was busy planning what to do with his windfall of a free day. I put the kettle on as I went past, not only does it get us tea but it helps to speed up the process of heating the boat up.

I was almost all the way to the bathroom when I heard Sam say. "I wonder where my sledge is."

Oh poot!

I hadn't actually told him that I'd had a little accident with his sledge at the end of last year. I'd had the stunning idea that I could load it up with coal and drag it over the flood defences. Unfortunately one of the ropes had snapped and the sledge had rushed off down the hill carrying my coal with it. This, in itself, hadn't actually been much of a trauma but when it reached the bottom of the hill it ran into a metal box that we used to keep tools in. The coal had been fine, it had just flopped off the sledge and lay in the snow waiting for someone to pick it up. The sledge hadn't faired so well; old and tired it had positively disintegrated on impact; bits of painted wood had littered the snow over a five-foot radius. Ever one to see the good side of anything; I'd gathered what bits I could and had burnt it on the fire.

"I think we'll have to buy you a new one, Sam," I said.

Sam wasn't particularly impressed that I'd used his sledge as fuel and told me so over and over again on our trip down to Ely. I had to admit to feeling a little guilty which is probably why he got a much better sledge than he might otherwise have.

Once back home he shot out with new sledge in tow. Almost knocking Janis over, as he scampered out he shouted back at apology.

"Well, he looks happy," Janis commented as she stuck her head through the door.

I nodded. "Any day off school is a good day, even if it's actually a rubbish day it still feels like an unexpected gift."

Janis managed to dissuade Mortimer from eating her ears and then shovelled him off the end of the sofa and refused to let him back on again. The dog, banned from loving mutilation, sulked in his basket.

"Coffee?" I waved the bottle of rum at her. "Are you driving again today?"

I'd completely forgotten that Janis wasn't as au fait with my rum and coffee habits as some other people and realised that she might see me as a complete lush. She looked taken aback for a moment but slowly a grin spread across her face and she nodded. "What a good idea," she said.

By the time we'd finished our first coffee and were well down our second, Sam had trailed sadly back into the boat. "I'm bored and lonely," he said. "Come out and sledge with me."

I was just about to open my mouth and reel off a complete list of why that would be a bad idea when Janis said, "OK then."

"What?"

"Don't be such an old fuddy-duddy," she said. "Lead on, Sam, I haven't sledged for years, but I'll give it a go."

As they left, Mortimer and I stared at each other. "I don't know why you're looking at me in that smug way," I told him. "If I'm going down you're going down with me."

Ten minutes later and we were all standing on top of the flood defences. Mortimer who had been rootling around in one of the log collections came and stood next to us. He was shivering. We all stared down the steep slope; it seemed a long way down to the bottom.

Sam handed the ropes of his new sledge to Janis. "Go on then," he said. He gave her a big smile. He obviously wasn't expecting her to rise to his challenge. He was sadly mistaken.

"All right." Janis settled herself onto the sledge and began to gather up the ropes.

Mortimer stared at the big red plastic sledge. His ears pricked up and his eyes flattened which is never a good sign. Step by step he deliberately advanced on the red sledge that was, by now, teetering on the very edge of the long run down to the hedge that bordered the field beyond.

"Mortimer!" Janis eyed the dog as he stalked toward her, mouth open, teeth showing. "What's he doing?" She dug her feet into the snow and prepared to stand up out of the way of a dog that was definitely looking more than a little purposeful.

As she tried to stand up the sledge moved, only slightly, but that was enough to drive Mortimer from stalk to attack. Bounding across the snow he grabbed the edge of the saucer-shaped sledge in his mouth and without fear of being run over he pulled the plastic toy, with Janis still on board, over the edge of the hill and away down to the gully running at the bottom.

Janis screamed as Mort's teeth closed around the plastic and she didn't stop screaming until she was face down in a pile of snow at the bottom of the hill. Mort, the sledge between his teeth, tore around and around with his prize. It took the combined might of both Sam and myself to retrieve it. Then we went looking for Janis.

There really wasn't much of her to find. While Sam and I had been chasing the dog she had managed to flip over and was now lying on her back, half buried in snow, staring up at the trees. She raised her head and glared at us. "Well, that was a little faster than I would have liked," she said. "That dog of yours is completely insane." She lay back in the snow her whole body shaking with laughter.

I looked down at the *insane* dog and he stared up at me. His big golden eyes were wide and completely blameless. Tail wagging, he shuffled closer to the sledge that I was holding out of his reach. "I wonder if he'd do it again," I said.

Well, as the whole activity was dangerous and more than a little stupid of course he would. For the next hour, Janis, Sam, and I were Mortimer-propelled around on the sledge. Eventually Janis had to leave because her customers had turned up to pick up some sofa cushions. They'd been watching our ridiculous antics as they walked across the flood defences and it really didn't take much pressure from us for them to join in. Mortimer was in his element.

"Doesn't he mind doing that?" one of the other neighbours enquired as she wandered up to join us.

"Evidently not," I said. "I'm not telling him or forcing him, he's not tied to the sledge he's just pulling it along with his teeth. I think he's enjoying it almost as much as we are."

With a bit of pressure we managed to convince this new neighbour (I didn't even know her name) onto the sledge and Mort happily dumped another person face first into the snow. I began to wonder if this really was the best way to meet new people. Well they'd certainly remember us.

That night both Mortimer and Sam slept very, very soundly.

Apart from the joys of dog-propelled sledging, the rest of the month was a hard slog. As expected, the water froze and it became a daily grind to drag big bottles of water and twenty-kilo bags of coal over the frozen ground. Because the boat was now so far away, every little trip became an exercise in load-carrying logistics. Boat maintenance now went from half an hour a day to just over three.

It didn't seem to matter how much wood we cut, we were always just running out and a bag of coal lasted no more than two days. Getting out of the boat to go to school or work became more and more difficult and a lot of time was spent scraping cars. I was desperate to see some sign of spring after the year we'd had but knew full well that nothing would change for at least eight to ten weeks.

It seemed as though the weather was affecting not only everybody but everything. One Saturday morning in late January, Sam, Geoff, and I, packed up to the ears with shopping bags, washing, gas canisters, and anything else we could conceivably need, trudged our weary way to the car. Sam, given control of a huge bag of washing, muttered imprecations against the woman who had let the pile get this big. Spotting his sledge buried under the wood pile he stopped for a moment and eyed the washing bag and then studied the sledge. I turned to glance at Geoff, he grinned, we knew exactly what Sam was thinking but in the still January morning you could almost hear the cogs turning in Sam's head.

Eventually, he dumped the bag of washing into the snow and slid down the slope toward the wood shed. Grabbing his sledge he slipped and slithered his way back up the hill. Once at the top he triumphantly balanced the bag of washing in the middle of the sledge and experimentally pulled it a couple of metres to see how the whole thing handled. Evidently it was to his satisfaction and giving me a wide smile he sauntered over and held out his hands for the bag I was carrying. "Madam," he said. He gave me a florid bow. "That bag looks heavy, please let me carry it for you."

I theatrically fluttered a gloved hand at my throat and flapped my eyelashes at him. "Oh lawks, sir," I said, "that would just be too too kind of you."

I handed him the bag and, giggling, he squashed it onto the sledge and walked away dragging the whole thing easily over the compacted snow at the top of the flood defences.

Geoff watched him go. "Is it only me that can see imminent disaster?"

I shook my head. "Nope, any moment now." I thought for a minute and turned back to Geoff. "It seems a little mean not to warn him," I said.

Geoff gave Sam's retreating back a sad look. "But it would be so funny."

I laughed and called out toward boy and sledge. "Sam, I'd keep that in the middle of the track if I were you, there's no telling what the ground's doing at the edges."

Sam turned round and gave me a "look". "I think I can pull a sledge, Mother."

Geoff's beard split into a big happy smile. "There," he said, "parental duty done, you warned him. Can I watch and laugh now?"

We both stood and watched as Sam hit a patch of ground that sloped sharply away from the river. Sure enough, as expected, the sledge slid over the edge and carrying a load that weighed a fair amount dragged Sam with it into the deep snow on the other side of the flood defences. The scream from our rather surprised son seemed to hang in the cold air. We watched as the bags of washing fell from the sledge and flung their contents with gay abandon all over the snow. It looked as though a herd of brightly coloured skiers had met some untimely demise.

Geoff snorted a laugh. "I supposed we'd better go and dig him out."

I nodded. "I'm glad he tried that when the washing was dirty," I said. "I might have been a bit miffed if all that had been cleaned and dried." I trudged through the snow after Geoff. "At least he won't make the same mistake on the way back."

Geoff came to a sudden halt, causing me to bump into his back. He turned to face me with an incredulous look. "You have actually met our son, haven't you?" he asked.

I gave him a small push; unfortunately it wasn't hard enough to send him the same way as the washing. "Don't be mean," I said.

It took us about ten minutes to gather up clothes, son, and sledge and we watched as a rather wet and demoralised teenager pulled the sledge with a little more care over the final part of the walk.

We loaded everything into the back of the car and Sam sat gibbering, wet, and cold in the car while we cleared the snow and ice from the windows.

"Are you all right?" I glanced into the rear-view mirror.

He nodded, his teeth chattering. Finally he got his mouth to work and asked. "How long will it take for the car to warm up?"

I laughed. "Not long. I'll put my foot down and that will help the engine warm up." I pulled carefully out of the snow-filled car park and on to the cleared road.

Geoff frowned. "What's the matter with this car?" He leant forward, listening to the engine. "It doesn't sound very good."

I bit my lip, the last thing we needed was the car to fail on us. Hoping it was just as cold and miserable as the rest of us I put my foot down, maybe a little extra gas would clear whatever blockage seemed to be causing the car to cough and splutter. At the junction the car settled down to a nice even tick-over. I shrugged. "Seems all right now," I said. I put the Kia in gear and tried to pull away. Nothing happened, the car just coughed and choked.

Geoff waved a hand at the ignition indicating that I ought to turn it off. "I think I'd better have a look," he said.

It was getting nicely warm in the car now and I really didn't want to stand outside. "Do you need any help?"

He smirked. He knew very well that I wanted the answer to be no.

A couple of minutes later he emerged from under the bonnet and tapped on my window.

I rolled it down, wincing at the blast of frigid air.

"I think you'd better come and have a look at this," he said.

Grabbing my coat, hat, and gloves I wondered what he'd found. It had to be something fairly obvious otherwise there would be no reason to show it to *me*. Despite my luck with the generator I was no mechanic. I stepped out of the car and peered into the engine compartment. For a moment I couldn't work out what I was looking at and then the whole sorry mess seeped into my brain. "What the hell has happened to all the HT leads?"

Geoff grabbed my phone from my pocket and proceeded to take pictures. "I think we have either mice or a single mouse that's been living in our engine," he said.

Every rubber cover on every HT lead had been eaten away. The car wouldn't fire properly because the sparks weren't contained in any way, they'd just been bouncing off the underside of the bonnet. Tiny little shavings of rubber and plastic covered almost every available flat surface of the engine. When we looked hard we could follow the dastardly little rodent's progress as it had made a meal of almost every bit of insulation that was showing.

"So what do we do now?" I picked up a palm full of rubber shavings and dribbled them back on top of the block. "Where's the mouse?"

Geoff shrugged. "I have no idea but I should think it's taken refuge in the side of the engine compartment. We're lucky that we didn't get far from the car park," he said.

"Why?"

"I think I need to go and get some insulating tape." He closed the bonnet and, pulling his hat down around his ears headed back toward where his van was parked.

About half an hour later and the engine of my poor car looked like a Christmas present that had been wrapped by a three-year-old. Silver insulating tape was wrapped around every electrical component in an effort to keep each one from interacting with its neighbours.

I looked in at his efforts and laughed. "Very pretty."

Geoff frowned. "I don't care what it looks like," he said. "I just hope it works."

It did and we headed to the motor parts shop in Ely. We bought new HT leads and lots of other bits and bobs. In the coffee shop Geoff studied the bill and shook his head. "We should have fed the little chomper on filet mignon and champagne," he said.

I looked up, confused. I'd been communing with my cream covered hot chocolate and hadn't really noticed what he'd been doing. "Why?"

"It would have been damn well cheaper to buy him a decent meal." Geoff sighed and, after balling up the receipt, he shoved it deep into his pocket.

He hates unnecessary expense and I expected him to be grumpy for the rest of the day. He wasn't, Sam and a sledge full of clean washing fell down the hill again on the way home and that went a long way to cheering him up.

The deadline for all boats to leave our previous marina came and went. Elaine and Dion had been planning to leave on the very last day and then join us at the new place. We kept an eye out for them but they never showed up, it was a little worrying, but we were used to people taking their sweet time so we weren't unduly alarmed. On Sunday afternoon I got a phone call from Dion.

"We've got a bit of a problem," he said.

It turned out that only three hundred metres out on the main river and their engine had gone kablooie. Luckily they had broken down merely yards away from where Bill and Drew were currently moored so they'd been towed across the river and settled into the unoccupied space behind The Blue Boar.

Geoff looked up as I was chatting to Dion. "Is everything all right?" He mouthed the words at me. I shook my head and waved a hand to indicate that I couldn't hear very well. "What's going on?" He mouthed at me again and poked me in the shoulder with his finger. "Hang on, Dion," I said. "Geoff wants a word." I handed the phone over to Geoff — it was just easier that way.

I listened to Geoff asking all the same questions that I would have asked: did they need a tow here? Did they need a lift anywhere? Could we pick up any engine parts for them? When he'd received the negative to all these questions he said goodbye and turned my phone

334

off. "I don't know why you gave the phone to me," he said. "*You* could have asked them all that."

I resisted the urge to poke him in the belly button and instead asked, "So what's wrong with their boat?"

Geoff frowned. "I didn't ask that."

"Is Drew going to have a look at it for them?"

Geoff chewed his lip. "I don't know."

"Are they still planning to come here?"

He stared at me. "You're just making these questions up now, aren't you?"

I nodded and went to make tea.

About a week later and I was having coffee with Bill. I hadn't realised how much I missed everyone I normally hung about with until I saw her stagger, windswept and rain-soaked through the door of an Ely café.

We chatted for a while about where everyone had gone and what had been happening with Elaine's boat, then she reached into her pocket and pulled out a folded page of newsprint. "I don't suppose you happened to see this, did you?" She carefully unfolded the paper and placed it in front of me. "I assumed you hadn't which is why I saved it for you. I assumed that if you *had* seen it we would have heard your howls of rage all the way to Cambridge."

I laughed and studied the article she was showing me. The picture was the same one that had been taken the day we'd tried to talk to a reporter about the early changes at the marina, however there was a new headline: "Owners can refurbish marina despite protests by boaters". Confused, I glanced up at Bill.

She reached over and tapped the article. "Just read it," she said. "It's another triumph for understatement."

I shrugged and read on. There was a paragraph about the plans being confirmed and they got the numbers of boating families affected wrong. It did appear to point out our major issue that, with that number of boats hitting the system, it would be difficult to find moorings for everyone.

There was another paragraph stating again that the plans for the refurbishment had been given the go-ahead and, reading, I began to wonder what the whole point of this was. I glanced up at Bill who was watching me closely over the top of her glasses. She was obviously expecting a reaction about something.

The next paragraph had Mrs Owner saying how they understood that we were upset (upset? UPSET?) by the decision to have us all off the land and they did sympathise.

A grin began to spread across Bills face as I gave a derisive snort. "It gets better," she said.

The next paragraph had me grinding my teeth in pure rage. It stated: "The majority of them have all gone now and it actually hasn't been as stressful as we all thought it would be."

Bill laughed as I crumpled the page in my fist. "Yeah," she said. "That's the bit."

I had to take a couple of moments to get my mouth to work. I took some deep breaths and concentrated on drinking my coffee. Eventually I couldn't be quiet any longer. "Not stressful?" I glared at Bill who grinned happily at me. Obviously I was reacting almost exactly as she had. "*She* didn't lose her job, *she* didn't have to move her child to a new school, *she* didn't have to completely refit the electrical system of her domicile to the tune of a couple of grand."

On each word my voice rose just a little more and, as I noticed women at other tables turning to look at us, I clamped my teeth together and forced myself to calm down.

Bill used a little force and rescued the crumpled newspaper from between the fingers of my fist. She stroked it straight again and folding it put it safely back into her bag. "I think I'd like to keep that as a memento," she said.

"Of what?" I could hear myself snarling but couldn't seem to be able to stop it. "Complete ignorance?" I stared into my empty coffee cup. "People who had lived on boats for more years than I gave up that lifestyle because she hurried them into leaving at precisely the very worst time of year. People had to sell their boats. Elaine and Dion now have a boat that isn't working. You don't have a mooring at all, Donna and Steve's isn't really ready yet, Lewis can't find one he likes, and we have one that is barely liveable. God knows what's happened to half the others. Half of them are still stuck in the floods." I banged the mug down on the table. "And to top it all off none of us can actually get off the system because they did this in the depths of winter when the locks are undergoing maintenance and the weather is so bad that those that do work are actually silted up and closed. And while we've all been running around like

337

headless chickens trying to get our affairs in order, she's been sitting there congratulating herself and thinking that it hasn't been *stressful*?" I took a deep breath and forced my voice to drop an octave or three. "I'm just trying to work out exactly what the issue is here." I glared up at Bill. "What would you vote for? Complete ignorance, greed, or Narcissistic Solipsism?"

Bill laughed and then reached over and patted my hand. "You look a little wild around the eyes, dear, and you've started ranting in multiple syllables," she said. "Would you like another coffee?"

I nodded and wondered if I had any rum in my handbag. While Bill was at the counter I read through the rest of the article, there wasn't anything else exciting. I had to admit it might be a misquote, it wasn't like a reporter hadn't got it wrong before. I couldn't imagine how anybody could be that blind. By the time Bill came back with two large hot chocolates covered in cream and sprinkles I'd calmed down again.

"I took the liberty of ordering something naughty," she said. "Have you calmed down yet?"

I huffed a laugh and began poking the thick cream into the chocolate with the back of my spoon. "I have to hope . . ." I watched as the cream bobbed to the surface of my drink like a snow-covered iceberg in the middle of a liquid midden ". . . that the paper got it wrong and that she's as furious with them as I was last time I read an article about the marina."

"Would you even go back if you could?" Bill asked.

I shook my head. "No, I don't think so, but Sam would, he still thinks of it as 'home' and he's definitely mourning the change."

There really wasn't much to say after that and the conversation moved on to more cheery topics.

As January slowly wound to a close very little changed and life became really quite hard work. The month started well enough but the waterways system was still trying to cope with the vast amounts of water that had been dumped into it the previous year. Stuck where we were, close to Denver Sluice, our little bit of river was one of the first to be affected when the Environment Agency tried to get rid of the flood water. Within hours the river would drop by as much as two foot and *Minerva* would settle onto the bottom of the river and tilt alarmingly to port. This made day-to-day living very difficult and we would stagger down the boat, the floor beneath us dropping away to the river side. If we hadn't come off the bottom by the time we wanted to sleep, both Sam and I would cling to the edge of our respective beds lest we inadvertently roll over and get tipped onto the floor. Geoff, who slept next to the wall, wasn't quite so affected. During the night however, he would roll across the bed until he was pressed up against my back. Determined not to be pushed onto the carpet, I would roll over and push him back across the bed and try to keep him in place with either hands or feet. Suffice to say none of us were happy with the amount of sleep we got and the whole family was a little grumpy and tired.

Trying to cook while the boat was like this was another trial. Baking was almost impossible. Every cake I created came out of the oven at an angle, burnt and crispy where the mixture was only a couple of millimetres thick and uncooked on the other side where it was deeper. Crockery slid from the kitchen work tops and I spent a lot of time clearing up spilt drinks. This odd, slightly drunken, existence lasted for about two weeks before yet another freeze set in and the river finally stayed at a decent level.

For the rest of the month, snow, hail, and wretched howling winds battered the boats and their inhabitants. We waited for it to howl itself out but the weather showed no signs of letting up and every day became a battle against the elements. Heads down against the wind, we would drag whatever we needed for that day to a car that was frozen solid. I would spend most of my days dragging necessities such as coal, gas, diesel, and groceries back again. The pipes that carried the drinking water to the boats froze for nearly two weeks and we had to start borrowing bathrooms from friends that didn't live in the boondocks. Even Geoff's cheerful and stoic personality started to crack from the strain.

"I'm really not sure I can do this for much longer." He sat on the sofa and winced as he stretched his muscles. The deep cold played havoc with various old motorcycling and re-enactment injuries and after taking the last of the paracetamol he stoked up the fire and handed me his TENS machine. I stuck the little sticky pads to various muscles and then turned the machine on to its highest setting. He sighed with relief as the little machine sent electrical pulses through his back and shoulders.

His statement surprised me; he was usually the biggest advocate of the boating life. I could always be relied upon to find something to moan about but he was usually happy with our rather vigorous lifestyle. "You're not thinking we should sell up, are you?"

He looked up and shrugged. "If we have to stay here then I think I might consider it."

Silence fell and, needing time to think about this, I got up to make tea. I looked around our boat. It was warm and cosy and, compared to the world outside, it was a positive haven of snug living. I had to admit it was the outside world that was letting us down.

Eventually, I handed him a mug of tea and an early hot cross bun and studied him. It had been seven years since we started this little escapade and we'd made a lot of changes. Children had grown up and left home. We now had a grandchild and, all too soon, Sam would be gone as well and it would be just us. We were so close to being able to relax and mooch about I didn't want to lose it all now and I was fairly sure that Geoff didn't either. He looked tired. Sitting on the sofa, still in his work blues, he winced every time the TENS machine sent a particularly enthusiastic pulse through his sore muscles. We hadn't seen the sun for months and his extended hours were taking their toll, he looked sallow and grey, I was fairly sure that I didn't look much better. With no water we'd concentrated on making sure that our bodies and all our clothes were clean but the washing up only got done every two days and I know the mess was certainly getting me down. Eventually I plonked myself down beside him. "But we don't have to stay here," I said. "You were never that enamoured of the place before we even got here."

"But you like it, don't you?" He stared down into his mug. "It could be quite nice when the summer comes."

I snorted. "I like Janis, the rest I could live without. You'd still have an hour's drive to work and we'd still have a long walk to the car." I thought quickly, Geoff absolutely hated doing anything for himself, the man was a complete martyr. It was one of the reasons I adored him. "Anyway, you know we have to get out of here before spring," I said.

Geoff looked up at me and frowned. "Why?"

I shrugged as though it was obvious. "Too much plant life around here." I got up and gathered up the mugs. Wandering down the boat I placed them on the teetering pile of washing up. "Those trees are going to give off a huge amount of pollen in the spring. Sam will just become one wet pile of gripes and moans." I caught a mug as it slid with a clatter toward the floor. "No, I never wanted to stay here for good. It was only going to be a pit-stop for a couple of months."

Geoff grinned at me. "You are a terrible liar, you do know that, don't you?"

I nodded. "If you don't like it here and it's making you sad, we go. That's really all there is to it. We didn't give up a static life just so that we could take on another one. We only stayed in the last marina for so long because it was convenient."

I wasn't lying to him about moving, that really was one of the things I loved most about my life. There are many downsides to this lifestyle and each season has its own challenges. However there is *never* any need to stay in a place you don't like, you don't have to put up with neighbours you don't like, you don't even have to put up with a rubbish view if you don't want to. There is always the option to move.

After our little conversation Geoff was much happier and, with something to look forward to, a little of the winter gloom lifted.

CHAPTER
FOURTEEN
And On...

At the end of February Elaine and Dion limped down the river to join us. Their boat still wasn't fixed but they were happy to have a mooring and with spring just around the corner were content to wait for better weather before they attempted to rebuild their engine.

We, however, had had enough and were just waiting for Salters Lode lock to clear before we were planning to be away.

Eventually, at the beginning of April, we got the news that boats were, once more, moving through the middle levels. Geoff confirmed this with a phone call and at his big smile I started thinking about what we needed to pack up.

Spring was definitely dragging its heels but the day we left the wind had dropped and the sun was shining. Sitting on the front deck watching the world go by I really couldn't think of anything I'd rather be doing.

It was as though the gods of boating were smiling on us that day and the whole trip was just textbook from start to finish. We'd been through Denver Sluice and Salters Lode on three previous occasions. Being so long our boats always caused a problem and today was expected to be no exception.

Geoff had spoken to the lock-keeper only the previous morning and it was planned that we would go through the locks as the very last boat of the day. This was evidently to keep us on high water. There was every chance that we would have to sit in the lock pound at Salters for the afternoon waiting for the water to go down naturally but it was something we were happy to do.

Making excellent time we pulled up at the moorings outside Denver at about twelve o'clock. Sitting in the sunshine with a cup of coffee we watched as a sparkly new boat began to pull in behind us. The lady sitting in the front looked a bit harassed.

Placing my coffee cup on the ground I stood up and held out an arm. "Sling us your rope if you like," I said.

She gave me a great big smile and threw her rope to me. It was a good throw and I picked it up and wrapped it around one of the mooring bollards. Geoff walked to the other end of the boat to do the same.

The gentleman on the tiller swung it the wrong way and the boat's backside headed out toward the centre of the river. I looked up, wondering why the boat, that had been coming in so nicely, now seemed to be on a nose first collision course.

The lady on the front looked a little embarrassed. "First time out," she shouted over to me.

With shouted instructions from Geoff they finally moored up and joined us for coffee. It really was their first time out with their brand new boat. They'd moved on to it while it was being finished and it was now on its maiden voyage to its home moorings.

"Do you mind if we go through with you?" Julie stared up at the huge gates of Denver Sluice.

I was just about to laugh and say, "Oh you don't want to go through with us, we don't know what we're doing." When it occurred to me that we *did* know what we were doing. It came as a bit of a shock.

After seven years of getting it wrong, sometimes quite disastrously, we were quite comfortable taking our great monster from place to place. I thought back over the latest trip. We'd turned her around with only about four foot to spare, we'd manoeuvred her into a fairly tight mooring space. I was no longer worried about going through the big locks.

Julie looked a little worried by my silence. "We won't if you don't want us to."

I shook myself out of my reverie and laughed. "No, that's fine. Sorry, I was just thinking about the trip here. Of course you're welcome to go through with us."

After making plans to meet them in half an hour for lunch at the pub we went our separate ways. I was still mulling this latest revelation over.

We'd managed to get a very dilapidated boat through a frankly hideous year and had ended up with no proper mooring and no electricity but we'd survived. We knew when things weren't right, when the engine note changed, when something smelled bad, when she was badly ballasted and we now knew what to do about it. I'd managed a minor repair on the generator in sub-zero temperatures and kept everyone warm and fed. Geoff . . . Well, Geoff had fixed everything else. Bless him. I could change gas bottles over and fill her with water and pump out. I was more than a little surprised to work out that there wasn't anything I was worried about any more.

I remember back to when we first decided to live on a boat, everything had seemed so alien. I couldn't remember, try as I might, when this life became "acceptable" and our old, normal, life began to seem like the one to avoid.

Fortified by this new found knowledge and a couple of glasses of beer I prepared to face the locks that I had previously done everything I could to avoid. Quite frankly I found myself looking forward to it but that could have been the beer.

Both boats pulled into the huge lock at about three o'clock. Due to the large banks of silt we were warned to come out one at a time and to make sure we stayed firmly to the right. The lock doors closed and the water levels began to change. The metal walkway high above dropped water on us and I grinned as Julie squeaked at the cold drips and the overpowering smell of mud and water plants that always marked a lock for me.

As the big doors lifted I could see why the keeper had asked us to stay to the right. A tall digger with an extraordinarily long arm stood silent above us on newly created banks. The Environment Agency had obviously had to do a lot of work to create this channel through which we now travelled.

Sam, wondering at the odd moon-like landscape through which we now travelled, stepped out of the doors and joined me at the front of the boat. He'd obviously just had a shower and he leant over the side so that the wind could dry his hair. Five years ago I would have wrapped a rope around his foot but now I knew it was unlikely he'd fall overboard and let him get on with it.

"What on earth is that?" He pointed to a rounded, slick grey hump that emerged like a plague island from the centre of the river.

I explained about the silt movements that had been going on because of all the flood water and he shook his head.

"When you said there was silt I imagined that maybe the river was a bit shallow," he said. "I didn't expect there to be hills of the stuff."

I nodded. "It's been a bit of an extreme year."

Sam ducked back inside the boat and emerged a couple of minutes later with a mug of coffee.

I must have looked confused. "It's for you," he said. "You didn't get to drink your last one."

I stared at the mug of coffee and then looking up, studied my son. When had he changed from being pudgy selfish child into a casually thoughtful young man?

He looked worried. "Don't you want it?"

For the second time that day I had to shake my thoughts away. "I'd love it, thank you."

Sam sat down on the side of the boat and looked happily smug. Obviously brownie points had just been earned.

I was just finishing the last mouthful of coffee when we approached the sharp left turn into Salters Lode.

348

Sam was seeing it for the first time. "Have we got to turn into that tiny little channel?" He stood up and peered over the front of the boat.

I nodded. "Yep, and with a boat this big it's a right pain in the ar —"

Geoff cut across me. "Give me a shout when I hit the wall, will you?" he called.

I gave him a thumb-up and leaned, with Sam, over the front. We both watched the approaching wall of tyres with some trepidation.

There was hardly a bump as Geoff brought us slowly and expertly in. Pushing the nose against the tyres, he swung the back end around and then we drifted slowly into the lock pound. We didn't have to wait, within ten minutes we were out and on our way again. Perfect.

We'd planned to stop for the night at the lock moorings but, as they were full and we had a fair amount of daylight left, we decided to press on so we waited for Julie and her husband to come alongside to tell them what we were up to.

We said our goodbyes and they went on ahead. Determined to make their mooring by nightfall they were going to be much faster than we were likely to be. Sure enough within half an hour they were lost to sight.

By five o'clock we'd found a mooring at the strangely named place of Gady Dacks and pulled in for the night. It was wonderful, quiet, empty and just long enough that *Minerva* took up the whole thing.

As the sun was setting we amused ourselves by sitting out on the mooring to eat our dinner.

Geoff, full of pudding and tea heaved a happy sigh and stared down the river in both directions. There was nothing and nobody to see, idyllic. He turned to Sam with a big grin. "I don't suppose you want to change schools again, do you, Sam?"

Sam spluttered into his ice cream and looked at his dad. "No," he said. "I really don't."

He was just about to launch into a full argument about how much he liked his new school and how it was going to be GCSEs next year when I nudged him into silence. I knew Geoff was joking but I knew why.

"He's joking, Sam," I said.

Sam subsided with a huff of exasperation.

"He just means that it's so nice to be travelling again that he doesn't want to stop." I had to agree the thought was terribly tempting.

Sam grinned and pushed his hair out of his eyes. "I knew that."

We all sat in silence and watched the sky darken. Eventually Geoff got to his feet. "I suppose we'd better close up for the night before we get a boat full of flies," he said.

An hour later and we were all sprawled across the sofa watching *Dr Who*. When the program had finished we turned the telly off and Geoff got up to make tea.

Sam watched him for a moment and then turned to me with a worried look. "Where would we go if we kept going, Mum?" he said.

I shrugged. "I really fancy heading for home, Sam."

He looked confused and I realised that, to him, this was home. The inside of the boat was what he called home and the outside really didn't matter to him. I clarified, "I'd really like to head toward Worcestershire and Birmingham."

He shook his head. "Why?"

"Well it would be nice to go full circle, it's where we started from after all." I thought about it for a moment. "Nanny and Granddad are there, your aunt, your cousins, and loads of old friends."

Sam looked down at his feet for a moment. "I could change schools again, if you really wanted to do that," he said.

"What?" I pulled him into a hug, he was really getting too big for hugs. "No. Two more years and you'll have your GCSEs and then we can think about where you want to go for your A levels. I can wait another two years, especially if you're in a school you really like."

Sam nodded slowly. "I think I'd quite like to do my A levels in Worcester." He frowned.

"What's the matter?" I pushed him away to study his face. "Don't worry about it, it's going to go really quickly."

Geoff wandered up and handed me a mug of coffee. "What's going on?" He grinned at both of us.

I took the coffee. "I was just explaining to Sam that we're happy to wait for him to finish his GCSEs before we move on."

Geoff nodded in agreement. "Of course we are," he said. "I was only joking, we fully expect to stay here for the next couple of years while you're studying."

"It'll be nice actually," I continued, "the girls are doing their own thing, your dad's got a job he enjoys so maybe we can have a little peace and quiet for a couple of years. Maybe we could even get *Minerva*'s paint job finally done. We might, just might, get a summer this year."

Sam peered up at me through his hair.

"I'm really looking forward to just spending some quiet time living on this boat. We've got some decorating and bits and pieces to do but she's nearly finished. You're studying for your exams, we're just going to puddle on till you've finished and nothing . . ." I glared up at the ceiling. "NOTHING, exciting is going to happen this year. We'll all just carry on as normal."

Sam looked down at his feet. "Can we go to the cinema soon?"

"Huh?" I was always taken aback by his ability to change the subject so quickly. "Erm . . . yes if you want to."

"I do like the school," Sam said. "I'm really happy with my options for my exams but there is another reason I like it there so much."

I buried my nose in my coffee and stared down the river, happy and contented at the view and the complete lack of anything even vaguely representing a problem. "What's that then?"

"Can I bring a friend to the cinema?" Sam studied his trainers.

Oh, we were back to the cinema again were we? I nodded. "Yes if you'd like to, who is it?"

352

His voice was muffled beneath his hair. "Well, there's this girl . . ."

I took a deep breath in, swallowed coffee and began choking and spluttering. *That* scenario did not represent a nice quiet life. I could hear Geoff laughing over the sound of my coughing and all I could think was . . .

"OH NOOOOO!!"

Other titles published by Ulverscroft:

NARROW MARGINS

Marie Browne

Faced with the loss of everything following the collapse of the Rover car company, Marie Browne moves her long-suffering husband Geoff, chaotic children and smelly, narcoleptic dog onto a houseboat in search of a less stressful, healthier, alternative way of life. Strapped for cash, the family buys a decrepit seventy-foot barge called *Happy Go Lucky*, which had been run as a floating hotel. Outdated and in need of a complete refurbishment, Happy becomes their floating home as they negotiate the trials and tribulations of life in the slow lane.

NARROW MINDS

Marie Browne

Having saved her family from financial ruin by moving onto a houseboat in search of a less stressful, cheaper way of life, Marie Browne, her tea-fuelled husband Geoff and their children find themselves sucked back into normality. With a new job, a new rented house and a mountain of bills, they are pretty much back where they started, and the children are threatening mutiny. Facing perky postmen, ice-skating cows, psychotic villagers and outraged rodents, they're running out of time, their financial situation is getting desperate, and there's every chance life has conspired against them to make sure they never get back afloat. Until they find that the answer to their dreams lies with *Minerva*, a narrow boat even more run-down than their first . . .

THE STY'S THE LIMIT

Simon Dawson

Years ago, after a drunken misunderstanding, Simon Dawson gave up his job in the city, moved to the wilds of Exmoor and became an accidental self-sufficient smallholder surrounded by animals. But now his life is changing all over again: horror of horrors, he's getting older. Enlisting a cast of best friends — including Ziggy, a panicked soon-to-be father; Garth, an annoying teenager; and the General, a rather handsome pig — to work through their age-related angsts, a plan is hatched to help each other mature (or immature). Hilarity and heartfelt discoveries ensue — all with a fair dose of pigs, chickens, goats and animal madness along the way.

I LEAP OVER THE WALL

Monica Baldwin

At the age of twenty-one, Monica Baldwin, daughter of Prime Minister Stanley Baldwin, entered one of the oldest and most strictly enclosed contemplative orders of the Roman Catholic Church. Twenty-eight years later, after a prolonged struggle with her vocation, she left the convent. But the world Monica had known in 1914 was very different to the world into which she emerged at the height of the Second World War. This is the account of one woman's two very different lives, with revealing descriptions of the world of a novice, the daily duties of a nun, and the spiritual aspects of convent life. Interwoven with these, as the author is confronted with fashions, politics and art totally unfamiliar to her, are the trials and tribulations of coping with a new and alien world.